Praise for

JOURNEY TO TRUE SELF

"In *Journey to True Self*, Dr. Anne Deatly guides you to the depth of your inner wisdom where you can see the world through a different lens. What a beautiful and powerful book to illuminate your path."

  Marci Shimoff, #1 New York Times bestselling author, *Happy for No Reason and Chicken Soup for the Woman's Soul*

"Anne Deatly takes an understanding of Energy Medicine and masterfully places it within a higher spiritual context. We are proud to recommend this book."

  Donna Eden and David Feinstein, Ph.D., co-authors of *Energy Medicine and The Energies of Love*

"Anne Deatly's Guide is a revelation! Lucidly written, meticulously researched, and radiant with deep insight. I recommend it to everyone trying to make sense of this world."

  Carolyn Godschild Miller, Ph.D., author of *Creating Miracles: Understanding the Experience of the Divine and Creating Miracles: A Practical Guide to Divine Intervention*

"What if we could experience pure love, freedom, understanding, and compassion, free from unresolved emotional issues? Anne Deatly describes how all of this and more is possible when we identify ourselves with our True Selves, and welcome experiences of spiritual awakening that are characterized by enjoying a peaceful state of living, regardless of what is happening. Journey to True Self invites us to experience our True Selves, which are far more magnificent and uniquely inspired than we've ever imagined."

  Cynthia Sue Larson, author of *Quantum Jumps and Reality Shifts*

"Dr. Anne Deatly has written a remarkable book, a book that is a gift to humanity and our planet. We are at a crossroads, and the sooner humanity learns to act from the truth of who we really are, the sooner we can ensure that we—and our planet—survive to be the gift to the Universe we are meant to be. May each reader of this wonderful book find their True Self and begin that journey!"

  Dr. Vicki Matthews, Naturopathic Physician, Founding Director of Eden Energy Medicine Certification Program, and author of *The Five Elements of Relationships: How to Get Along with Anyone, Anytime, Anyplace*

"What do Socrates, Descartes, and Anne Deatly have in common? The recognition that understanding and knowing your true self is essential to developing your highest potential and living an authentic life. Anne Deatly's book is a guide to help you discover the hidden aspects of your True Self. Your journey begins with her book. I have learned from it, and you will too."

George J. Pratt, Ph.D, author of *Code to Joy and Instant Emotional Healing: Acupressure for the Emotions*

"Journey to True Self guides the reader on a path through ancient teachings, quantum discoveries, energy medicine, and sacred geometry, all leading to greater consciousness of one's own Soul. I felt my own inner frequency rising as I read, accompanied by deep insights. Meaningful prompts for meditation and practice further the learning. A wonderful book!"

Regina Bogle, M.D., author of *The Healing Light Series* and *Feeling Our Way: Embracing the Tender Heart*

JOURNEY
TO
TRUE SELF

Discover Your
Divine Magnificence

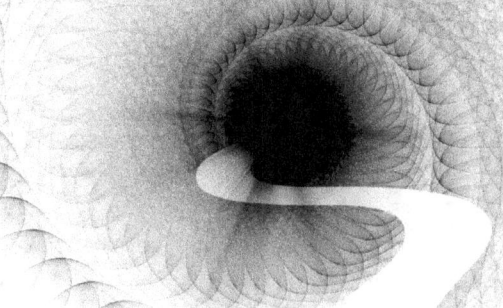

Your Divine Magnificence Trilogy

Anne M. Deatly, PhD

Sacred Dragon Publishing
Los Angeles, California

Sacred Dragon Publishing™
An imprint of Sacred Dragon Publishing Services LLC
Los Angeles, California
SacredDragonPublishing.com

ISBN: 979-8-9876749-3-2 Paperback
ISBN: 979-8-9876749-6-3 Hardcover
ISBN: 979-9-9876749-4-9 eBook

Cover Design: Amygdala Designs
Interior Design: Ryan Forsythe

The information presented in this work is the author's opinion and does not constitute any health or medical advice. The content of this work is for informational purposes only and is not intended to diagnose, treat, cure, or prevent any condition or disease or is meant as a substitute for consultation with a licensed practitioner.

Publisher's Cataloging-in-Publication (Provided by Cassidy Cataloguing Services, Inc.).
  Names: Deatly, Anne M., author.
  Title: Journey to true self : discover your divine magnificence / Anne M. Deatly, PhD.
  Description: Los Angeles, California : Sacred Dragon Publishing, [2024] | Series: Your divine magnificence | Includes index.
  Identifiers: ISBN: 979-8-9876749-3-2 (paperback) | 979-8-9876749-6-3 (hardcover) | 979-8-9876749-4-9 (ebook)
  Subjects: LCSH: Spirituality. | Self-actualization (Psychology) | Energy medicine. | Quantum theory. | Consciousness. | Geometry—Religious aspects. | Religion and science. | BISAC: BODY, MIND & SPIRIT / General. | BODY, MIND & SPIRIT / Healing / Energy. | BODY, MIND & SPIRIT / Inspiration & Personal Growth.
  Classification: LCC: BL624 .D43 2024 | DDC: 204—dc23

Printed in the United States of America

Dedicated to my children,
Kate and Bill.

May you find your Spiritual Journey
in your own time in your own way.
I love you deeply.
I will always BE with you.

TABLE OF CONTENTS

ILLUSTRATIONS

FIGURES

TABLES

AUTHOR'S NOTE

Throughout this book, I refer to specific experiences with clients and friends to show the validity and authenticity of the healing practices, energy work, and Divine revelations contained in these pages. The events shared are my truthful and best recollection. Without exception, the real names and personal details of these individuals have been changed to protect their identities. I have also taken great care to ensure that everyone has given consent to have their healing stories and fictionalized information included in this book.

I have used capitalization throughout the book to draw attention to the significance of the myriad ways the Divine is part of our life experience. Words like Consciousness, Source, Soul, Self, and the Universe are also capitalized because I believe they all represent aspects of the Divine. BEing is used to represent our Soul aspect from the perspective of a Divine state of being.

The use of the information in this book is only to help you on your Spiritual Journey. I don't claim that this will help everyone, even though it has helped me and others. Please follow your own guidance system in engaging with the content of this book.

Preface

From a spiritual perspective, we have at least eight types of missions in our physical life. The first mission is to understand that life is a Spiritual Journey to discover who we really are and why we are here on Earth. The second mission is to meet specific challenges and learn, grow, and evolve to be our True Selves, or Souls, in the physical realm. Facing challenges helps us become the best versions of ourselves and learn how to live our best lives. A third mission is to accomplish the specific purpose that our Soul intended to help us evolve and make an impact on the world. Our fourth mission is to learn about Divine Love—to understand Divine Love, experience Divine Love, extend Divine Love, and become Divine Love.

The fifth mission is to become a beacon of Light and understanding. We are invited to radiate our Divine Light to help others learn, grow, and evolve. Our Light helps illuminate our own path and the path for others. We can use our light to extend loving kindness, compassion, and benevolence on our journeys. The sixth mission is to help others awaken to their Spiritual Journey. The seventh mission is to live from our Soul, our True Selves, own our Divine Magnificence, and BE our Divine Magnificence.

Lastly, the eighth mission is to come together in peace and join as ONE humanity to raise the vibrational frequency of the Universe together to make the world a better place for all. All these missions are equal opportunities for our life on Earth.

At first, this list may seem overwhelming. But as you progress on the journey to your True Self, you will see how each new mission is a natural unfolding that builds on the growth and understanding developed to that point. Each unfolding brings new ideas, concepts, and perspectives that help us accomplish these missions, or at least some of them, almost concurrently without any effort. You will discover secrets you never knew before. You may make one shift or understand a deeper meaning of one aspect that helps you move forward on several missions simultaneously.

Nonetheless, these missions are easier to navigate if you know the bigger picture of your life. That is why I wrote this book. I wish I had known about the bigger picture of the Universe and my place within it long before I was catapulted into a new reality. While I am forever grateful for all of the life lessons that came from being tossed in head-first to navigate a new paradigm for living, I hope that sharing what I have learned from experience, research, and lots of Soul-searching will make your journey easier by knowing the breadth and depth of what to expect on the road ahead.

Until my life was turned upside down through grief and loss, I wasn't seeking a Spiritual Awakening. I was doing all the right things to live a Spiritual Life—actively engaging in a church community, praying, reading scriptures, and being in spiritual direction groups. I didn't know there was more. But the unexpected and tragic death of my significant other, Michael Angelo Ludas, in 2008 thrust me into asking hard questions about why such things happen and *why are we here* that can only be answered through a Spiritual Journey.

As Mike prepared for the next stage of his journey, he continued to be his caring, fun-loving, and curious self. Although I knew Mike's death was imminent, I wasn't prepared for the profound feeling of loss and the way my life spiraled into a whole new reality when it happened. I didn't go to work that day and stayed close to Mike's bed. When his breathing changed that afternoon, I alerted his three children and three siblings to be with him in his last moments. We all held hands around his bed and told him how much we loved him. This loss would leave a gaping hole in all our lives. It was a loving and compassionate send-off for a truly and deeply wonderful man.

Seeing Mike finally free of metastasized colon cancer, I felt overwhelming relief knowing his suffering was finally over, along with bouts of desolate grief, not knowing how I could continue without his love and joy surrounding me in the physical realm. Although he shared love and joy with everyone, he shared his life with me from deep in his heart in a rare and beautiful way.

Mike had a fierce curiosity and was quick to ask hard and insightful questions—questions without obvious answers. He was extraordinary in his thinking and believed in more than just the physical earthly experience. He was on a Spiritual Journey, even if he didn't express it that way. I know that now. A couple of weeks before he transitioned, Mike shared that he was excited about the next phase of his life—meaning his death. I remember him saying, "I am sorry you can't go with me. I am going to get all the answers to my questions. I know it has something to do with the String Theory."

I now understand this was an invitation for me to explore quantum physics.

Losing Mike to colon cancer was my initiation into transformation through aligning with the Divine and the Spiritual Realm—my first quantum breakthrough. Among the many things I have learned since then is that colon cancer indicates an energetic imbalance in the large intestine meridian. This meridian feeds the large intestine or colon and carries the energy of *letting go*. Mike couldn't let go of certain situations in his life, which likely contributed to his developing colon cancer. Emotional states are connected to our disease states.

A few days after Mike died, I woke up *knowing* there was a healing modality that could have saved Mike's life. I cannot explain this *knowing*. I certainly didn't have it when we were putting all our faith in the medical community. My curiosity about this claircognizance set me on a life path of discovery to find that healing modality. I was reading Wayne Dyer's *Power of Intention* at the time and set an intention to discover how to be optimally healthy. Sometime later, I started hearing about energy healing, Healing Touch, and Energy Medicine over the course of a few days.

I didn't know anything about energy healing. So, I searched the internet for answers and clarification. I found *The Energy Medicine Kit* for $20 and ordered it. The kit came with a CD, DVD, guidebook, flashcards with exercises, and a small, clear glass, faceted crystal on a red thread. As a PhD studying viruses, my immediate reaction and misperception was this wasn't for me since it couldn't possibly be scientific and most certainly couldn't have the answers I wanted.

As I was separating the package contents for recycling, I noticed a flyer announcing that Donna Eden, the pioneer of Energy Medicine, would be teaching in Australia, Norway, and Wales over the next six months. I was incredulous at this widespread interest in Energy Medicine. Reading further, I saw that Donna Eden was doing an Omega Institute workshop the following weekend near where I lived. My whole body shook.

In that moment, I was stunned that my body shook. My body was clearly encouraging me to attend the workshop. But I was confused because scientists don't believe the human body talks to us. But how else could I explain what just happened *to me*? I had never experienced anything like this. If my body was telling me to go, I definitely wanted to find out WHY.

After several minutes of silence and knowing something miraculous just happened, I was on the phone registering for the event. It was the first of many to follow, illustrating that we are being guided in life—even if we don't consciously realize it. Listening to my body resulted in another quantum breakthrough in my life.

One of the first things that Donna Eden explained at the weekend workshop was that there is an inner wisdom that guides the body to heal itself. There it was! It was exactly what I was looking for: a healing modality that could have saved Mike's life. I was on the edge of my seat the entire weekend. I was learning a whole new perspective on life. I wanted to know more.

Two weeks after that workshop, I was sitting in my first class of the Energy Medicine Certification Program. I was embarking on a miraculous new adventure that would transform me, my life, and my career in the most magnificent way I could ever have imagined. I studied Energy Medicine for four years—another quantum breakthrough. I felt a strong magnetic pull to help people transform their lives through Energy Medicine. I left my science career and opened my new business, **E Quantum Breakthroughs**.

Several years later, I started writing this book, which was another quantum breakthrough on my journey. You might say I am the least likely person to write a book about your True Self and Divine Magnificence. Working as a PhD scientist for decades, trained to be a logical, left-brained critical thinker, I did not accept anything without physical proof or evidence supported by data—statistically significant data! Before Mike passed, I wasn't consciously connected to the Spiritual Realm. The pathway into the higher level of BEing had not opened for me yet. I didn't know the depth and wasn't aware there was so much more.

No journey starts in a vacuum or even in a moment. It's the culmination of all that went before and the start of what's to come. That's especially true for a Spiritual Journey as a lifetime of endings and beginnings along the path to discovering our True Self. From an early age, I had a sense there was more to life than the physical world around me and more than just this one life. I recall times when I felt like I had just woken up and said to myself, "It's me, it's me, it's me." I was remembering a past life and reassuring myself that I was present in this one.

I was also fascinated with words like *eternity* and *forever* as something to be explored. I repeatedly said the words as if saying them would somehow help me understand their meaning. I never told anyone about these experiences because I didn't want anyone to tell me I was wrong. I wanted to hold onto this belief in something more.

I was also fascinated and resonated with the concept of miracles. Decades later, and from a scientific perspective, I remember thinking a miracle is real; we just don't understand scientifically *how* it can be real. I hope you can take this same approach as you read this book. There is a lot about the Spiritual Realm that we still don't understand, but not understanding doesn't mean it isn't true.

After Mike's death, I started living my life as a Spiritual Journey to know the truth of who we are as Divine Creator BEings. This journey is about tuning into the higher vibrational frequencies of our True Selves and discovering our Divine Magnificence and the wisdom of the Universe. From a spiritual perspective, the significance of our time here on Earth has more to do with our Spiritual Journey than success, fame, material goods, or wealth of the physical realm. We are here to align with the Divine and pursue our Divinely guided missions for this life. An important mission for us is to grow and evolve our Souls. The whole Universe grows and evolves with us when we grow and expand.

Why am I writing a book on your True Self and your Divine Magnificence? I call it a Divine Invitation. In the stillness of meditation, I heard the call to go deeper in exploring the Divine than I had dreamed possible. It was a clear message from somewhere, both inside me and from the beyond—*write a book about wisdom*, this book, and others to come. I carefully considered this call to action. Writing a book would be a conscious, deliberate commitment to discover how to align with the Divine and share the wisdom and knowledge I gained to benefit others. But the decision was made, probably long before my conscious awareness, and I am dedicating my life to fulfilling that call.

Given my background in science, it was natural that my book would include researched material to give depth and expanded perspectives. I also share personal stories about how the challenges, roadblocks, and *aha* moments helped me learn, grow, and evolve on my journey of discovering higher levels of living and BEing. As you progress on your own journey, you will have different roadblocks and challenges and grow in different ways. But the destination is the same—to know and become your authentic True Self.

In realizing the truth of who you are, you will begin to understand the truth of the infinite abundance and potential available to you. It is yours to tap into. I invite you to open to new possibilities and opportunities. Say *yes* more often. Understand that you don't know everything. There is a force more powerful and more loving than you could ever imagine. You are more magnificent than you could dream. You even have a built-in guidance system in your double helix DNA molecule—the blueprint of your physical, energetic, and Spiritual Life.

You are meant to accomplish something only you can do. You are celebrated in the Spiritual Realm. Allow the Divine to express as you. It's your free will choice to allow the Divine in you to flourish.

I offer this book as a bridge that you enter from the perspective of the physical realm, encountering new concepts and wisdom spanning science, energy healing, quantum physics, spirituality, sacred geometry, Divine Human Potential, and Consciousness along the way until you reach the other side and cross into the Spiritual Realm.

Each section of the book is intended to enlighten and awaken you to progressively higher levels of thinking and BEing in the world, reveal truths and untruths, and unlock your unlimited potential for love, happiness, and abundance. As a Divine BEing on a journey of discovering your Divine Magnificence, you are loved and supported beyond your wildest imagination.

Embrace the mystery of this magnificent Universe. Be in awe and wonder about your unlimited potential. Trust and surrender to the Universe. The Spiritual World is cheering you on to discover who you really are and what you came here to do.

I am honored to be a guide on your Spiritual Journey. I am excited to begin this journey together.

Live radiantly!

If You Only Knew

If you only knew your true potential and ability.
If you only knew the wisdom within your Soul.
If you only knew the energy flowing in and out to support revitalization.
If you only knew how closely the Divine is to you.

If you only knew the Divine Plan for your life.
If you only knew the mission to evolve your Soul.
If you only knew that people in your life are Soulmates.
But perhaps not just your spouse.

If you only knew the Divine Language of the Universe
Guiding you on the intended journey and goal.
If you only knew stars and planets align for you.
If you only knew and listened to your intuition.

If you only knew and connected to your Higher Self.
The Divine part of you existing in dimensions beyond 3D.
If you only knew the perspective of eternity and eternal life.
If you only knew you come from pure unconditional love.

If you only knew there's only one you for good reason.
If you only knew your Divine Power.
If you only knew the Divine Intelligence permeating all your cells.
If you only knew the radiance flowing to you and from you.

If you only knew you were designed for specific intentions.
If you only knew there is nothing random in our Universe.
If you only knew sacred geometry plays a significant part
In who you are and where you are.

If you only knew you are a treasure, a Divine Gift.

If you only knew your journey is to align deeper with the Divine.

If you only knew you're a channel for grace and love.

If you only knew you're made from celestial molecules.

If you only knew…

what

    would

        you

            do

                differently?

Anne M. Deatly

LIFE IS A SPIRITUAL JOURNEY

Success is Not the Goal

In our 3D world programming,
Life is hard and stressful.
We run the hamster wheel of life
Not really getting anywhere.

We're anxious and overwhelmed
Just like most other people.
We think this is the life we should live.
We focus on the problems.

We are not free but tied to our jobs.
Trying to make it through, pay the bills.
We struggle and force ourselves into what we think is right.
But still not getting anywhere.

We focus on success and increasing our income
More money will bring us freedom.
We are trapped by possessions and paper
We are blocked or stuck in limiting beliefs.

If we open up and see, there's much more
The truth is we are unlimited
Our potential is beyond our understanding.
We just have to believe.

Life is really a self-discovery path to find our True Selves.
The True Self is the Soul or the Divine indwelling Higher Self.
The Self that subtly guides and nudges you.
The Self holding your Inner Wisdom, Divine Power.

Our True Self knows what's our best and highest good.
And who we really are with unlimited potential.
Our True Self knows our Divine Plan and Mission
To make a specific difference in the world unique to us.

Our mission is to evolve our Souls,
To learn from specific challenges and help us grow.
To embrace all situations, events, opportunities,
To exponentially expand in Consciousness.

Expanding Consciousness is a universal benefit.
When we expand, we bring others with us.
We model a new way of BEing and doing.
We send out more positive vibrations.

More positive vibrations come back.
People sense joy, peace, and love from us
And feel at peace with us and now within.
What goes out comes back.

Success is not the goal.

Anne M. Deatly

Life is a Spiritual Journey

We are all Spiritual Beings having a human experience. Deep within our Innate Wisdom, most of us know this. But when our Soul enters the physical form of a human body, we lose our conscious connection to this inner aspect of our BEing. As a result, we forget our original mission for this life, the Divine Mission we so carefully chose to accomplish in this lifetime. One explanation for this profound forgetting is free will, which allows us to choose how we experience our human life as we are living life. According to Dr. Michael Newton in his book *Journey of Souls: Case Studies of Lives Between Lives*, free will is how we choose our specific life path and the challenges we need to learn and grow.[1]

Unfortunately, in this free will experience, we tend to get caught up in the physical details of our lives that mostly distract us from our original Divine Mission. One could say that we are two beings: a spiritual BEing and a physical being. Most of us are primarily concerned with our physical being because we haven't yet come to the part of our life journey that has called us to connect with our Spiritual BEing. Reading this book suggests you are ready to make that connection or already have and are ready for a deeper dive to explore this other part of you. If we truly understood our spiritual aspects and the higher purpose of our existence, I believe we would naturally be drawn to intentionally living from the Soul, not just the physical body, the ego. As a result, people would identify more with their Spiritual Selves and less with their physical selves.

Living life as a Spiritual Journey changes things. Along the way, we may discover a treasure of secrets about ourselves and the world around us that can profoundly affect our sense of purpose, meaning, and happiness. As these secrets are revealed, we can pause to examine, explore, ask, listen, meditate, journal, dive in, and see how their wisdom can transform our lives at every level as we are ready to accept them.

I am deeply grateful for this opportunity to serve as a guide and fellow journeyer, helping you uncover the treasure of secrets within you and provide insights for connecting you to the wisdom of the Universe.

> When I accepted that my life is a Spiritual Journey, everything changed. I had lived my life for more than 50 years without conscious awareness of a connection to my Soul or Divine Mission. Then, I was guided to learn about Consciousness

and the truth about who I really am. I now know why I am here and am putting together why I've had specific challenges and obstacles to overcome. It all adds up. There is a reason for it all. It became clear that my greatest challenges most likely reflect my life mission or how my Soul wants to evolve.

I suppose I always had an inkling that there was more to life than growing up, getting married, raising children, having a job to earn money, and then retiring. I used to ask myself, is this all there is? Am I just existing for the paycheck to pay my bills?

Don't misunderstand me here. I had a great childhood and a fun family. I had a great career, and I raised two wonderful children who have both been great teachers for me. But I knew something was missing in my life. I knew there was something that I didn't understand about my life and my purpose.

Deep down, I knew there was something wonderful that I hadn't learned yet. As I reflect, it must have been my Soul raising these questions for me to ponder. The beautiful thing is that I have always believed in miracles.

Some fundamental questions about life are: *Where are we all going? Are we moving toward an objective in life, a real destination, like heaven, or is the journey the most important part of our life?* To me, life is a journey of self-discovery. The path is found within. We aren't going to end up in a physical destination like going on a vacation. No milestones or journey markers indicate that we are on the right path to our destination. Instead, it is a path that reveals who we really are and the incredible potential we have as humans. It can lead us to experience different vibrational frequencies and higher levels of Consciousness when we are ready. It can make us wiser and more in tune with the flow of the Universe.

When we reach that part of the journey where we become curious about our life journey and begin to understand that we are Spiritual BEings having a human experience, it's possible to connect with our Divine Mission—our reason for BEing. No checklists confirm that we are accomplishing our Divine Mission. It is not an engineering project or a mathematical equation to solve. It is a process of growth opportunities through challenges. All of what happens to us is really *for* us.

But before we can even conceive of our Soul and Divine Mission, we must fully embrace and realize that we are more than our physical form. I suggest that our Soul is actually our natural state of BEing as an energy body that, on some levels, is more important to our happiness and health than our physical form. Understanding that our Spiritual Self is an energy body invites us to understand how our energy body functions and how it exists in the Universe.

Everything is Energy

Everything communicates and manifests through invisible energy fields that regulate the Universe. We are energy beings and live in an energy Universe. A sea of energy surrounds us and is us. But what do we know about energy?

Emerging scientific studies are finding compelling evidence that everything in the Universe is energy. The study of quantum physics is based on this concept. However, from a scientific and cultural perspective, we have been taught to focus on the physical world of what can be known through physical and sensory perception. In other words, only the physical aspect of the world matters. Yet, according to quantum physics, there is a physical and non-physical world working in tandem. We live and function within both worlds as aspects of our shared reality—mostly without realizing it.

Most of us have been taught Newtonian Physics, which views reality as limited to only what can be observed by our physical senses—what we can see, hear, smell, taste, and touch. This way of thinking significantly limits us and holds us back from the true and full potential of our existence within the Universe.

Our ability to see, hear, feel, sense, and taste energy is rarely examined in scientific laboratories. Yet, I firmly believe we connect and communicate energetically through intuition beyond sensory perception.

> Until 2010, I was a skeptic who believed the world is limited to what our five senses detect, living from my intellect. I thought the most important thing was to study and learn intellectually in order to grow. Now, I think very differently. Today, I believe that living an extraordinary life is the result of living from our

heart and our Soul. Living an extraordinary life comes from learning experientially, which gives us wisdom. If we open up and connect to our Souls, we will be guided to our Divine Purpose. We will be shown our magnificence and who we really are at our core.

In school, we were mostly taught to think of energy as the ability of an unseen force to make things work. When a force is applied to the object, it moves; when we exert energy, we move. In this view, there are two main types of energy: potential and kinetic. Potential energy is the energy of position. It has the ability to move, but it is not actively moving, having only the potential to do work. Kinetic energy is the energy of movement. Kinetic energy is potential energy that has been released and moved. A subset of kinetic energy is vibrational energy, along with rotational and translational energy. We will focus on vibrational energy here.

This non-physical aspect of our world is even more powerful than the physical world. It holds amazing potential for all of us. One way of understanding the non-physical world is that it functions as a Life Force existing within us, through us, and around us. It is the most significant aspect of our lives and our BEingness. Yet many of us dismiss the possibility of an unseen Life Force Energy, even though we are quite happy using microwave ovens, cell phones, computers, and radios, which all use unseen energy available to us in the Universe.

Before we explore the nature of Life Force Energy, let's look at how we commonly experience unseen energetic forces in our lives. If we can accept the existence of these invisible forces, perhaps it is easier to open up to the possibility of other types of unseen energy at work in our lives. Here are some examples of unseen energies we take for granted in our everyday lives.

Dogs can hear at a higher frequency than humans. The higher-frequency sound exists even though our human ears can't hear it.

Different radio stations exist at different frequencies; we just need to tune into the right frequency to get our favorite radio station. However, all stations are available all the time.

Modern technology uses Wi-Fi for wireless communication that directs a specific energy frequency associated with our cell phone number so no other phone will receive the call.

Light energy or solar energy from the sun can burn our skin even though we cannot perceive the radiation particles interacting with our skin that cause it to burn.

We flip a light switch, and a light turns on. We see the light bulb illuminate but not the electrical energy that causes the illumination.

We can feel emotions like love, anger, grief, or fear. Even though these energies are emotional, we feel them in our physical bodies. We can also sense these emotions in the space around us, even if we haven't witnessed an event causing these energy reactions. We even know what emotion we are experiencing based on how it feels in our body. For example, love feels very different from fear or anger because they have different energy frequencies.

When we get an X-ray, there is no physical sensation of X-ray energy flowing through our body, but we see the results of the X-ray energy in our body when the image is produced.

With all these examples of energy functioning in ways we are familiar with—sound waves, wireless communication, solar energy, electrical energy, emotions—it stands to reason that just because we can't see other types of energy doesn't mean they don't exist.

The fact is, we exist in a sea of energy. All space contains energy. Our whole Universe is energy. There is no place in the Universe where energy is absent. Energy may actually be the Unified Field Theory of Everything that Einstein was studying when he died. Physicists are working to prove that the invisible energy in our Universe is the Unified Field Theory of Everything. As the renowned scientist Nikola Tesla observed, the secrets of the Universe reside in understanding energy, frequency, and vibration. [2]

As energy, everything in the Universe vibrates at one frequency or another. Nothing is at rest. This perpetual state of vibration is the Universal Law of Energy and Vibration. What looks like open space is filled with Life Force Energy we cannot see. Everything vibrates—but at different rates or frequencies of vibration.

As energy beings, we vibrate at a specific frequency based primarily on our mental and emotional state. Although our physical body is denser, more compressed energy than our energy fields, our overall vibrational frequency has most to do with our thoughts, feelings, and beliefs. We will look at this in more detail, but, essentially, thoughts and feelings related to more negative states of mind like fear, anger, panic, grief, and worry have a lower vibrational frequency that can also be experienced in our physical body as pain, tightness, or soreness. In contrast, more positive mental states like love, peace, and joy have a higher-vibrational frequency that makes us vibrant, and our experience of life flows more easily and effortlessly. Our life has a positivity that attracts more positivity.

The Science of Energy as Formless and Form

To better understand how energy works on a scientific level, let's turn to a brief introduction to quantum physics and the beginning of our Universe. According to present-day physicists, a period of inflation occurred 13.8 billion years ago. During that time, a subatomic particle, perhaps an electron, heated up to a very high temperature and expanded quickly. This subatomic particle and Universal Consciousness were likely expanding together as one. Or perhaps Consciousness already existed. Likely, there was no Big Bang or explosion. There was only a cosmic soup of energy expanding. Nothing physical as we know it today existed at the moment of conception of the Universe. Most likely, only energy existed.

Everything physical we know and see today came from that original cosmic energy soup. Everything physical in the Universe came from *no-thing*. Everything comes from the invisible world of energy.

But what about the subatomic particle? Isn't that a physical form—matter, not energy? According to the String Theory, Superstring, or M Theory, the foundational basis of everything in the Universe is a string of energy. These strings have different vibrational frequencies that become different subatomic particles and potentially exist as physical particles. In other words, formless energy becomes matter.

This concept of energy and matter being interchangeable is expressed in Albert Einstein's famous scientific formula, $E=mc^2$, where E = energy, m = mass or matter, and c^2 is a constant of light. Basically, this formula means that energy equals mass or matter, and mass or matter equals energy. Energy and matter are the same. Therefore, energy is all there is in the Universe. A subatomic particle, such as an electron, can exist as either energy or matter as it changes from one vibrational state to another—from a wave of energy to a particle and back to an energy wave. One becomes the other.

This concept of wave-particle duality is the foundation of quantum physics. One of the most famous experiments in quantum physics proving wave-particle duality is the double-slit experiment conducted by Thomas Young in 1801. Young's experiment directed a light beam through two openings or slits onto a flat screen behind the slits to determine whether light was matter or energy. The premise was that if the light is a particle, it will go through only one of the slits and land in one place on the surface behind it. However, if the light acts as a wave, it will go through both slits simultaneously and interfere with or enhance each other, causing a repeated pattern of dark and light on the screen. In Young's original experiment, the light beams produced a repeating pattern of light and dark, confirming that light is a wave. The interference pattern of light and dark proved the light was going through both slits simultaneously, which is only possible if light was a wave.[3]

A century later, in 1905, Einstein showed that light is made of particles with his famous photoelectric effect experiment. When Einstein directed a beam of light at a metal surface, the photons or particles of light affected the atoms of the metal when the light was at a specific frequency, like ultraviolet light. Incandescent light did not show the same effect. The photon's frequency was sufficient to extract an electron from the metal. The collision with the metal produced a photoelectric effect—a phenomenon in which charged particles are released from a material when electromagnetic radiation is absorbed. Einstein received a Nobel Prize in 1921 for this work since it solved the burning question about the wave-particle duality of light. The photoelectric effect represents an interaction of light and matter not explained by classical physics, which described light only as an electromagnetic wave. In this experiment, Einstein proved that a beam of light was a collection of discrete energy packets or photons.[4]

In 1924, Louis de Broglie, a French scientist, proposed in his doctoral thesis—the de Broglie hypothesis—that all matter has wave-particle duality. This idea that an electron has wave-particle duality was confirmed in 1927 by Clinton Davisson and Lester Germer in the United States and George Thomson in Scotland.[5] In these experiments, a double-slit experiment was performed with electrons to understand further how this wave-particle duality relates to matter. Just like light, electrons proved to exist as particles and waves and behaved in the same manner as light.

So, when is the electron a particle or a wave? Surprisingly, further experiments in this wave-particle duality showed that it is dependent on the observer. In other words, the behavior of these subatomic particles depends on the interaction of the person observing the experiment. In 1998, a research team at the Weizmann Institute of Science in Rehovot, Israel, published a paper in *Nature* about this *observer effect*.[6] The published results were fascinating—the more the subatomic particles were observed, the greater the effect on the experimental results. The conclusion was that observers affect the observed reality. When the subatomic particles act like waves, they can pass through both slits and meet on the other side in an interference pattern. They discovered that interference only occurs if the experiment occurred in the absence of observation. When an observer begins to watch the particles going through the openings or slits, the results change significantly—the electrons are forced to go through the openings as particles, not waves. Therefore, observation produces the particle aspect of the subatomic particle.

Further, the experiment showed that results also varied depending on the amount of observation. When the observer's capacity increased, the interference pattern weakened. When the capacity to detect electrons was reduced, the observer effect decreased, and the interference pattern increased. Even a passive observation of quantum phenomena, including changes to the equipment monitoring settings, changed the result of the pattern projection.

All these studies are important in contributing to the growing body of science confirming that everything is energy. Further analysis in quantum physics and quantum mechanics explains that electrons exist in an area of likely locations according to their wave functions. In other words, all possibilities exist at the same time. When the electrons are observed, their wave function collapses, revealing the real location of the electrons. The electrons return to the haze or sphere of probabilities after the observation. The state of the system changes when observed.

What does all this tell us, and what does it say about our relationship with energy?

It tells us that we, as observers, are integral to the reality we perceive. Our mere presence as an observer likely affects what is happening in and around us. In other words, we are creating our reality. We can affect the collapse of the wave aspect to bring something into form. This phenomenon, called the *observer effect*, suggests how a conscious mind can directly affect reality. Understanding this concept will also help us to understand how we create or manifest the events of our lives. Physicist John Wheeler from Princeton University referred to the Universe as a Participatory Universe.[7] Others are now calling it a human Universe.[8] In other words, the Universe is at least co-created by the Consciousness of humans.

This realization is the underlying principle of quantum physics. Non-scientists and physicists continue to be surprised that light and subatomic particles exist in both wave and particle form and that an observer can affect the results of experiments. If we are mindful that knowledge and understanding of these scientific experiments are ever-changing and expanding, we can be open to what is generally accepted and remain curious about what is yet to be discovered.

If we can truly be open, these concepts can empower us. We can benefit from being the co-creators of what we want rather than the victims of what is happening to us. We will have to experiment with events in our lives to see if these concepts work for us. We can use these concepts to direct our observation through prayer, visualization techniques, or setting intentions to experiment and determine if we can consciously create what we want rather than what we don't want. We will cover how to consciously create what you want in later sections.

Universal Laws

In addition to these scientific studies, there are also broader natural laws that govern the Universe. These laws represent the overlap of spiritual laws with scientific laws and operate whether we realize it or not. These parameters and conditions allow structure and give order to the Universe. Everything that happens will always happen in accordance with these laws. Therefore, we benefit tremendously from understanding these laws and how the Universe operates.

Our understanding of these laws can be traced back 5,000 years ago to the Hermetic Teachings of Hermes, an Olympian deity in ancient Greek mythology, also known as the Soul guide. Even though the birth of the mystic teaching dates back five millennia, all nations have borrowed from these teachings. For thousands of years, these teachings have strongly influenced different philosophies worldwide and represent the cumulative understanding and use of ancient civilizations, including Greek, Roman, Chinese, Indian, Chaldean, Medean, Japanese, Assyrian, Persian, and Egyptian.[9]

The Kybalion

The Kybalion is a book that conveys the teachings of Hermes Trismegistus through three initiates of his teaching. In it, three initiates point to seven principles upon which the entire Hermetic Philosophy is based.[10] A brief explanation of these principles is helpful to give a greater perspective on this broader concept of energy at the universal level.

> *The Principles of Truth are Seven; he who knows these, understandingly, possess the Magic Key before whose touch all the Doors of the Temple will fly open.*[11]

The Principle of Mentalism

The ALL is MIND: The Universe is Mental.[12]

Spirit is all aspects of physical matter, the phenomena of life, and energy. The ALL is Spirit, which is beyond our knowing and ability to define. The ALL, as Spirit, is a universal, infinite, living mind. Our world or Universe is a mental creation of the ALL. Your mind is One with the Universal Mind. Your mind projects your Consciousness, and you manifest from your mind. According to the Kybalion, with these teachings as the Master Key, the student can unlock the mental and psychic temple of knowledge.[13]

Relatively more recent science has confirmed the one-mind concept. Erwin Schrodinger, an Austrian physicist and Nobel Prize winner who studied quantum physics, said, " In truth, there is only one mind."[14]

The Principle of Correspondence

As above, so below, as below, so above.[15]

All physical, mental, and Spiritual planes of existence correspond to each other. What we learn on one plane can be applied to another plane. There is harmony, agreement, and correspondence because ALL is Mind; nothing is separate from the other. The invisible and physical are inextricably connected.

The Principle of Vibration

Nothing rests; everything moves; everything vibrates. [16]

This principle of energy and vibration explains the differences between matter, energy, mind, and Spirit in terms of rates of vibrations. Everything is in varying degrees of vibration, from the ALL to the smallest aspect of matter. The highest vibration represents the highest level. Spirit's vibration is at such an infinite rate of magnitude, force, and velocity that it is practically motionless. At the other end of the scale, the vibrations of other forms of matter have such low-vibrational frequencies that they, too, appear motionless. However, there is a continuum of vibrational frequencies between these opposites where there is detectable movement. [17]

The Principle of Polarity

Everything is Dual; everything has poles: everything has its pair of opposites; like and unlike are the same; opposites are identical in nature, but different in degree; extremes meet; all truths are but half-truths; all paradoxes may be reconciled.[18]

The Principle of Rhythm

Everything flows, out and in; everything has its tides; all things rise and fall; the pendulum-swing manifests in everything; the measure of the swing to the right is the measure of the swing to the left; rhythm compensates.[19]

The Principle of Cause and Effect

Every Cause has its Effect; every Effect has its Cause; everything happens according to Law; Chance is but a name for Law not recognized; there are many planes of causation, but nothing escapes the Law.[20]

Nothing happens by chance. Once understood, we can create what we want, rather than what we don't want.

The Principle of Gender

Gender is in everything; everything has its Masculine and Feminine Principles; Gender manifests on all planes.[21]

Since these Hermetic Principles have been tested and used for several millennia, they are now accepted as Universal Laws. However, they are only understood individually to the degree one is ready to receive them. There are other well-known and accepted Universal Laws that I will discuss as the need unfolds. The first is the Universal Law of Perpetual Transmutation of Energy.

The Universal Law of Perpetual Transmutation of Energy

We have already briefly looked at the Principle of Vibration. We now refer to this law as the Universal Law of Energy and Vibration or the Universal Law of Vibration. Another Universal Law related to energy is the Universal Law of Perpetual Transmutation of Energy. This law is based on the premise that everything is energy, and energy is always moving. Everything physical comes from invisible energy. Energy is always moving to become physical. Energy becomes manifest. Mike Dooley, the author of *Playing the Matrix, Beginners Guide to the Universe,* and *Notes from the Universe,* says, "Thoughts become things."[22]

In his book, *As a Man Thinketh,* James Allen expresses that we become what we think about.

> *Mind is the Master power that molds and makes,*
> *And Man is Mind, and evermore he takes*
> *The tool of Thought and shaping what he wills,*
> *Brings forth a thousand joys, a thousand ills,*
> *He thinks in secret, and it comes to pass:*
> *Environment is but a looking glass.* [23]

So how does something formless, like our thoughts, become form?

Another way to think about how energy moves from invisible formless to visible form is to think about the cycles of nature. When leaves grow on the branches of trees, they go from formless to form. When they fall from the branches, they degrade and become part of the Earth, changing from form to formless. In the winter, snowflakes form and then return to formless when they melt. A cloud is transmuted to rain, snow, or sleet. The concept that one becomes the other is evident.

As Mike Dooley and James Allen expressed above, humans also change energy from formless to form as it moves through us, and our thoughts change from an idea to a manifest form. Any idea or vision held in the mind is always moving into the physical. The body moves into action, which produces manifestation as part of our creative process. So, be careful of your thoughts; they manifest!

Surprisingly, this can happen despite the vast differences in space because everything in the Universe is linked together.[24] Another term for this is nonlocality. "Nonlocality exists, not because of extremely fast messaging back and forth at the subatomic level, but because separation does not exist."[25]

Every word and every thought has power and will manifest. However, the lapse of time between when we create something with our thoughts and the manifestation of that creation in our lives makes it difficult to see the correlation between our thoughts and creations. So, it helps to have an open mind that can see past the need for immediate proof of our creative power and make the connections as they arise.

Our life is a projection of our thoughts. We participate in the creation of what happens in our lives. What we think about expands and is created into form.

The Universe is Consciousness

Consciousness is probably one of the hardest terms to define. There are lots of ideas about Consciousness. The idea that the Universe is Consciousness is accepted but not well understood through science. I think of Consciousness as Universal Energy, the Divine Mind, the Intelligent Mind, the ALL, and the Creative Mind.

It is interesting to consider that all the material we can see is just a small fraction of the Universe. The rest is invisible and mysterious.[26] As Albert Einstein espoused, any committed scientist will become a believer in an evolved and higher-functioning Spirit through the pursuit of scientific answers according to Universal Laws.[27]

In his book *The Living Universe: Where Are We? Who Are We? Where Are We Going?* author Duane Elgin states that the Universe is a living system because it is unified, energy flows throughout it, it is continuously being regenerated, there is sentience or Consciousness throughout, freedom is its foundation, and it can reproduce itself.[28] In other words, the Universe is both energy and Consciousness. Elgin explains Consciousness as sentient. Elgin points out that the word Consciousness comes from the word "con-scire," which means "that with which we know."[29] Clairsentience is the ability to perceive and know beyond knowledge and the five senses. In other words, Consciousness has the ability to perceive and feel beyond the physical. There is sentience in all levels of the Universe, including atoms, molecules, single-celled organisms, plants, and animals.

According to Elgin, sentience is a foundational characteristic of the Universe. When we take into account humans, there is the "most direct evidence that consciousness is not confined within the brain; it is, instead, a field property of the universe itself."[30] Sentience is an awareness that doesn't come from the intellect or perception; it is a feeling of awareness. A living Universe is one unified field. A living Universe is a completely interdependent system that is perpetually revitalized and re-energized by Life Force Energy, which is Consciousness. This Consciousness has a mental capacity with a self-reflective ability. Systems at all levels of existence have the capability of freedom of choice or free will. [31]

For another point of view, Elgin turns to physicist Freeman Dyson, who believes that matter from the quantum level perspective is active, not lifeless, or inert. Intrinsic, natural, and fundamental in every electron is the ability to make choices to discern the best of alternative possibilities.[32] All matter is Consciousness.

Max Planck, the developer of quantum theory, regarded Consciousness as fundamental and matter as a derivative of Consciousness. We have difficulty understanding Consciousness, but everything that exists is inherently Consciousness. In 1931, Max Planck said, "I regard consciousness as fundamental. I regard matter as derivative of consciousness. We cannot get behind consciousness. Everything that we talk about, everything we regard as existing, postulates consciousness."[33]

In a 1944 lecture, Planck remarked further that in his research on atoms, he discovered that all matter begins from and exists only through a Life Force vibration. This Life Force vibration activates the subatomic particles of an atom to vibrate. Intrinsic in this Life Force is the capacity to integrate and unify all aspects of the atom to function like a minute solar system. Max Planck proposes this Life Force represents "the existence of a conscious and intelligent Mind. This Mind is the matrix of all matter." [34]

In the book *What is Consciousness? Three Sages Look Behind the Veil*, Ervin Laszlo, Jean Houston, and Larry Dossey add their wisdom to the concept of Consciousness. Jean Houston says, "Consciousness is the quantum field of the cosmos: the basic reality of the world."[35] Larry Dossey adds Consciousness is "eternal, infinite, and one."[36]

Beyond our individual Consciousness, there is an extensive Consciousness that unites all Consciousness, all minds, and all individuals into a shared existence.[37] Ervin Laszlo contributes that his Consciousness is the same as the Consciousness of all living beings. Furthermore, his Consciousness, though local to him, is a nonlocal manifestation or expression of a mind beyond space and time. Laszlo also realizes that his Consciousness is an intrinsic and infinite part of this nonlocal mind.[38]

The Universe as Consciousness relates to the immutable Universal Law of Correspondence that holds there is harmony, agreement, and correspondence between the physical, mental, and Spiritual planes. There is literally no separation in the Universal Field because everything is mind. The only difference is the rate of vibration. The same pattern is expressed in all the planes from the visible physical plane, from the smallest subatomic particle to the largest planet, and the invisible Spiritual realm. This Universal Law allows us to understand creativity from the Universal Mind perspective to comprehend how we create our reality. We can understand the results in our external physical lives by understanding our internal lives. Similarly, our inner world can be revealed to us by looking at what is happening externally in our lives.

Here are some analogies to help explain this concept.

Similar to a computer, Consciousness responds to what we put into it—ideas, analogies, thoughts, feelings, and beliefs in the moment. Consciousness also responds to our past conditioning, programming, experiences, and how we were raised. Consciousness takes these data and produces an output, which results in, or creates, our awareness and experiences through the lens of our BEing. Input = Output.

Consciousness is *like* a mind and has been referred to as the Intelligent Mind, Nature's Mind, and Divine Mind. Neurologists and neuroscientists don't yet understand how our minds, or brains, think. Likewise, physicists and scientists studying Consciousness do not yet know how our minds interact with Consciousness. However, I predict that scientists will eventually discover a direct connection between our minds and Consciousness and that the Divine Mind, or Consciousness, may even regulate and enhance our minds.

The paradox is our perception that our brains and our minds are the same. But they are not the same. Our brains are made of brain tissue and nerve cells located in the skull. Our brains are separate and individual.

In contrast, the mind is a mental aspect that does not have physicality and likely operates in our energy fields. I include the conscious, subconscious, and superconscious minds to all be in our energy fields. Our mind is part of our Consciousness, but our Consciousness transcends our minds. What if the mind experiences life and the brain interprets those experiences through images or understanding, making your body an expression of the experience of your mind? Consciousness has many layers of awareness extending into the deep layers of wisdom held within us. Most of us are unaware of this deep wisdom within our energy fields or are not connected to it.

Another way to interpret the concept of our minds connecting to Consciousness is that electrons or subatomic particles vibrate within and around us. I believe there's no separation between the vibrations of these particles within us and around us. Scientists are already starting to find the connections between the human mind and Universal Consciousness. The work of Vitaly Vanchurin proposes that the Universe is a huge neural network that regulates and connects everything around us.[39] His model includes String Theory as strings of energy passing from one neuron to another and connecting them in a network. According to Vanchurin, neurons in the Universal Consciousness connect to the neurons in our brains through these strings of energy. This concept would explain why I think we're all connected to Universal Consciousness and, through that, connected to each other. Our minds exist united in Consciousness, the Oneness.

To think and communicate, neurons release neurotransmitters that generate electrical impulses in our physical bodies. These electrical impulses are like waves and propagate the impulse to thousands of other neurons. This propagation cascade leads to a thought. Thoughts are generated when neurons experience electrical impulses. Therefore, energy affects the physical aspects of the brain. However, the effect may not be limited to the physical brain. The energy of Consciousness must interact with our brains or nervous system to produce thoughts in our minds. Those thoughts create our lives. In *The Science of Getting Rich*, author Wallace Wattles explains Consciousness as a thinking substance.[40] The energy of Universal Consciousness interacts with our minds and creates what we think about. Therefore, our thoughts, feelings, and beliefs create what is happening in our lives because of the Universal Law of Cause and Effect.

Consciousness is eternal. We are Spiritual BEings having a human experience. Every living person and creature in the Universe is Consciousness. Our spiritual aspect uses a physical form to interact and communicate. Our spiritual aspect is our energy body or non-physical body and transmits energy to communicate.

Consciousness is our Life Force Energy. Different names for this Life Force Energy include chi, prana, and ki. Similar to the scientific meaning of energy, which measures vibrational frequency, Life Force Energy is also detectable as a vibrational frequency. But it is understood and experienced as sensations rather than through scientific measurements. Our Life Force Energy exists in multiple dimensions simultaneously and has existed in multiple incarnated lives.[41]

Likewise, our Consciousness exists beyond the death of our physical bodies evolving over time and requiring different life experiences to achieve higher states of awareness.

Consciousness can also be viewed as thoughts, feelings, and beliefs we send out that interact with Universal Consciousness and attract matching energy and experiences. In this way, Consciousness acts like a mirror reflecting results that resonate with what we transmit to the Universe.

When I started putting together various concepts of spirituality and Consciousness, it became clear to me that Consciousness is Divine Energy. I was taught that God is always everywhere, as is Consciousness. There is no space in the Universe where energy, Consciousness, or the Divine is absent. Likewise, there is no space in the Universe where any one of us is absent. There is no place in the Spiritual Realm where I stop, and you start. However, we can be disconnected from what is all around us. A good analogy is that Divine Source Energy is like electricity in a house. The electricity is always on, but to illuminate our home, a lamp, for example, must be plugged into the electrical current and switched on to work. We are like the lamp; we must be plugged in and switched on for the light to shine from within us. We have to plug in as conscious and awake BEings to connect with the flow of Divine Source Energy. As stated in the Kybalion, "the lips of wisdom are closed, except to the ears of Understanding."[42] In other words, we must be ready to connect with and understand the gift of illumination.

We are part of Universal Consciousness regardless of whether or not we are plugged in. The evolutionary journey calls us toward connecting to and operating in harmony with this ever-present source of Life Force Energy.

We Are Energy Beings

The Life Force Energy

Life Force Energy or nine energy systems
Each comes in one at a time
In an organized, sequential way
To support the new individual to BE and grow.

Unfertilized eggs exist with an Aura,
Bright colors and loving energy.
The ovum moves along fallopian paths
Hoping for a complementary partner to activate and develop.

The Aura is both biofield and bio-shield.
It attracts people, events, situations, and opportunities,
Matching the vibration of the person,
Filtering out, protecting from unwanted negativity.

All energy systems, specialized aspects of the torus
A golden light with purple edges,
A vortex of energy with a central vertical channel,
Or Taiji pole, the energetic core.

After fertilization, Electrics come in.
At conception, an electric spark activates a beat
Pulsing energy in rhythm with the Earth.
This resonance becomes the heart.

Electrics—the spark of life,
Bridging all energy systems in time.
As the densest energy,
The most electric organ, the heart.

Ten Radiant Circuits come in next.
Yin and Yang Bridges, Yin and Yang Regulators,
Belt Flow, Penetrating Flow, Central, Governing
Spleen and Triple Warmer—all sacred energies.

This Inner Mom system first surrounds a growing blastocyst.
This energy bolts and jolts spreading everywhere.
This energy helps form the body—electricity and life,
Showering healing energy and JOY.

Vibrations and pulses bring new light
Along with joy and euphoria throughout
Creating circuits to connect within and without
Connecting the physical with the invisible.

Hyperlinking to connect, creating harmony, balance, and order,
Unfathomable intelligence seemingly ALIVE.
Ecstasy, enlightenment, elation, exaltation,
Exhilaration, excitement, exultation, jubilation.

Chakra energy is next to evolve.
Disks, vortexes, or wheels spiraling around
Spinning first as a circle, then spiraling
Seven layers of each with specific themes.

Psychological, physiological, and Spiritual
All contained in this system,
Specifically spiraling for each person's needs
Forming connections to this life and past.

Seven major embodied chakras—upper thighs to crown
Plus, eight morphogenetic chakras above and below,
All represent different dimensions of life.
Numbers four to fifteen being our wisest Higher Self.

Memories, events stored safely within
Each layer, every chakra, remembering life phases.
The truth is known in each layer within
Wanting to let go for improved energy flow.

Then fourteen Meridians evolve from RCs*
Forming pathways and grooves—no beginning nor end,
Supplying each organ with energy renewing,
Flowing defined paths each a unique function.

Matching organ's needs both day and night,
So perfectly in tune and alignment throughout.
Weaving optimal health with energy flow
With resulting harmony, peace, and glow.

Triple Warmer meridian responsible for survival
Regulating flight/fight, adrenals, hypothalamus too.
Plus, immune system, together with Spleen,
Also, existing as sacred Radiant Circuit.

Triple Warmer needs calming—any stress, a life threat.
Also keeps our habits, the good and the bad
Allergies, addictions, temperature changes.
And metabolism plus weight loss. too.

Hypervigilance, overwhelm, anxiety, fear
Insomnia, insecurity, and overprotection.
Emotional shock plus PTSD.
Triple Warmer can block us from being free.

The Five Rhythms system of water, wood, fire, earth, and metal,
Matching nature in flow and natural effects,
Formed from the auric bands is the
Rhythm of flow through all energy systems.

Our primary rhythm pulses throughout
A baby vibrating Earth energies around it,
The baby aligns with one rhythm—personality,
Physically guiding walking, talking, and behaving.

The Grid—skeletal structure of an energy body.
All systems fit within its embrace,
Like a car chassis surrounding all,
Chakras connect the Grid to the Aura.

The Grid encompasses emotional, Spiritual, structural,
Comes into the body when enough mass is present.
It is truly foundational and stabilizes all energies
Holding structure until traumas cause damage.

The Celtic weave, a predominant auric structure.
Infinity signs weaving all systems together
Enhancing vitality of the whole energy body,
Attracting like opportunities, events, situations for growth.

Each energy system unique—all work together
To bring vibrancy and resilience to the physical form.
You really can't live without these energy systems.
Why not bless them—tap into their intelligent brilliance?

Anne M. Deatly

* *RC refers to radiant circuits.*

We are energy BEings, just as the Universe is energy. Every atom of our being consists of subatomic particles, strings of energy extending from every cell to each of our organs, forming our energy body, which is organized into different energy systems. We really are more of an energy field than a physical form. So, while it might be easier to identify with our physical being, understanding and identifying with our energy being is a game changer.

Our energy body is the part of us that lasts forever—an eternity. We could call it our Soul, Spirit, True Self, Higher Self, or Divine Self. There is no exact or agreed-upon terminology, so we can choose how we want to honor and respect this magnificent aspect of ourselves. The energy body has a vibrational frequency related to our thoughts, feelings, and beliefs in each moment. We transmit this vibrational frequency into the Universe as ripples in the sea of energy Consciousness, and we receive back the vibrational frequencies from the energy around us. This constant receiving and transmitting of energy connects us to everything in the Universe, making us part of Universal Consciousness, the Divine Mind.

How do we learn about our energy aspect so we can identify with our energy being as easily as we identify with our physical being?

The first step in identifying with our energy BEing is understanding that we have an energy body and knowing its role. I present this introduction to Energy Medicine and balancing the nine energy systems as a foundation for preparing the energy body to connect and receive energy from Universal Consciousness. When we open our energy fields to optimal flow, we naturally open up to the flow of the Universe. Opening up to optimal energy flow massively transformed my life and my ability to understand our existence beyond its physical aspects.

In her book *Energy Medicine: Balancing Your Body's Energies for Optimal Health, Joy, and Vitality,* Donna Eden describes nine energy systems that comprise the human energy body.[43] Table 1 lists these nine energy systems and their respective functions. Although each system has a specific function, they are interconnected and work together. Each system has its own way of flowing through our bodies and its own way of amplifying the energy in our energy body. In general, these energy systems support and regulate our physical, mental, emotional, and energetic well-being.

Our body sends messages of pain, tightness, or soreness to let us know there is an energetic excess, blockage, or disconnection in that location. Medical doctors prescribe medications that may relieve the physical symptoms but do not address the core energy imbalance that is the root cause of these symptoms. Alternatively, energy healing aims to correct the energy flow where it is blocked or disconnected and restore balance that will alleviate the root cause of the pain or suffering. According to Donna Eden, Energy Medicine is the study of balancing and optimizing the flow of energy in each energy system by detecting imbalances and correcting them to enable the body to heal itself and achieve optimal health and potential.[44] Eden shares that our bodies were designed to heal themselves. Tapping into the body's healing force promotes health. Together, the personality, Soul, and physical body want to heal. Every cell has the wisdom and strength within to heal. "Healing is an inside job."[45]

According to Eden, optimizing the energy flow of the nine energy systems helps to balance the body, and then the body can heal itself.[46] Our nine energy systems operate within principles that direct the flow and function of energy. Energies do not want to be stuck; it's important that the energies have space and can move within our energy fields. The nine energy systems flow in different patterns. Someone like Donna, who sees energy, can distinguish which system may have an issue by these patterns. All these nine energy systems are connected and support each other to make one energy body. The state of energy flow in the body reflects in our physical health, well-being, and quality of life, including our Spiritual Life. The good news is that the energies can be modified and repatterned for optimal flow. Energies that have been disconnected can be reconnected.

Ideally, the energy body is open and clear, so fresh energy can fully revitalize it continuously throughout the day. If the energy body is closed or blocked, or our energy systems are disconnected, the energy body cannot be optimally revitalized, resulting in various types of discomfort or dis-ease. Energy body systems can become closed or obstructed in response to a variety of common life experiences, including these:

- Stress and anxiety
- Imbalanced emotional issues, such as fear, anger, panic, worry, or grief
- Negative thoughts or thought patterns
- Misguided paradigms of life: seeing and living from negative beliefs
- Self-limiting beliefs
- Karmic imprints
- Emotional shock or analogical states of mind when time seems to stop
- Irregular energy: abnormal, blocked, or sub-optimal flow of energy in the body
- Doubt or lack of confidence
- Disruptive environmental forces such as cold, wind, heat, damp heat, dampness, or dryness

Table 1: Basic Functions of the Energy Systems in the Energy Body

Energy System	Basic Functions of the Energy Systems in the Energy Body
Aura	The aura is a container for all energy systems of our energy body. It is a multilayered energy system for protection. The more structure the aura has, the stronger it is. The stronger the aura, the healthier we are. The aura has two main functions; to protect us from harmful energies or negativity and to attract what we need/want in life.
Electrics	The electrics energy system, the densest energy system, connects all the energy systems as if an electrical thread were flowing through each system.
Radiant Circuits	The radiant circuits are also called joy generators or psychic channels. They are the energies of exhilaration, euphoria, ecstasy, gratitude. Radiant circuits have divine intelligence and connect energies together through circuits and bridges.
Chakras	The chakras are energies flowing in spirals over specific areas of the body to energize the physical, psychological/emotional, and spiritual aspects related to those areas of the body. Each chakra has a specific theme to support us. Each chakra has seven layers representing different phases of our lives.
Meridians	The meridians govern energy flow to all the organs and systems. The meridians flow in specific pathways and have specific recurring functions.
Triple Warmer	Triple warmer governs the systems of the three burners in traditional Chinese Medicine. Triple warmer is responsible for our survival. It has the capability to conscript energy from other systems except the heart. Triple Warmer is both a meridian and a radiant circuit.
Five Rhythms	The five rhythms govern energy flow to all the organs and systems and hold the emotions in balance. The five rhythms are water, wood, fire, earth, and metal.
Grid	The grid is the energetic "skeletal" structure of the energy body and the foundation of the energy body. All the energy systems fit within the grid.
Celtic Weave	The Celtic weave is an energy system within the aura that helps weave all nine energy systems together in figure 8 patterns.

Table 1 Source Note: Donna Eden with David Feinstein, PhD, *Energy Medicine: Balancing Your Body's Energies for Optimal Health, Joy, and Vitality*, (TarcherPerigee, 2008), 109-241.

The Nine Energy Systems

Donna Eden suggests a toroidal energy field, or torus, surrounds the human body. This torus is not one of the nine energy systems; rather, all nine energy systems come from the torus. The torus connects these energy systems to Divine Energy. One example of how to visualize this energy field is through a simple experiment of putting iron filings on a piece of paper and holding a magnet underneath the paper. As the iron filings begin to interact with the magnetic energy, they vibrate and eventually form the shape of a torus. The fundamental pattern of energy flow in the Universe is the torus. Everything with an electromagnetic field around it, from our cells to galaxies, has an associated torus, including the Earth, all living beings, and our hearts. Probably, the Universe also has a torus or is a torus.[47]

The **Aura** is the outermost energy system in our energy body and is referred to as a space suit. Every unfertilized egg has an aura around it. Once the egg is fertilized, the aura surrounds the new being forming from the egg. From that point forward, the aura acts like a suit of protection around the entire energy body to ensure that unwanted or negative energies do not enter the body's energetic field. The aura also functions as a broadcast signal and receiver, attracting or magnetizing positive energy of what we want or need to learn, grow, and evolve. The other energy systems and the environment all feed the aura. Aura is most intimately associated or connected to the Celtic weave and the electrics systems.[48]

The **Electrics** system is activated immediately upon conception and is a pulsing rhythmic electric beat that resonates with the Earth. This electric beat eventually becomes the heart. The electrics is a separate energy system but part of all the other systems, like an electric thread linking all the energy systems. The electrics are responsible for the pulsing and rhythmic movements of energy throughout the body—down to the cellular level. Electrics specifically feed the meridians and stabilize the interactions and interconnections of all the energy systems.[49]

The **Radiant Circuits** are one of the first energies to support the growth, perhaps as early as the blastocyst stage. The radiant circuits are formed from the pulsing of the electric beat. There are ten radiant circuits, or joy generators, each with a unique role in generating joy in the energy body. There is a mysterious and profound intelligence in these radiant circuits. When activated, they do not have set pathways. Instead, they jump to anywhere within the energy fields that need repair or support to correct an energetic imbalance. They can create circuits to bridge, connect, and activate specific energies in distress or are disconnected. Their main function is to harmonize all the energy systems. Radiant circuits are involved with the energy of emotions, specifically positive ones—from awe to spiritual awareness and Divine Connection. Radiant circuits affect all energies in the body.[50]

The **Chakra** energy system is composed of energies focused on a person's physiology, psychology, and spirituality. Chakra energy spirals around certain centers of the body like ripples in a lake. The chakras sit in the area of the central vertical channel or energetic core as well as in front and behind the physical body. The chakras receive information about the individual from the organs and other energy systems. The chakras also broadcast information to the other energy systems to orchestrate bodily functions, especially hormonal functions. The seven main embodied chakras are root or base, sacral or womb, solar plexus, heart, throat, third eye or brow, and crown.

The main function of the chakra system is to fuel the organs and the endocrine glands situated in their flow pathway. Chakra energy flows in spirals around the central vertical channel, counterclockwise if energy is being released and clockwise if energy is being integrated. Chakras also store the major memories of our lives based on the type of life experiences or themes associated with each chakra.[51]

> The **Root Chakra** holds the energy of survival and connection to our tribe, ancestors, and place in the world. This energy is important for grounding. This chakra is aligned with the base of the spine and sacrum.
>
> The **Sacral or Womb Chakra** holds the energy of creativity, productivity, joy, awe, and wonder. This Chakra is right below the navel.
>
> The **Solar Plexus Chakra** holds the energy of self-esteem, personal power, identity, and ego. This chakra is between the sternum and the navel and spirals over all the organs between the two areas.
>
> The **Heart Chakra** holds the energy of love and connection. This chakra is located over the heart, chest, and lungs.
>
> The **Throat Chakra** holds the energy of integration and expression. This chakra spirals over the throat area. The throat chakra consists of seven chambers—one for each of the seven chakras. The throat chakra integrates the information of all the chakras to express one truth with one voice.

The **Third Eye or Brow Chakra** holds the energy of abstract and non-abstract perception, transcendence, and out-of-the-box thinking, seeing, and believing. This chakra spirals between the eyebrows.

The **Crown Chakra** holds the energy that connects to the Divine. This chakra is about four inches above the top of the head.[52]

The **Meridian** energy system also fuels the organs and energizes the body. They run along specific pathways and may be thought of as streams of energy flowing up and down the body. Meridian energy can be accessed through acupoints, acupressure, or acupuncture points to support the balance of the meridians. The meridians have specific repetitive tasks. The meridians feed the chakras, and the chakras feed the meridians. The radiant circuits also are intimately connected to the meridians. The flow of the meridians is optimal when the electrics are strong.[53]

The **Triple Warmer** system is a primal force energy. It has the dual nature of both meridian and radiant circuit energy systems. Triple warmer, as a meridian, has more capabilities than the other meridians because it has the extra responsibility for our survival. It mobilizes efforts to protect and sustain us throughout our life. Triple warmer is responsible for immune function, emergency responses, temperature, survival behavior, and habits. When we have a stress response, the triple warmer tries to keep us safe, sometimes by forming an energetic wall of protection that can make us feel stuck or paralyzed. As a radiant circuit, triple warmer is the sacred energy that brings us into the world and takes us out of this world.[54]

The **Five Rhythms**, or Five Elements, of water, wood, fire, earth, and metal comprise an energy system that reflects a person's emotional state. Each rhythm was named according to its behavior as that particular aspect of nature and its rhythm or flow. Each rhythm comprises two meridians, except for fire, which has four meridians. Each rhythm is balanced with yin and yang energy. The tension between the yin and yang energies creates this system's pulse or energy flow. As a new human being starts resonating with the vibrations of the Earth, it aligns with its innate natural rhythms, which leads to the evolution of its unique personality. The primary rhythm of an individual strongly imprints its nature on the expression and vibration of all the other energy systems, the physical body, health patterns, and personality.

Water represents the energy of inspiration, courage, flow, and hope when balanced. Its flowing energy expresses freedom and ease, flexibility, and adaptability. When we express the water rhythm, we are processors and deep, quiet, creative, wise thinkers. When imbalanced, this energy holds fear, hopelessness, or despair.

Wood represents the energy of growth, initiation, and activation. An expression of wood energy is optimism, romance, adventure, kindness, and being naturally active and driven. People who express wood energy are leaders who know why they are doing what they are doing. When out of balance, wood energy expresses as anger, frustration, irritation, and annoyance. An imbalanced wood individual may be critical and judgmental. Their positive side is that they are organized, systematic, and always get the job done.

Fire represents the energy of flames dancing in a fire. One characteristic of a fire-dominant person is they easily get distracted or diverted. They are all about joy, passion, and having fun. They are the people that make parties fun. They laugh and let go and can be themselves, all in the spirit of having a good time. Fire energy is about transformation. When out of balance, the fire energy is panic or hysteria.

Earth energy represents the embodiment of resources and giving. Earth energy is about taking care of others, nurturing, and compassion. People who are earth rhythm dominant care deeply and may like to bake; they are supportive, create comfortable homes, and tend gardens. When out of balance, earth energy is experienced as worry or being overly or under-compassionate.

Metal energy represents elegance, grace, order, refining, and swaying movement. Metal energy is about completion and ending. When balanced, metal energy is about letting go. When out of balance, metal energy is grief and holding onto the past.[55]

The **Grid** is like a container for all the energy systems. The chakras are in direct contact with the grid, and the radiant circuits also have an intimate relationship with the grid. One would think the grid energy would come into the body first, but the grid can't form until there is enough mass to form a grid around it. A broken grid can block joy and positivity. If a grid gets broken, the energy body does its best to keep the energy pieces close together, but there is likely a leakage of energy from that break. The energy body cannot repair this break, but an advanced energy practitioner can.[56]

The **Celtic weave** energy system is the last system that comes into our bodies and is intimately part of the aura. The Celtic weave energy consists of many energies flowing sideways in figure 8s or infinity sign patterns. The Celtic weave is like a basket weave or network of figure 8s, keeping all the energy systems woven together. The more figure 8s, the stronger we are, the healthier we are, and the happier we are. The Celtic weave helps stabilize the other energy systems, especially the radiant circuits and triple warmer. The main function of the Celtic weave is to interconnect all nine energy systems. Through the Celtic weave, the energy systems help and support each other.[57]

These nine energy systems are the infrastructure of the body's physical structure and intimately correlate with illness or health. They work together in a well-orchestrated symphony to create balance and harmony in the body. The body is a master at communicating where the imbalances are through pain and other symptoms that can easily be ignored. When an energy system becomes imbalanced, blocked, or disconnected, the other systems try to adapt and compensate for the imbalanced energy. The other systems can then become imbalanced when trying to affect a change in another system. This compensation leads to a domino effect in our energy fields. As a result, layers of imbalances can accumulate. That is why healing is not always instantaneous; each layer of imbalance must be corrected to establish resilience in the body.

Correcting energetic imbalances can bring the body back into harmony, allowing it to heal naturally. When energy freely flows in and out of our energy bodies, we are constantly being revitalized and functioning at our best. The quality of our energy flow correlates with the quality of our lives. Table 2 lists the energy imbalances related to the nine energy systems.

When life presents challenges, our energy body can become compromised. But we don't have to stay challenged or stuck. There are simple exercises and techniques to release stuck or blocked energy and keep it flowing. As renowned Hungarian research scientist and Nobel Prize winner Albert Szent-Gyorgyi stated, healing has been accomplished through shifting or moving energy in all cultures and medical traditions.[58]

Table 2: Nine Energy Systems and Their Energy Imbalances

Energy System	Nine Energy Systems and Their Energy Imbalances
Meridians	Health issues related to specific organs or systems, something unusual or chronic happening at a particular time of day, jet lag, pain in muscles associated with a meridian, phantom limb pain, or emotional issues.
Five Rhythms	Emotional imbalance: **water** is fear/hopelessness, **wood** is anger/frustration/irritation, **fire** is panic/hysteria, **earth** is worry or under/over compassion, and **metal** is grief/letting go.
Triple Warmer	Stress/reactivity, fight/flight/freeze, PTSD, overwhelm, anxiety, paralysis or feeling stuck, not feeling safe, needing protection, addictions, hypervigilance, lack of security, difficulty relaxing and enjoying life, sleep difficulties, chronic muscle tension, emotional shock, hormonal issues—adrenal and thyroid issues, immune system issues and autoimmune disorders.
Aura	Easily overwhelmed in the company of others, feeling small or ignored or invisible, chronic illness, high sensitivity to electromagnetic energies (wireless devices), excessive fright in life, sensing the veil between the physical and Spiritual Realm is very thin, appearing timid or shy, over-active triple warmer without obvious stressors, recently experienced disease, surgery, or autoimmune disorder, after a serious accident or near-death experience.
Celtic Weave	Weak auras, feeling disconnected, health and vitality are compromised, depleted, communication between energy systems is off, excessive stress, or pain.
Electrics	Fatigued or depleted, needing revitalization, nervous system disorders (MS or Parkinson's), heart organ issues, memory issues, disorientation, energetically disconnected, experiencing strange electrical phenomena, electrical irregularities in the heart, or resulting from an accident or surgery.
Chakras	Endocrine or hormone issues, when very ill, issues with a specific organ, issues related to the chakra themes: **root** (grounding, primal survival issues or connection to ancestral line), **sacral/womb** (creativity, productivity or reproductivity issues, connection to joy, issue with authenticity), **solar plexus** (personal power, identity, ego, guilt, paranoia), **heart** (love and connection), **throat** (not speaking up or standing up for oneself, not of one clear message, inability to stop talking), **third eye** (difficulty with the abstract, imagination, inability to tune into planes beyond the five senses), **crown** (spirituality is limited).
Radiant Circuits	Persistent negativity, blocked/stuck in negative habits, focused on past negativity, lacking joy, disconnected from Self, others, and the Divine/spirituality, and when life seems limited to the five senses and the physical realm.
Grid	Energy leaking, unstable, or stuck in the body, sometimes lacking joy, often been traumatized.

We Transmit and Receive Energy

We are energy beings communicating our vibrational frequency to the rest of the Universe in every moment of every day. We each vibrate at a different frequency depending on our inner world—thoughts, feelings, and beliefs. In this way, our energy transmits into the Universe, similar to radio waves emitting from a radio tower or sound waves traveling out from a tuning fork. Radiating outward, these waves of energy mix with the collective energy that ripples throughout the world as a great ocean of Universal Energy.

In the ocean of Universal Energy, we also receive the energy transmissions of others. But we only attract energy waves, or transmissions, that match the frequency of the energy we send out, so what we receive is a person, an opportunity, an event, or a circumstance that resonates with our frequency. This means we create what we experience in life through our energy fields and vibrational frequency. We magnetize or attract what happens in our lives. This resonance with like energy is the Universal Law of Vibration and Energy. This concept may sound like the Law of Attraction, but the Law of Attraction is a subsidiary law of the Universal Law of Energy and Vibration.

Simply stated, we attract life experiences that match the vibrational frequency of the energy we generate and radiate out from our own energy field. A lower vibrational frequency manifests experiences that have a more dense, heavy feeling. This energy drains life out of us. A higher-vibrational frequency manifests lighter, more joyful experiences. This energy uplifts us and enhances our life. Think about it. It couldn't happen any other way. It's scientific—like attracts like.

We Sense and Communicate Through Energy

In the universal exchange of energy, we constantly sense the energy around us, even if we don't realize it. We are sensitive to everything in our environments because energy communications impact our energy level and vibrational frequency. For example, perhaps you have walked into a room where two people are arguing and feel tension without hearing anything or seeing their faces. Or perhaps you have walked into a room and experienced a sensation of joy. The feeling of tension or joy in these examples is how our energy body senses, receives, and experiences the energy transmission.

Table 2 Source Note: Donna Eden with David Feinstein, PhD, *Energy Medicine: Balancing Your Body's Energies for Optimal Health, Joy, and Vitality*, (TarcherPerigee, 2008), 109-241.

In the same way we feel the energy transmission from others, they also feel and respond to our transmissions. We can affect someone's mood by our vibrational frequency. We can affect their vibration if we have a high vibrational frequency or influence them to vibrate at a lower frequency if we are vibrating at a low frequency. Knowing how our energy communication can affect others, we can be more conscientious about what we communicate.

We can also sense what others are thinking about us because we all have mirror neurons. These neurons help us mimic and learn from others. They also mirror energy transmissions based on what we think about others and what they are thinking about us. For example, when we think positively about someone, we send an energy transmission that allows them to respond in kind by reflecting that positive energy. Similarly, negative thoughts about someone send a transmission that the other person may sense and react to by transmitting negatively charged thoughts and energy. By understanding how we sense and communicate energy, we can become more aware of how we may be influencing what we are experiencing. Although we might think others are the problem, we can consider how we may be influencing what is unfolding.

Being aware of the energy we are communicating is one way we can significantly affect positive change in the world. By consciously communicating higher-vibrational energy, we can influence the vibrational frequencies of others, empowering them also to transmit higher-frequency energy to others. Together, we raise the vibrational frequency of our communities, cities, nations, and beyond.

Training ourselves to see ourselves and others in positive ways likely requires a radical change in perception. First, we must overcome the negative mind chatter of our ego minds. The ego mind is always comparing ourselves to others. The ego tries to show us how we don't measure up. But if we remember that we are all traveling on our own Spiritual Journeys and our Souls are trying to guide us in the right direction to learn, grow, and evolve, we will more likely think and behave differently. Although we are all experiencing our journey differently, our goal of evolving to a higher state of BEing is the same. Remembering this basic concept, we can consciously start thinking this way and not listen to our ego.

We all know people who struggle with depression, stress, anxiety, and fear, which are all low-vibrational frequencies. Life Force Energy is draining from us in these lower vibrational states, and we are weakening energetically.

Let's try an experiment to demonstrate how emotions create a physical response and how our thoughts directly relate to how we feel. Recall a time when you experienced a lower-frequency emotion such as depression, stress, anxiety, and fear, then take a moment and answer the following questions:

Where do you feel this emotion in your body?
What is the feeling? Can you describe it?

Now, recall a time when you experienced a higher-vibrational frequency emotion such as joy, exhilaration, excitement, or ecstasy and answer the same questions. Then ask yourself:

How did the lower-frequency and higher-frequency emotions feel different?

A positive thought most likely feels like movement, flow, and opening up; perhaps there is an experience of warmth in the body. We might feel this in the heart area or gut. Negative thoughts most likely feel like restriction, tightness, contraction, or blockage; they might even feel like being walled off, boxed in, or stuck. These sensations or feelings are how our body lets us know it is responding to the energy of the thoughts we send to ourselves—our thoughts tell our body how to feel. In the same way, our body responds to the energy and thoughts of others.

Our body is always letting us know how it is responding to our thoughts. In this way, our thoughts actually determine how we feel.

We Create Our Lives Through Our Energy

Everything starts with a thought. Thoughts lead to feelings; repeated thoughts lead to beliefs. Together, thoughts, feelings, and beliefs affect our vibrational frequency and the way we experience the world. Our lives are projections of our thoughts.

The Universal Law of Cause and Effect says there is a specific cause to every effect. Applied to our life experiences, we can understand this to mean that the vibrational frequency of our thoughts, feelings, and beliefs is the cause; what we experience, the circumstances, events, and the people we meet are the effect. In other words, we reap what we sow. Following this line of thinking, it only stands to reason that if we don't like the effects we are experiencing in our lives, we can change them by changing the cause—the vibrational frequency of the thoughts, feelings, and beliefs we are transmitting. It's a simple concept to understand intellectually, but it's a whole other level of understanding to actualize.

The empowering principle here is that the vibrational frequency we transmit through our thoughts, feelings, and beliefs is our choice. This is our sovereign domain, and we can learn to control our choices to match the vibrational frequency of what we want to create and manifest in our lives. The Universe does not place limits on what we can create. We do that to ourselves. The happiness and success we experience are ultimately based on our choice of vibrational frequency. We can choose to be grounded in love, abundance, and freedom and experience the effects as seeming miracles in our lives.

This new paradigm of thinking also impacts how we view health and well-being. Health is not just an absence of disease or unhealthy physical symptoms; it is also how we feel about our state of well-being and our perceptions of our vitality, strength, and Life Force.[59] Our inner sense of our overall health is largely measured by how much energy and stamina we have to do the things we want and how well we are accomplishing our goals. When we are vibrant and radiant, we are in balance and harmony with our dreams, desires, and where we are going on our journey. We are resilient and immune to seeing or associating with lower frequencies.

Energy is our ultimate power in life. It sustains us and enables us to reach our highest potential. But we don't always experience optimal energy; paying attention to the ebbs and flows of our energy level and addressing imbalances is another key to creating the experiences we want in life. For example, constant fatigue or low energy can signal that our body's energy systems are not flowing optimally, which could lead to other physical symptoms and disease. As author Deb Shapiro shares, our body speaks our mind through physical symptoms and disease states.[60]

Energy needs to flow optimally through our bodies without blocks or restrictions to maximize our potential power to manifest the experiences we want. When the body is not fully energized, it cannot achieve and sustain optimal physical and mental well-being. Similar to how thoughts, feelings, and beliefs impact our vibrational frequency, they can also affect the flow of energy within our body.

In my Energy Medicine practice, I have witnessed time and again that my clients are in a state of distress in large part because they are transmitting lower vibrational frequencies, causing them to experience low energy and lower-frequency opportunities, people, and situations. They perceive themselves as victims of the world around them, not realizing the degree to which they create these lower-frequency experiences through their own energy field. Fortunately, no one has to remain stuck in these lower-frequency experiences. It is relatively simple to raise vibrational frequency by changing our thoughts, feelings, and beliefs, as I have witnessed with nearly flawless results throughout my years of practice.

Understanding states of BEing is key to understanding our vibrational frequency. A state of BEing is the energetic frequency we most naturally match. It is who we are as our energetic baseline from which we can progress up and down in frequency. Each state of BEing has a different vibrational frequency. Dr. David Hawkins mapped out this concept in his *Map of Consciousness*, which shows the correlation between seventeen different states of BEing—levels of Consciousness—and their vibrational frequency measured on a relative scale of 1-1,000. In his book, *Power vs. Force: The Hidden Determinants of Human Behavior*, Dr. Hawkins explains how he created this map from thirty years of clinical research.[61]

The *Map of Consciousness* is divided into two major sections: one represents levels of Consciousness that relate to Power, strong and supporting life, and the other represents levels of Consciousness related to Force, which weaken us, as draining, anti-life energies—much like the feeling or difficulty of going through life trying to push a boulder uphill. Dr. Hawkins explains that Power is the power within— empowerment as in inner strength rather than power over others. Nothing outside of us has power over us.[62] As we move from lower to higher-frequency states of Consciousness, we become more empowered, stronger, and more resilient; we go from feeling powerless and victimized to feeling strong and empowered.

To better understand what Dr. Hawkins means by a level of Consciousness, let's look at the level of Consciousness named Love. This isn't referring to a few moments when we may feel love for or from another person. Instead, Dr. Hawkins is pointing to a vibrational frequency of Love as our primary, natural, or most consistent state of BEing—it informs how we think and act daily. It is a state of BEing love.[63]

Dr. Hawkins calibrated each level of Consciousness on a logarithmic scale of energetic power ranging from 1 to 1000. Level 1 indicates the Consciousness of mere existence, and 1000 is enlightenment—the highest level of Consciousness known on Earth. Any level of Consciousness less than 200 is destructive of life. Conversely, all levels of Consciousness above 200 represent expressions of empowerment.

The *Map of Consciousness* shows a progression of levels of Consciousness within the framework of Force, beginning with the lowest level of Consciousness—shame, at a relative vibrational frequency of 20. The next higher level of Consciousness is guilt, with a relative vibrational frequency of 30, followed by apathy-50, grief-75, fear-100, desire-125, anger-150, and pride-175. The progression of Consciousness levels within the Power framework begins with the relative vibrational frequency of courage at 200, followed by neutrality-250, willingness-310, acceptance-350, reason-400, love-500, joy-540, peace- 600, and finally, enlightenment, which ranges from 700-1000.[64]

At a relative vibrational frequency of 200, the Consciousness of courage is a critical point of truth and integrity that shifts us from destructive to life-affirming energy characterized by integrity, self-honesty, and real empowerment. The shift to the level of Love Consciousness signifies a shift from being mind-focused to heart-focused and opens the doorway to the Spiritual Realm.[65]

Another way of looking at the *Map of Consciousness* is that the levels of Consciousness above a relative vibrational frequency of 200 are creative and life-enhancing. At these levels of Consciousness, we have a greater capacity for expanding Consciousness. As a result, we are more connected with the natural flow of the Universe that supports life, creativity, innovation, growth, and expansion. This is where life is most exciting, as we are positively contributing to the Universe. We are open to learning more and BEing more. These states of BEing are about truth, integrity, and supporting life or *power*.[66] In contrast, levels of Consciousness below a vibrational frequency of 200 keep us in survival mode with a *force* approach to life that is destructive, weakening, and out of alignment with the natural flow of the Universe to grow and expand.[67]

According to Dr. Hawkins, we can choose to move up or down this scale by changing our vibrational frequency. Letting go of negative emotional issues, self-limiting beliefs, and subconscious stories that are trapping us in a lower level of Consciousness allows us to progress toward higher levels of Consciousness and eventually an optimal state of BEing.[68] This empowers us to see how changing our perceptions of ourselves and the world around us intimately affects our state of BEing. In Section Two, we will learn a technique to help us raise our vibrational frequency by letting go of low-vibrational frequencies stuck in our bodies.

Words Can Restrict or Open Our Energy Flow

In addition to thoughts, feelings, and beliefs, the words we speak also have a vibrational frequency. Just like thoughts and feelings, our bodies hear and believe the words we say, and the corresponding vibrational frequency of those words affects our health and well-being and the flow of energy in our bodies.[69] Therefore, an easy and important practice is to become more aware of our word choices so we are not inviting negativity or low-vibrational frequencies that can get stuck in our bodies, resulting in emotional imbalances or ill health.

In talking with a client before testing her energies, I noticed she was using the "F" word more than usual—like every other sentence. I didn't say anything at first, but I knew the low-vibrational frequency of this word could be influencing the energy flow somewhere in her body. Through testing, I discovered that her upper back was tight, which was a sign that energy was not flowing well there. She confirmed her experience of pain with my touch. Immediately, I sensed this was where the "F" word had gotten stuck in her body.

I held the area of tightness in her upper back and asked her to repeat the following words out loud: faith, illumination, wisdom, peace, joy, love, enlightenment, compassion, gratitude, and kindness. The idea was to superimpose high vibrational frequencies in her body to counteract the low-vibrational frequency that caused the tightness and pain. I retested her upper back, and the energy was now flowing well in her back. She confirmed that the pain and tightness were gone. She was in absolute shock to learn that her choice of words had caused energy to get stuck in her back.

Dr. Masaru Emoto is a Japanese scientist who discovered that human Consciousness expressed through spoken words affects how water crystallizes when frozen.[70] In his experiments, Dr. Emoto spoke words with various vibrational frequencies while holding a glass of water and then froze the water at very low temperatures for several hours. When he took the water out of the deep freeze, he used a microscope to watch the formation of the crystals as the water melted.

Dr. Emoto found that the water exposed to high-frequency words, such as love, joy, and peace, formed crystalline structures corresponding to the specific vibrational frequency of each word. In contrast, water exposed to low-frequency words, such as hate, war, and ugly, did not create a crystalline structure. Instead, the molecular structure of the melting water remained chaotic and disconnected. Since humans are at least 70 percent water, I suspect that the words we use must affect the water within us and our energy flow in a similar way.

Like thoughts, feelings, and beliefs, the vibrational frequency of words is also transmitted to the Universe. Knowing this, we have the opportunity to be more mindful of our word choices so their frequency will come back to us in positive ways. It is empowering to understand that we have control of our words and can use them wisely for our benefit and the benefit of the whole Universe.

What would change within us if we consciously spoke high vibrational frequency words to our glass of water before we drank it? I think it would positively affect our biology and chemistry, not to mention energy flow. Choosing high vibrational frequency words will improve our energy flow and health and raise the level of Consciousness of the Universe. Here are some words of wisdom from an article by Frank Outlaw in the *Canandaigua Daily Messenger*.[71]

> *Watch your thoughts, for they become words.*
> *Watch your words, for they become actions.*
> *Watch your actions, for they become habits.*
> *Watch your habits, for they become your character.*
> *Watch your character, for it becomes your destiny.*

We will explore working with your vibrational frequency in more detail in Section Two.

Exercises

Use these exercises to help you embrace what may seem new to you. Meditate, journal or both to go deeper with these concepts. These exercises are meant to help you integrate the concepts more deeply than just reading these concepts. Trust your inner wisdom and intuition to guide you to truths you can accept and apply to your life.

Exercise 1: Map of Consciousness Exercise

- What level of Consciousness do you want to experience in your life?

- What Views, Emotions, and Processes on Dr. Hawkins's Map of Consciousness do you want more of in your life?[72]

- If you aren't experiencing life at the level of Consciousness you desire, consider what changes you can make to raise your vibrational frequency and progress toward this goal.

Exercise 2: Meditation and Journaling

Meditate and journal on these questions for applying new ideas and concepts to your life and how you live your life.

- Meditate and write about the observer effect. How would knowing your observation of what is happening in your life change what is happening for you?

- What would change within you if you consciously spoke high vibrational frequency words to your glass of water before you drank it?

- What changes in your life with the realization that life is a Spiritual Journey?

- How would you now define success in your life?

- What do you think about Consciousness being like a neural network?

- What impact do you want to make as a participant and co-contributor of the Universe?

- Explain how the Universal Law of Perpetual Transmutation of Energy changes how you view the world.

- Knowing the power of words, thoughts, feelings, and beliefs, what would need to change for you to be a more positive contributor to the Universe?

Exercise 3: *What-if* Questions

Meditate or journal on these *what-if* questions for increased understanding.

- *What if* you could visualize and create a new outcome in your life? What would that be for you?

- *What if* you understood you are an energy being? How would you pursue understanding more about this energetic aspect of who you really are?

- *What if* the whole Universe was Mind?

- *What if* Consciousness is a living field that surrounds you, is in you, and serves a significant role in your life?

- *What if* we create our lives through energy?

SECTION TWO

OUR DIVINE PURPOSE

Our Divine Purpose

At the 30,000-foot view of life, we come into these human bodies with our Divine Purpose to accomplish something significant for the Universe and the evolution of our Souls. From this larger, higher perspective, we wouldn't have decided to come into the physical world unless there was a really good reason to do so that served a greater good and guided us on an evolutionary path. This Divine Purpose must be grand and important to make us leave the peace and unconditional love of the Spiritual Realm.

Our Spirits or Souls decide this Divine Purpose before we come into the physical form.[73] Although it is specific to our intention to grow and expand our Souls, it is also tied to the principle of the Universe to grow and expand. Whatever our Divine Purpose is, we chose it. It was not given to us. Whatever helps us grow will help the Universe grow. It is always a win-win in the Spiritual Realm.

Our Divine Purpose is related not only to our specific gifts and talents but also to our challenges. We agreed on the specific challenges we will experience as a means to learn and grow from them; we chose them to help us evolve in unique and specific ways that help our Souls reach their highest levels of expression. Whatever difficulties we have experienced or may be going through were chosen by us at a higher level of Consciousness. Hopefully, this concept puts the challenges we face in a better perspective and makes them easier to overcome. We are not victims of our circumstances because we chose the circumstances as the adventure to elevate our level of Consciousness. Our experiences happen for us, not to us. Our experiences are golden opportunities for growth.

But we live in a third-dimensional plane where the exercise of free will is paramount. This means that even though we have the opportunity to choose to accept and pursue our Divine Purpose, we also have the free will choice to experience life in a way that is disconnected from our Divine Purpose. The exercise of free will easily leads us off track from consciously living in alignment with our Divine Purpose because we get sidetracked by daily living. We get caught up in accumulating material things that appear to improve our lives, falsely thinking that the physical, material world is our only reality—our real life. But the material world is only one experience, or expression, of our multi-faceted lives. In my view, our Spiritual Life is our real life. Seeing our lives from a spiritual perspective is very different from seeing our lives from a physical perspective. It is fine to accumulate material things that improve our lives, but it is definitely not all there is to life. We are missing out if we just consider the physical material world.

Since we have free will, we can consciously choose not to pursue our original Divine Purpose, provided we know what it is, and switch it for another one if we find fulfillment in making some other significant contribution that provides a substantial opportunity for growth. The Soul wants to live a life that matters and positively contributes to the world. At a fundamental level, it is essential that our lives matter—that we add significance in our own unique way. But regardless of how we view our purpose in being here, at the core of our existence is a fundamental need to understand who we truly are and align our life with our True Self. This ever-present Self lies hidden underneath the illusions, complications, triggers, wounds, subconscious limiting beliefs, and childhood stories. Our True Self is our holiness, our sacredness, and our Divinity that we don't understand or even acknowledge for the most part and exists beyond fear, illusions, trauma, and suffering. The Divine created us to become our full potential Self, the highest version of ourselves, to realize our Divine Magnificence, and to accomplish our unique Divine Purpose.

Even though our True Self can get covered up by all the illusions of our daily lives, our Holiness and Sacredness, cannot be obliterated. No one can uncreate what the Divine created in us, including us. We are all ideas in the mind of the Divine. We are all created perfect and holy and cannot be made unholy.[74] We are undeletable files in the computer of our higher Consciousness. It is who we are at our core. Even if we act in a different or unholy way and think unholy thoughts, we are who we are; we are who the Divine created us to be.[75] According to *A Course in Miracles*, "Your sinlessness is guaranteed by God."[76] From the perspective of the physical realm, sin is an act or thought that changes who we are at our core. But this is an illusion from a spiritual realm perspective because we were created by the Divine and cannot be uncreated as anything separate from that. We can't alter who we really are. Therefore, sinlessness is guaranteed. The Divine sees perceived transgressions only as mistakes and offers forgiveness. [77]

Own this truth. We are all Divinely created. We need to own the light and goodness within us. Own the light within you. Do we each realize the power of this light? The only things we need to be saved from are the illusions about ourselves: we aren't good enough; we don't deserve success or love; we are bad, guilty, or unworthy. These are the illusions of our mistakes. Mistakes don't change or alter who we are. Mistakes are just opportunities for growth and learning.

If we accept our holiness, we accept who we really are. The Divine created each of us in holiness. This includes us—you, me, everyone, and everything. Our holiness is our salvation.[78] It represents our Oneness with the Divine, complete with unlimited power. Our true identity abides in the Divine.[79] We express the Divine through our holiness; we are the feet and hands of the Divine. We can solve all problems and bless the world with our holiness.

I am increasingly identifying with my Spiritual Self as I realize the two parallel universes of my life. One universe is my ego, which sees through my physical eyes and seems very real. My emotions are tied to this reality. The other Universe is the REAL world—the Ultimate Reality of the Spiritual Realm. This is a reality my body's eyes cannot see. At some point in my life, I truly felt that I did not fit into the physical world, even though I wasn't yet aware that there was another experiential reality. I heard others, like my clients, express the same feeling of not fitting in with the physical world they were experiencing. I thought perhaps we feel this way because we think we aren't good enough, smart enough, or whatever other not enough we have been told.

But when I thought more deeply, I came to an understanding that we are not really this physical person trying to fit into the world we perceive. Instead, there is so much more beyond our physical form. I now understand that we are Spirits or Souls inhabiting a physical body. Each person is on their own path of self-discovery to realize the Self beyond physical form. Feeling like we don't fit in is a part of awakening to the truth of who we are as a gift, bringing something new to the Universe, not outcasts who are deficient or lacking in some aspect.

With this new understanding, I am learning to detach from the world of the ego and see the world from a more spiritual perspective. In the world of the ego, I am not at peace. I am constantly assaulted by negativity, fear, and stress. I want to be at peace and have found my path to peace in seeing the world and my experiences through a spiritual lens. The ego teaches us it is a meaningless world, and the Soul shows us it is a meaningful world. I want to be in the energy of my Spirit, who guides me in a meaningful way and order. Recognizing my Holiness is a choice that makes all the difference in how I show up in the world. My empowerment is in how I use my Holiness or Sacredness. Do I use my Holiness to bless the world and make it a better place? I am different because I have chosen to bless the world and the people around me.

If I see the world through the perception of my Holiness, I will see the innocence and the truth all around me. These are new understanding eyes. My Holiness blesses everyone and everything around me because I see with these new eyes. I know with these wise, understanding eyes comes an unlimited power to heal. I can help people see both their Holiness and their illusions about themselves. I am present with the Divine in my Sacredness, and nothing comes close to my sense of Oneness with the Divine—not career, money, material things, fame, status, fortune—nothing.

I want to see through my Divine Eyes, think with my Divine Mind, and feel through my Divine Heart. I want to know Divine Love and Wisdom.

Nothing is Random

Nothing is random in the Universe. We are not random. Dr. Michael Newton confirmed this in his research. We are all part of the Divine Plan.[80] Our Soul accepted the Divine Plan and chose to come back to the physical plane. Our Soul selected a life with specific challenges in order to evolve in our own unique way. Particular challenges help evolve our Souls to the highest level, which contributes to uplifting the whole Universe.

The Universe is not random, either. Sacred geometry teaches us is that the Universe was designed intentionally in geometric proportions using perfect forms, the Golden Spiral, and the Golden Ratio. Since everything in the Universe is an aspect of sacred geometry, everything fits together in the natural world like a jigsaw puzzle. Skilled in geometry, the Divine created the Universe with perfect proportions resulting in ease in flow and beauty from one cycle to the next. The Divine carefully orchestrated a design to serve and support us all in the physical and Spiritual Realms.[81] This intentional mastermind also enhances the unification of the physical and Spiritual Realms.

Sacred geometry uses the Golden Ratio or phi (1.618), the Golden Spiral, and the Fibonacci sequences (0, 1, 1, 2, 3, 5, 8, 13, 21, 34, 55, 89, 144, and so on) for the design. The Fibonacci sequence is the result of adding each pair of numbers (0+1=1, 1+1= 2, 1+2=3, 2+3=5, 3+5=8, 5+8=13, and so forth). The Golden Ratio, represented by the Greek letter phi, φ is approximately 1.618. The Golden Ratio is an irrational number, like pi. Its actual value is 1.618033988764989.

The Fibonacci sequence of numbers relates to phi, φ. If we divide the pairs of numbers in the Fibonacci sequence, skipping 0, we get 1 / 1 = 1. The next pair is the 1 and 2; 2 / 1 = 2 (if we divide the larger number by the smaller number). As the numbers get larger, the ratio becomes 1.618. For example, 55/34 =1.6176, 89/55=1.6181, and 144/89 =1.6179.

As a result, there is harmony and symmetry throughout nature. Drunvalo Melchizedek, a well-known expert in sacred geometry, calculated that "the Earth is in harmonics with (in the phi ratio to) the Moon, and these ratios are found in the proportions of our human energy field and even in the very Egg of Life itself."[82] We can think of this concept as "man is the measuring stick of the universe."[83] For example, the Golden Ratio is the ratio of our forearm length to the length of our hand. The structure of our ears is a Golden Spiral. Leaf patterns and the number of petals on flowers follow the Fibonacci sequence of numbers. These designs and patterns are everywhere in the natural world.

Nothing is random, and everything in the Universe came from Consciousness. At the very beginning, when the Universe was expanding out from the Big Bang, there was only Consciousness. Authors Deepak Chopra and Menas C. Kafatos state their belief that Consciousness is the creator of everything and was present before the Big Bang. According to them, we all come from a cosmic soup of energy Consciousness. Consciousness is the ultimate field or quantum reality of all that exists in the Universe.[84]

This pre-creation Consciousness is pure potential. "Every possibility exists in seed form. These seeds are made of nothing that can be empirically measured."[85] Aligning with this concept of creation, our Divine Purpose is likely something we need to create from Universal Energy or Consciousness. We need to connect to a specific seed of possibility that opens up to our Divine Purpose.

How do we Create with Universal Energy or Consciousness?

The answer to this question is in the realm of the unknown. But let's review what is known that could illuminate possible answers to how we create something physical from the energy of Universal Consciousness.

The Universal Law of Perpetual Transmutation of Energy explains that the formless becomes form and then goes back to formless. These concepts show us that there is a connection between the physical aspect of something and the energetic aspect of it. Energy in the Universe is dynamic, always transmuting into and out of form. Energy cannot be created or destroyed, but it is perpetually transmuting.

Going back to the String Theory discussed in Section One, strings of energy with different vibrational frequencies are at the basic level of everything in the Universe. At the quantum level, different strings of energy or different vibrational frequencies become different subatomic particles that become a frequency or a wave. The same cycling or transmutation also occurs above the quantum level, as illustrated in the famous scientific formula $E=mc^2$. In this equation, E = energy, m= mass or matter, and c^2 is a constant of light squared.

Basically, this formula means that energy equals mass or matter, and mass or matter equals energy. Energy becomes mass, and mass becomes energy. Mass and energy are different states of the same thing. There is an ongoing cycle of energy transmuting into matter and matter transmuting back to energy. The formula also illustrates that a lot of energy is associated with mass or matter. The constant of light c^2 refers to the speed of light or 186,000 miles per second. The square of that number is 3.4596×10^{10}. Therefore, there is an enormous magnitude of energy in a small amount of matter. Because there is a significant amount of energy in mass or matter and matter and energy are the same, it might be possible that matter is just compressed energy.

In everyday life, how does the Universal Law of Transmutation of Energy apply to the way we create matter or something physical from energy? How do we connect to the energetic seed of possibility and align with that in the physical form? The answers to these questions are not clear. But here is a possibility.

Likely, the wave aspect of an electron is a haze or sphere of energetic possibilities until it is observed; then, it becomes a particle—a form of matter.

What if we considered the seeds of possibility as waves of possibility? What if we *observed* or visualized the possibility in our minds, and it would materialize from the haze of possibilities? What if our energy bodies exist as a haze of different possibilities or states? What if we have the potential to transmute our state of BEing or level of Consciousness?

Authors Deepak Chopra and Menas C. Kafatos view humans as different states of Consciousness. According to this perspective, we exist in different states or potentials similar to electrons and other subatomic particles. What you are most familiar with is being a separate, individualized, unique physical body in the physical realm. What is hard to imagine is that in the quantum reality or Spiritual Realm, you exist only as an energy form. Because you are comprised of electrons and other subatomic particles, you share the qualities of the wave-particle duality; you can exist as a wave-energy form or a physical being—different aspects of the same vibrational frequency. In your wave aspect, you exist nonlocally or everywhere as part of the whole Universe. The particle or human physical body aspect of you is localized to a specific location.[86]

We can change our lives or our level of Consciousness by transmuting to a different aspect or state in the haze of possibilities that exist in our Consciousness. We are invited to be open to that possibility. We are invited to be open to change. We make these changes through Consciousness. It seems unlikely that we exist in different states as humans, but what if there is a haze of possibilities available to us to choose from? We could consider one state in the physical realm and one state in the Spiritual Realm. But both states are connected when we realize that we are each on a journey to become our highest potential Self. We are changing, learning, growing, and moving toward our higher states of BEing, in which our Consciousness level and vibrational frequency are evolving. We are evolving in both the physical and Spiritual Realms simultaneously because we cannot have any Spiritual experiences here without a physical form to make it possible.

Transmuting to a different aspect of ourselves from the haze of possibilities in Consciousness may also explain instantaneous healing or the placebo effect. Perhaps we can collapse the wave of our optimal health rather than continue to exist in an unhealthy state. We all know people who have had cancer one day, and then at the next doctor's visit, the cancer is no longer there. Maybe that happens because the person visualized or observed themselves in an optimal healthy state free of cancer. By observing, they collapsed that wave of possibility, and it materialized into physical form.

If this is how it works, what if we apply this concept to transmuting to a state or level of Consciousness to accomplish our Divine Purpose?

To pull down the energetic aspect of ourselves that aligns with our Divine Purpose, perhaps we need to be in the energy of the Divine Purpose. Perhaps we need to vibrate at the same frequency as the new path we want to align with. Perhaps we could start aligning with the energy of the Spiritual Realm. Perhaps we need to study or start visualizing life from the Holy Spirit or our Higher Self's perspective. Could we just start observing or visualizing the state we want to transmute into?

Trying to understand how the physical comes from an energetic wave, authors Deepak Chopra and Menas C. Kafatos explain that the observer in quantum physics is a unique concept and difficult to believe that observation of an event can be enough to elicit physical particles from the invisible.[87] They define this in physics terminology as the collapse of the wave function in the haze of possibilities that extends without limits as opportunities in all directions and changes shapes from the invisible to the visible, the particle.

Understanding the Universe in these terms, we live in a realm of full potential and possibility that can transform from the invisible to the visible. The collapse of the wave function is a form of transformation or even transcendence. The belief is that all of this happens within the mind. Therefore, Kafatos and Chopra state that more research is needed to understand and "to prove that the mind is not just one factor in the cosmos but the factor that underlies how everything in creation behaves."[88] Universal laws, like the Law of Perpetual Transmutation of Energy, are based on science and spirituality. However, even from a scientific perspective, there is a growing discourse in quantum physics literature that suggests the third-dimensional reality we experience is an illusion in certain aspects. The shifting from one transmutable state to another in quantum reality happens within Consciousness.[89]

According to *A Course in Miracles,* true reality from the spiritual realm perspective is what we experience in the vibrational frequency called love. We can't see love as a physical thing, but we can experience it. *A Course in Miracles* invites us to see the world around us differently—that everything has a spiritual aspect and function. If we could see through the lens of love, we could dispel illusions and discover the truth[90]. Everything in life is a call to love. Unfortunately, our experience in the third-dimensional physical world draws us into forgetting who we are and why we are here, resulting in an experience of lovelessness, pain, and suffering. But we have a choice of how we experience our world depending on where we focus our attention. If we identify mostly with the physical body, we exist in a perverse comfort zone in which the ego that controls our physical body wants us to avoid love. This is because the love vibration moves us into identifying with our higher Consciousness, or True Self, which means the death of the ego as the primary controller of our life.[91] The Divine intends for us to be messengers of love and discover the heart of the Divine within us and in others.[92]

Fear is the opposite of love, a major theme in *A Course in Miracles*.[93] Fear is a low-vibrational state that blocks us from our full potential. Fear is probably the number one thing that holds people back from BEing their True Self. Fear also keeps us disconnected from the Divine and the truth of our Spiritual Identity because it solidifies trust in only our ego self when we could be trusting in the Divine. When we trust in the Divine, we have a deep connection to all our inner power to create and experience a joyful and meaningful life, including alignment with our Divine Purpose. There is nothing to fear if we are aligned with the Divine.[94]

Awakening and enlightenment are remembering who we really are; this is the journey I am inviting you to take with me—discovering who we really are and our Divine Purpose. Discovering our Divine Purpose likely means creating something in form out of the formless. But everything is provided for us if we trust.

Our Spiritual Journey Leads Us to Our Divine Purpose

Everyone has their unique path and journey for shifting from an ego-driven life to connecting with their Divine Purpose. The Spiritual Journey that led me to my Divine Purpose was rather dramatic.

Shifting away from an ego-driven life requires a fundamental change in how we create our experiences. In our results-oriented and or *doing-driven* world, we are trained to believe that we have to do something and take some action to get the desired result. Action equals a specific result, and action represents the essence of life. But as we move toward alignment with our Divine Purpose, we begin to experience the BEing world. Rather than only taking result-oriented action—in an unconscious way, we simply align with our True Self and BE that expression of our Self.

While taking conscious action and BEing, we allow life to unfold naturally in Divine Right Timing and Order. BEing equals the perfect experience of our Divine Purpose and Spiritual Journey. BEing, rather than just doing, is a magnificent way to live without stress and anxiety. In BEing, we are co-creating with and being guided by loving forces within and beyond us that allow us to trust and surrender. In BEing, perhaps we are observers collapsing that particular wave of possibility. We are open and ready to receive and accept whatever appears on our path, which usually is not what we expect. Even challenges become gifts, deepening our connection to our True Selves and Divine Purpose.

If we don't know our Divine Purpose yet, we can set the intention to figure it out at the right time and in the right order of events in our lives. We were all infused with specific Divine Soul Energies to help us connect to our Divine Purpose or Divine Mission. We can trust that we will know when it is time to know.

After obtaining my PhD in microbiology at Vanderbilt School of Medicine, I worked in a research lab studying viruses until 2012. As I shared in the Preface, just after Mike died in 2008, I woke up one morning knowing that there was a modality that could have saved Mike's life. At the time, I was reading *The Power of Intention: Learning to Co-Create Your World Your Way* by Wayne Dyer.[95] So, I immediately set an intention to discover this new modality. I had been totally absorbed in the medical and scientific communities and wasn't even aware of these alternative healing modalities. About two years later, I started hearing about Healing Touch, Energy Medicine, and energy healing from different people within a short time frame. So, I did an internet search and found "The Energy Medicine Kit" and ordered it.[96]

When I received the kit, I was delighted to find a guidebook, CD, DVD, and a stack of flashcards with exercises. Then, I opened a small compartment and discovered a clear faceted crystal on a red thread. My critical thinking mind immediately decided that I was not interested in any modality that used a crystal. I dumped the kit in the garbage and, in separating items for recycling, found a program announcement showing that Donna Eden, touted as the pioneer of Energy Medicine, was traveling all over the world giving talks. In the next six months, she was going to Australia, Norway, and Wales. I was incredulous that there was that much interest in this kind of modality around the world. I also saw an announcement for a workshop the next weekend offered by the Omega Institute in New York City, just a few miles from my home.

Just as I finished reading the blurb about the Omega Workshop, my whole body began to shake. I stood there in amazement at the realization that my body was telling me to go to the workshop. As a scientist, I didn't believe our physical bodies spoke to us, but there was no denying what had just happened. After a few moments, it occurred to me that this shaking may be the result of setting the intention to discover a healing modality.

"Could this be the modality that could have saved Mike's life?"

I called the number on the announcement and got a ticket for the workshop.

One of the first things that Donna Eden said in the workshop is that energy medicine allows the body's innate wisdom to heal itself. It felt like she had read my mind asking, "How could Energy Medicine have saved Mike's life?"

That workshop was amazing. It opened me up to a whole new world of understanding the Universe. I was literally on the edge of my seat, experiencing something so far out of my realm of possibility, critical thinking, and limitation. It was like I was being invited into a whole new reality that offered peace, joy, and fulfillment. I was being transformed. There was a force way beyond me that was opening this new door. That is all I can say to explain what happened to me. There are no words that fully grasp my experience.

The more I learned, the more I was determined to get more training in this energy healing modality. At the end of the weekend workshop, the speaker explained the Energy Medicine Certification Program, which started in two weeks. The speaker explained that there was a prerequisite to attend a five-day program. I immediately enrolled in a five-day program but was told I had to wait a year to attend the Energy Medicine Certification Program training. I was very disappointed because I had the momentum to get started right then.

Thinking about what to do, one part of me was urging me to call Donna Eden's company, Innersource, to see if I could enroll in the certification program that started in two weeks. But another part of me kept telling me that I didn't have the prerequisite, so I couldn't attend. I went back and forth like this for a few days until I realized that I couldn't lose anything by calling to determine whether there was any possibility of me getting into the next class. When I called, the person I spoke with told me that if I ordered a DVD set of a five-day program and agreed to take the program test, I could enroll in the certification program. Ecstatically, I agreed and enrolled in the certification program that day.

I was incredulous! That part of me urging me to make the phone call was right. Did that part of me know there was a possibility? I was even more intrigued now about what I was discovering about my urging voice inside me.

Reflecting on what happened, I realized I had discovered my Divine Purpose without even trying. Energy healing could not be further from studying viruses. The introduction to this healing modality felt like Divine intervention, indeed.

Living From Our Purpose

As we progress through life, we work on specific goals and desires to learn, grow, and evolve. Learning to live from these desires helps us to accomplish them. Living from a desire means that we think and feel how we would BE if that desire were our reality in the present moment. From this perspective, we make decisions based on BEing in our new reality rather than what we perceive as our current reality. In other words, we match the energetic level of experiencing the desire in the physical realm and, quite literally, tune into the new reality.

We must envision and feel that change to be our truth in the present moment. The Universe mirrors our internal world to us. We reflect the world, and the world reflects us. If we change our inner BEing, our world changes. The world responds differently to how we are now BEing. This seems like a mystery until we know the truth and wisdom of how the Universe really operates.

> When I started getting clear about my next burning desire, I discovered it was to be a respected Spiritual Influencer, changing people's lives. As I became more and more passionate about that reality, I started stepping into those shoes or the energy of experiencing that life. I started creating quotes about how I see that world to post on social media. I started to write verses on different topics related to Consciousness, spirituality, and quantum physics—some are included in this book. I also started getting serious about writing a book. I started creating videos called "Divine Wisdom Moments" that I post on YouTube. It became more of a calling to a new place rather than a struggle to get there. I got clear on the desire, made a decision, and committed. I visualized what my life would look like, then took conscious action from a different level of BEing. I was energetically rising to the higher-vibrational frequency and level of Consciousness to know what action to take. Then, everything started to unfold naturally.

Taking inspired and conscious action is key when interacting with the Universe because it creates momentum and energy for aligning with our desires. By actively engaging at the level of frequency of that desire, we tune into that specific seed of possibility, vibrational frequency, or level of Consciousness to BE that BEingness. When our heart is also aligned with our desire, it is easier to see and follow the new path and take the steps that lead to fulfilling our desire in the physical world. This is especially true if your burning desire is also your Divine Purpose.

Here are some ways we can live our Divine Purpose by aligning with it now:

- Be clear on what your burning desire is and why.
- Visualize yourself receiving that burning desire and BEing that burning desire.
- Feel what it would be like to be in that reality now.

- BE in the energy or the spirit of the burning desire.

- Tune into the vibrational frequency of the desire.

- Engage and imagine what your five physical senses would be experiencing in that new desired state.

- Take conscious action to create forward movement and momentum for achieving your burning desire.

- Make decisions from this new perspective and state of BEing.

- Align your heart with the burning desire.

- Be committed.

- Do whatever it takes.

- Follow your intuitive guidance.

A Divine Purpose for All of Us

In addition to our personal Divine Purpose, we all share a common Divine Purpose. That purpose is to share the love of the Divine with others and think the way the Divine Intelligence thinks to bring in more love. In our lives and experiences, many of us are pulled away from thinking and acting through love and even programmed to use our minds without it. But we have free will and can choose differently. We can choose to switch out of what we have been told or programmed to think by others, which keeps us disconnected from experiencing and sharing love. When we choose to fulfill and live our common purpose to express Divine Love, we close the gap between lovelessness and love in Universal Consciousness.

In his book, *The Divine Matrix: Bridging Time, Space, Miracles and Belief,* Gregg Braden explores Universal Energy and shares the story of a Tibetan abbot who described Universal Energy as the energy of compassion.[97] Although we more commonly think of compassion as an act or thought in the moment, Braden understood the abbot to mean that compassion is also a powerful vibrational frequency that pervades the Universe. Understanding that we have a collective purpose to express Divine Love within the Universal Energy of compassion sheds a whole new light on the real purpose of our human life. It gives a new perspective for answering deep questions about our existence.

Living From the Heart

If we are to extend love to all as our Divine Purpose and realize compassion in all we do, we must live from our hearts rather than just our minds. This invites us to have a better understanding of the heart and love. Love energy naturally flows to us and from us through our hearts. Living from your heart means BEing in tune with what your heart wants, aligning with that, and BEing in the vibrational frequency of Love Consciousness or higher. We see the world through the lens of the heart, through the lens of love and connection.

Experiencing the heart as the energy of love is a state of BEing, not doing. Experiencing the heart as love energy is BEing who we are authentically. The main premise of *A Course in Miracles* is to become enlightened, meaning to transition from living in fear to living in love. Love is real, and fear is an illusion. Love is who you are.[98]

Similarly, Dr. David Hawkins's *Clinically Proven Map of Consciousness* illustrates living in fear means living in a low vibrational, weakened state.[99] On the other hand, love is a high vibrational frequency that enhances inner strength.[100] This type of love, however, is much more expansive than the kind of special love we feel for families and friends; it is BEing open-hearted and loving everything and everyone. It is the desire to see, witness, and discover the love in everyone. It is seeking to see or witness the love, rather than guilt and imperfection, in ourselves and others.

Forgiveness is also a big part of transitioning from fear-based to love-based living because it allows us to see every living being as innocent and a Divine Creation rather than observing how they have hurt us or are behaving. Sometimes, we expect people to be a certain way to meet our needs. But everyone is living their own journey according to their Divine Purpose, not ours. Sometimes, we want or need something from others that they are not willing or able to give us.

But just because we see the love in others and remember that they were Divinely created doesn't mean they won't act from their non-Divine aspect—their shadow self or false self. When that happens, we can know or remember their Divine Nature and love them regardless of their behavior, raising their frequency and perhaps helping them rise above their shadow or false self. Although we must allow them to make changes in themselves in their own time, we can still be powerful allies in helping them transition out of fear-based or low-vibrational living. Their mirror neurons can mimic our mirror neurons.

Going beyond accepting and respecting people for who they are and that they are on their own journey, we must look for the love within them. Knowing or believing in the love within others may be difficult if we don't see the love within ourselves. Learning to love ourselves may help us love others and accept that they were created in Divine Love—just like us. According to philosophers, a basic need in life is love and connection. However, as much as we may want to experience this in our lives, judgment often interferes with fulfilling this need.

If we judge others, it is likely we also judge ourselves by focusing on our imperfections rather than truly loving ourselves. We may hold perfectionist standards for others as we do for ourselves. When we are in judgment or criticism of ourselves or others, we are not living from our heart. We are not in a state of Love Consciousness. Instead, we may be coming from a place of fear or lack imprinted on our inner child as a response to conditioning or programming in early childhood. For example, fear of losing the love and connection of our parents can create a reactive mode for survival in childhood that becomes embedded as a conditioned response later in life.

Fear and love are opposing concepts. Fear is a low-vibrational frequency, and love is a high vibrational frequency, as indicated in Dr. Hawkins's *Map of Consciousness*.[101] While we want more love, rather than fear, in our lives, most of us need reprogramming or rewiring of neural pathways to transition from fear to living from love. Fortunately, there are tools to help with this neural pathway rewiring. But we can start at the level of Consciousness. A simple way to create more love in our lives is to send more love out into the world. Be at the vibrational frequency of love, operating from Love Consciousness. Look for opportunities to be loving. Focus on evidence of love all around us. There are opportunities every day to send love to people. Love is even expressed through a smile. Witness love and BE love. Experiencing life from the heart connects us to the love frequency, allowing us to act from love and radiate love frequency. Our world naturally unfolds from love frequency.

We associate love with our heart organs, and, indeed, the vibrational frequency of love emanates from the heart. Similarly, we associate higher truth and wisdom with the heart, which corresponds to heart and Soul energies emanating love and wisdom. Connecting to our heart wisdom allows us to be the best versions of ourselves and increases our overall intelligence. Heart intelligence goes beyond logic and analytical thinking and helps us access and integrate other aspects of our innate abilities, such as intuition, creativity, and direct knowing. When heart intelligence is engaged, our awareness expands beyond linear, logical thinking, opening us to more possibilities and solutions without stress because our perspectives and perceptions are more open, adaptable, creative, complete, and far-reaching.

To discover and align with our Divine Purpose, we most likely need to raise our vibrational frequency. To live more fully from the heart, we must be in the high-frequency energy of compassion and transmit that into the Universe. A new way of BEing opens up new possibilities to help us in this discovery. As Gregg Braden discovered from a Tibetan abbot, the energy of the Universe is compassion.[102] Therefore, if we want to be aligned with the energy and flow of the Universe to discover and align with our Divine Purpose, we must connect to and BE in compassion energy, which is truly unconditional love. I explore being in flow with the Universe to help us align with our True Self for living more fully from the heart, loving unconditionally, and BEing compassionate in the next book in this series.

The Heart Organ

If the Life Force Energy of the Universe is compassion, we may need to learn how to vibrate at that same level of love and compassion. To accomplish our collective Divine Purpose, love and compassion must be our vibrational state of BEing. Let's explore how we can reach these vibrational states by illuminating the heart and heart energies.

The heart organ and heart energies are truly amazing. Electric, magnetic, electromagnetic, and subtle energies support the optimal functioning of the heart. All the energies work together to resonate with compassion. When the energies are each balanced and supporting each other, and the mind is set on benevolence, the energy of love and compassion is transmitted. To better understand how to work with heart intelligence and the energies of love and compassion that flow through the heart, it's helpful to understand the energies that support it. Many energies support the functioning of the heart organ, underscoring its significance in multiple aspects of our lives and the need to optimize its activities. The heart energies not only support the physical functioning of the heart but also the psychological, mental, emotional, and spiritual aspects of the heart organ.

On the physical level, this fist-sized cardiac muscle contracts and expands to keep the blood pumping. The heart keeps us alive by pumping blood throughout our whole body via the circulatory system. Oxygen and nutrients are distributed to all the organs through the blood as it circulates throughout the body. In addition, the blood also removes CO_2 and waste, which helps to sustain the organs. The deoxygenated blood returns to the heart and gets shunted to the lungs for re-oxygenation. The heart beats 100,000 times daily and pumps five or six quarts of blood per minute—equivalent to 2,000 gallons per day. It never stops beating for our entire lifetime and never gets time off.

The heart starts pumping at 21 or 22 days after conception with the help of electrical energy. The electrical wave of energy in the heart is about 50 times the amplitude and 1,000 times the strength of the brain's electrical energy, making it our most electric organ. There is so much to be in awe of about this amazing organ that I recommend thanking it regularly for all it does.

> When I am driving alone on a long trip, I make it a point to acknowledge each organ in my body. I thank each organ for what it does for me to live radiantly and vibrantly. Thank you, thank you, thank you. I even put my hand over the organ as I talk to it. When I do this, I get a feeling that I am smiling on the inside! It may sound weird, but this little exercise can produce magnificent results. Try it!

Surprisingly, heart tissue comprises not only heart cells but also every cell type in the brain and in the same proportions. The heart is the area of the body that processes deep emotions and stores our values—what is important to us at the level of our desires—and our connection with others. In this way, memories are stored in the heart's cells. There is a story in *The Heart's Code: Tapping the Wisdom and Power of Our Heart Energy* by Paul Pearsall, PhD, about a ten-year-old girl who was murdered. Her heart was transplanted into the body of an eight-year-old girl.[103] After the transplant, the eight-year-old girl woke up with nightmares revealing the murder of her heart donor in such vivid detail that she was able to identify the murderer. With the heart organ being the only connection between the two girls, this was powerful evidence of cellular memory in the heart. But we still have much to learn and understand about how heart memory works. Knowing that the heart contains brain cells is not enough to illuminate how the heart stores and retrieves memories. This is partly due to a lack of understanding about exactly how the brain creates and stores memory but also because the energy of the two organs is vastly different. Perhaps because heart energy is involved with heart functions, heart energy is also involved with the heart's memory functions.

What are Heart Energies?

The heart has several different energy systems supporting it. The heart is the most electric organ, so the electrics energy system supports heart functions. Subtle energies also support the heart, including the heart chakra. An electromagnetic field surrounds the heart and extends about eight to ten feet from the body in the shape of a torus. By comparison, the brain's energy only extends about two to four feet from the body. This is significant because it means that heart energy picks up stimuli from the environment before the brain does. Also, according to the HeartMath Institute, the heart, rather than the brain, is most likely the core regulator of the physical body. It transmits information to the brain, making the brain more like a relay station, sending out information from the heart rather than detecting the information firsthand.[104]

The Energetic Heart

For a heart to be radiant and vibrant, it must function optimally, pumping blood and keeping us alive, have the vibrational frequency of Love Consciousness, be in energetic connection with others, and have a connection with the Soul. An open energy flow in the heart is important for longevity. The heart is crucial not only to our physical life and well-being but also to our emotional and Spiritual well-being. According to Dr. W. Brugh Joy in *Joy's Way*, "the magnificence of the heart perspective of awareness is the direct connection to the Divine aspects."[105]

To sustain these critical functions, the heart needs optimally balanced energy to keep it going 24/7/365. To ensure this optimal balance, several different energies regulate the heart's physical, emotional, and spiritual aspects, including the heart meridian, heart chakra, heart electrics, heart neurovasculars, heart neurolymphatics, and the fire rhythm. These different energies are discussed below.

Heart Meridian Energy

The heart meridian's electromagnetic energy helps regulate the physical functioning of the heart. The heart meridian starts at the top of our underarms and runs along the inside of our arms. If we extend one arm up positioned with the palm facing toward the center of the body and the thumb facing up, the heart meridian is on the side of the arm closest to the body or on the bottom of the raised arm. We can use the electromagnetic points on our fingers and hands to enhance or add energy to and strengthen the heart meridian. Take the opposite hand with the palm side toward the body and place it at the base of the underarm. Move that hand from the underarm straight up the inside of the arm and off the little finger. Since the heart meridian is on both sides of the body, repeat on the other side of the body. That is a quick way to strengthen the energy flow in the heart meridian. Tracing the meridian forward brings more energy to the heart. We never trace the heart meridian backward because we never want to remove energy from the heart organ.

Knowing how the heart meridian flows, we can understand that when we hug someone, we are actually embracing them with our heart meridian energy! I believe this also relates to compassion.

The heart meridian also supports the emotional and spiritual aspects of the heart. The heart meridian, when balanced, can open up and transmit compassion. It is essential that the heart has an optimal balance of energy to function in all aspects—physically, mentally, emotionally, psychologically, and spiritually.

Heart Source Point Energy

To balance energy in the heart organ, you can rub the heart source point, which stores extra electromagnetic energy as a backup reserve for the heart organ. The heart source points are on the heart meridian on the palm side of each wrist crease, where each arm and hand meet, and are in line with the little finger. Because this energy is easily accessible through the skin, rubbing this point sends energy directly to the heart organ to balance the energy within. For example, rubbing each heart source point will balance high or low blood pressure—the key word is balance.

Heart Chakra Energy

Energy flows into our bodies from the Universal Life Force constantly. There is an ebb and flow of energy into and out of bodies when the energy is in optimal flow and balanced. This ebb and flow is true for the heart chakra as well. The heart chakra's subtle energy feeds the heart and all the other organs and body parts near the heart, including the lungs, breasts, pericardium, thymus, shoulders, arms, upper thoracic vertebrae, and ribs. It also supports us psychologically and spiritually. For example, it can carry broken-hearted energy and grief when imbalanced. If this low-vibrational frequency energy is not cleared, it can cause congestion and block the normal flow of this chakra energy, impacting its ability to function optimally in support of other organs and energy systems.

As already discussed, the heart chakra also stores memories. All chakras are like filing cabinets storing the significant events in our lives. The heart chakra stores significant memories related to love and connection. The heart chakra flows over the heart area as spiraling energy moving clockwise or counterclockwise. If the heart chakra is releasing energy, it flows counterclockwise. It flows clockwise if it integrates new energy, such as memories of recent events. There are seven layers of the heart chakra representing seven phases of our lives. If we were traumatized at any phase of our lives, the unresolved emotional issues—stored as energy—are likely stuck in the layer associated with that phase of life.

To clear the heart chakra of congestion from unrequited love or broken-heartedness, put your left hand over your heart with your fingers pointed toward the right side of your body and circle your left hand counterclockwise in the direction your left fingers are pointing. The electromagnetic points on the left hand and fingers pull out the congested energies in the chakra. Your left hand should be two to four inches off the body, and the circles should extend out to the full width of your body. To entrain the heart chakra energy to your hand, go slowly, taking about five to seven seconds to make a full circle. Keep circling your left hand for two to three minutes or until the energy feels less dense or congested. The congested energy will collect on your left hand. Clap your hands together several times to remove the congested energy from your left hand. After the congested energy has been released, circle your right hand clockwise to help integrate the remaining energy in the chakra. To do this, put your right hand over your heart with your fingers pointing to your left side and circle your right hand clockwise for one to two minutes using the same technique used for the left hand.[106]

Heart Electric Point

The heart electric point is a way to access the heart's electrical energy to enhance or balance the heart organ's electrical component.

> *The Electrics are a sort of 'live wiring' for the heart's electrical rhythm and the pulsing that travels to and from each cell, giving the electric charge to our very aliveness, nature, and rhythm.*[107]

As the most electrical organ in the body, medical doctors and cardiologists use EKGs or electrocardiograms to measure heart health by the level of electric impulses signaling the heart to contract and relax. A deficiency in electrical energy can prevent the electrical impulses from reaching the heart's lower chambers, weakening the heart's pumping action and causing fatigue, dizziness, and fainting symptoms. This is called bradycardia. In contrast, tachycardia results from excessive electrical energy that causes the heart to beat too quickly.

With either bradycardia or tachycardia, working with the heart electric point can revitalize the heart's electrical energy. The heart electric point is located at the intersection of the top of the left underarm and the left nipple. To use this point for enhancing or balancing the heart electrics, place a 3-finger notch—thumb, index, and middle fingers of your left hand—over the heart electric point. At the same time, place your right middle finger along the right groin line and up against the right side of the pubic bone. Hold these two points simultaneously for 5-20 minutes and imagine connecting them to revitalize the heart's electrical energy.[108]

Heart Neurovascular Point

The heart neurovascular point is at the top center of the head at the baby soft spot.[109] When there is a restriction of energy at this point, an energetic channel between the nervous and vascular systems is restricted. Place a 3-finger notch—thumb, index, and middle fingers—on this spot to release or balance stuck emotional energy, such as broken-heartedness or grief. The electromagnetic points in our fingers magnetize energy to the heart's neurovascular point, causing it to open and release any restriction. After holding this point for several minutes, you may feel an emotional release because the trapped emotional energy is no longer stuck.

Heart Neurolymphatic Points

The heart neurolymphatic points are on the right and left upper chest area below the first clavicle.[110] They represent the energetic connection between the lymph system and the nervous system. Rubbing these points will activate the flow of the lymph system and release stuck toxins or emotional energy. If this area is sore, it may be an indication that toxins or emotional energy are stuck there. To release tenderness, toxins, and stuck emotional energy in this area, rub, thump, or tap this area to get the energy moving. It may require daily rubbing for a while to release all the stuck energy in this area.

Heart Meridian in the Fire Rhythm

One of the nine energy systems described in *Energy Medicine: Balancing Your Body's Energy for Optimal Health, Joy, and Vitality* by Donna Eden with David Feinstein is the five rhythms or five elements of water, wood, fire, earth, and metal.[111] This energy system holds the energies of emotions. Each rhythm is a synergistic collaboration of two or more meridians. When the rhythm is balanced, the emotions are in balance or are in control. When the rhythms are not balanced, the emotions are imbalanced or out of control.

The fire rhythm consists of four meridians: heart, small intestine, triple warmer, and circulation/sex or pericardium. When these four meridians collaborate well, the fire rhythm is balanced. When the fire rhythm is imbalanced, the emotions of panic and even hysteria are expressed. This imbalance can result in panic attacks, which can be felt in the heart organ, presumably due to an imbalance of the heart meridian or circulation/sex meridian affecting the heart rate. Imbalanced emotional issues related to stress, reactivity, or anxiety are associated with triple warmer and circulation/sex meridians and may also play a role in panic or hysteria; they are capable of being reactive in an imbalanced way. The heart meridian will also be affected if any of the meridians are imbalanced in the fire rhythm. These four meridians are supposed to support and collaborate with each other, but if one is imbalanced, it can affect the other three meridians. It only takes one of these four meridians to be imbalanced to cause the fire rhythm to become imbalanced.

To balance the fire rhythm, hold the fire neurovascular points. Place one hand at the back of your head behind your eyebrows and one hand on your forehead and hold them in place for five minutes.[112] It is best to lie down and prop up your elbows on pillows to fully relax into this technique. By placing your hands in these two areas, you open up the flow in the energy channels connecting the nervous system and the vascular or blood system and release the restriction caused by unresolved emotions.

The Heart May Be the Core Regulator of the Body

As discussed previously, the heart tissue comprises heart cells and proportionally every cell type in the brain, making it one of the three brains in our body—head, gut, and heart. These three brains must be synchronized and coherent for optimal health and well-being to create a harmonious body and powerful mind.

The heart and gut brains communicate with the brain in our head, supporting brain development, reducing depression and sadness, increasing happiness and sense of well-being, and many other functions. Heart-brain communication occurs through the release of chemicals in the blood sent to the brain and electrical signals transmitted through the vagus nerve and spinal cord. As the tenth cranial nerve, the vagus nerve is the longest nerve in the body, starting behind the ears and ending at the anus and enervating every organ. It updates the brain on the well-being of all the organs. In addition, scientists have discovered neural pathways between the heart and brain that facilitate or inhibit this electrical activity. For example, deep, slow breathing exercises stimulate the vagus nerve, which benefits the heart and gut by reducing blood pressure and improving heartbeat rhythm.

The heart is also an endocrine gland that produces hormones and releases peptides that help with blood pressure and improve the functioning of the kidneys. These same peptides also stimulate the pituitary gland to release hormones like oxytocin, the *love* or bonding hormone. Oxytocin stimulates happy feelings in the heart as well as compassion towards others.

From a Consciousness perspective, the experience of the heart is BEing—not doing. BEing heart-centered is something we become. In Section One, I introduced the *Clinically Proven Map of Consciousness* by Dr. David Hawkins, which places love in the top portion of the map as a relatively high vibrational frequency.[113] Experiencing life from the heart connects us to the love frequency allowing us to act from love and radiate love frequency. Our world naturally unfolds from love frequency. In this state, we can feel compassion toward ourselves and others.

Here are some additional interesting facts that may help with understanding the heart may actually be the key regulator of our physical bodies.

- The heart is developed before the brain. As illustrated in Table 1, we can see that after the aura, which surrounds all unfertilized eggs, the electrics system is the first energy system to enter the newly developing zygote. Electrical energy begins to pulse and develops into a physical heart.[114]

- The heart's electromagnetic field is by far the most powerful produced by the body. For example, it's approximately five thousand times greater in strength than the field produced by the brain.[115] The heart's field not only permeates every cell in the body but also radiates outside of us, measured up to 8-10 feet away with a magnetometer, a sensitive device for measuring magnetic fields.[116] A person can be "brain dead" but still live. But if the heart no longer functions, we die. [117]

- The heart does not need to be directly connected to the brain to beat.[118] When doing heart transplants in humans, the nerves connecting to the heart are cut to remove the physical heart from the donor. When this heart is transplanted into the recipient, doctors do not connect the nerves in the heart to the nerves in the brain. The heart operates and functions well even though it is not directly connected to the recipient's brain.[119] This fact is amazing and understood from an energetic perspective.

- Scientific discovery has also revealed that the brain doesn't make all the decisions for the body. The heart receives the intuitive information before the brain processes and decodes the information.[120] The heart sends information to the brain, and the brain responds, affecting the person's behavior. Also, the heart doesn't always respond to information from the brain directly.[121] These discoveries further suggest that the brain is not the core regulator of the body. [122]

- According to scientific research at the HeartMath Institute, there are four ways the heart communicates with the body and the brain: neurologically, biochemically, biophysically, and energetically. The communication pathways are different as the heart communicates neurologically through the flow of nerve impulses through the body. The expression and messages from hormones and neurotransmitters help the heart communicate biochemically. Pressure waves support heart communication through biophysical pathways. The heart communicates to the brain and body through electromagnetic field interactions.[123] In these four ways of communication, the heart significantly guides and influences how the brain and all organs function.[124]

- Research by the HeartMath Institute and others shows that the heart sends more information to the brain than the brain sends to the heart.[125]

- HeartMath experiments on research participants demonstrated that focused attention on their hearts induced synchrony between their hearts and brains through energetic interactions.[126]

- Being the strongest generator of electrical currents in the human body, the heart helps the other organs and physiological systems to entrain with its rhythms.[127]

Heart and Emotions

The heart organ is also affected by emotions. Different emotional states affect the heart in different ways, like the beating of the heart or the heart rhythm. Different emotional states affect cognitive and emotional aspects. During stress and anxiety, the heart patterns are chaotic and irregular. They look like jagged lines on a machine monitoring the heartbeat chart. These erratic heart rhythm patterns produce erratic neural signals between the heart and the brain, inhibiting the intelligible functions of thinking, remembering, learning, reasoning, and making important decisions.

The more stable or smoother the heart rhythm patterns, the more optimal the memory, decision-making, learning, positivity, clarity, and emotional stability become. Maintaining positive emotions affects whole body health and significantly enhances our perceptions—how we think, feel, and act.

Feeling joy, gratitude, and appreciation profoundly influences how our body functions to achieve optimal health. However, negative emotions are real and should not be ignored or repressed. Acknowledging our negative reactions to events and people is important and authentic. However, we must focus on resolving those emotions so they don't become stuck in our energy fields. Then, we can perceive situations differently.

I believe that the Divine created the heart and heart energies to be so strong and significant because of their importance in extending and sharing the love frequency to uplift the vibrational frequency of our world and the Universe. In this competitive and survival-focused world, it is easy for us to get stuck in our heads. We analyze, think, compare, judge, learn, and grow intellectually. Along the way, it is easy to disconnect from our heart energy and communication.

The HeartMath Institute provides methods for optimizing heart and brain connectivity and efficiency for optimal health, which they call heart-brain coherence. Heart-brain coherence is when the heart, mind, and emotions communicate energetically and are aligned to achieve resilience. In this state, the energy is used optimally for intentions and peaceful, harmonious results.[128]

In coherence, the heart and brain energetically act on the same wavelength enabling us to feel whole in body, mind, and Spirit. Heart-brain coherence helps balance our emotional state. It aligns the head and heart to facilitate higher brain function, which appears to create a direct link to intuition or super-high-speed intelligence.[129] Stress causes heart-brain incoherence, resulting in negative effects on the heart and the brain organs. Our nervous system and heart rhythms are no longer synchronized. Our hormones suffer from this imbalance. Incoherence prevents us from performing well and living a quality life. As a result, our health is less than optimal.[130] To address this health issue, the HeartMath Institute has developed specific techniques to increase heart-brain entrainment by specifically altering the emotional state. These emotional shifts result in a change in how the heart communicates with the brain. When the brain and heart are in alignment and attuned to each other, our bodies function optimally.[131]

The practice of heart-brain coherence is accepting life unconditionally as it is in the present moment. The more we accept ourselves and our lives, the more unity we have within ourselves, and the more we become one with the Universe. If we accept what is happening in our lives, we can let go of negativity. We can take action aligned with our hearts—more heart-centered actions. We feel we are enough. The more we accept that everything happens for us, we know everything will be okay. We have less resistance, are more relaxed, and experience deep inner peace. With this deep trust in ourselves, our personal power, and inner peace, we find nothing to stress about or fear.

When the heart and brain are in coherence, we are more in touch with our feelings and less thinking. We can connect to our true essence—who we really are. By aligning with the heart's intentions, our energy naturally focuses on taking heart-directed action. We are vibrant and energetic. We are more creative. We allow space in our minds to spend more time in imagination and creativity.

Creativity and joy extend to all areas of our lives. When our minds and bodies are aligned with our Souls, we accept and embrace our emotions. We are not resistant to experiencing all aspects of our deep, intelligent hearts. We have a new freedom. It becomes easier to face and resolve core inner conflict. We become resilient to what is going on around us. We maintain emotional intelligence. Once we trust our hearts, we have optimal mental health. No person or outside circumstance can break through this trust. We can be strong and survive no matter what happens. Our physical health also improves, including our immune systems. Stress hormone levels decrease, and we can enter into the parasympathetic mode of the autonomic nervous system. Overall, our heart health and wellness improve.

We also have a deeper emotional connection with ourselves and others. The more compassion and trust we have for ourselves, the more compassion and trust we can have for others. We can be more authentic, honest, and transparent. In general, the quality of our lives improves overall. Life is easier, more joyful, and has a deeper meaning. We become optimally healthy, vibrant, and radiant.

We can learn to embrace all that happens to us and even bless everything. Bless the people and the events that cause us pain. They are the open doorways to growth, acceptance, and new wisdom. We must experience all aspects of life to truly experience ourselves and the depth of who we really are. We don't know the later effects of what is happening in the moment. If we think negatively or doubt the good the experience can bring, we are in judgment based on fear conditioning of our childhood that is blocking a positive outcome. We are not in our hearts. Decide to see and live from the heart. The heart wisdom knows what is for our best and highest good. Bless everything, and let the heart and mind merge in coherence to bring the highest potential into reality.

Understanding the negative results of living in heart-brain incoherence and the benefits of living with heart-brain coherence helps us live a life through the lens of the heart. When the heart and brain are working well together in coherence, an optimal state of health and well-being is possible and even likely.

How Do We Achieve Heart-Brain Coherence?

A simple way to bring the heart and brain into coherence is to place our hand over our heart while taking slow, deep breaths and intentionally connecting the two energies as we breathe into the connection.

Another simple exercise is FREEZE-FRAME, described in the book *The HeartMath Solution* by Doc Childre and Howard Martin.[132] The name FREEZE-FRAME refers to stopping at a specific frame in a movie, with our lives being the movie and the frames being specific moments in the movie of our lives.

The exercise helps to shift perceptions and attitudes in the present moment, enabling the heart and brain to move from incoherence to coherence in these ways.[133]

- Developing awareness of whether you are enhancing or draining your energy.

- Accessing the core values and power of the heart and heart intelligence.

- Balancing the sympathetic and parasympathetic aspects of the autonomic nervous system.

- Reducing stress.

- Enabling clear decision-making.

- Balancing our state of awareness.

Shifting perceptions and attitudes in the present moment allows us to be an observer as we stop what we are doing at a critical time to help us make a different decision or respond differently to specific events or people. In particular, it invites us to realize when we are responding to stress with stress and shift our perspective to decrease or eliminate any stress response. We can use this simple technique to bring awareness to any moment of the unfolding movie of our lives and shift into heart-brain coherence.[134]

If we recognize we are going into a negative energy state, as in stress, we can choose to reframe how we perceive the situation. By shifting our attention to our heart and breathing through it, we engage its energies. To experience this more optimally, I recommend putting your hands over your heart to connect more fully with the heart's energies. You may feel tingling in your hand as it acknowledges the connection to your heart. Once you feel the energy shift, you can deliberately focus on something positive in your life by visualizing a movie clip of that positive time or event in your mind's eye. This shift puts us into a higher level of Consciousness so that we can perceive the situation from the heart's perspective. With the heart energies fully engaged and open to receive, ask the heart a question on how to perceive this situation differently and how to respond for a more positive outcome. Our heart or intuition will give us the answers if we believe we will get the answers.

BEing Our Best

To align with our Divine Purpose, we may want to raise our state of BEing to be our best. BEing the best versions of ourselves means aligning with the highest vibrational frequency available to us or, at least, aiming in that direction. BEing our best means we completely understand we are as the Divine created us.

We can tap into that aspect of ourselves and come from that True Essence. We can live from that True Essence. It means we are resilient and unaltered by negativity, fear, anxiety, stress, or upset present in our external environment. We can start living from our desires rather than someone else's. Living our best life and BEing our best is not for anyone else to determine but us—the Soul part of us. BEing our best is an intention that sets us on a path to discover who and what BEing our best really means as part of becoming our best Self. Our intention is to BE in heart-brain coherence and emotional intelligence. Our intention is to break through all negativity and negative thought patterns from past conditioning or programming.

Setting these intentions creates the momentum or the energy for something new to happen and transmits it into the Universe to receive its response. BEing our best means we are in flow with the Universe. Being in flow with the Universe means that life unfolds naturally for us with ease. We understand that life is happening for us and not to us. We live from our hearts in a miracle zone aligned with our Divine Purpose and Mission; life feels almost effortless.

BEing our best also means that we have vibrant and optimal health. We are radiant and shine our light on the world. Our high vibrational frequency is expressed in everything we do and everyone we connect with. People love our energy and tell us that positive things happen after they have spent time with us. We raise other people's vibrational frequencies—even people we don't know.

Giving and Receiving

Aligning with our Divine Purpose may mean we become more aligned with the flow of the Universe to allow the journey to be natural and peaceful. Many cycles in the Universe ebb and flow together to maintain balance. The cycles of nature reflect this flow like the tides, yin and yang rhythms, the in-breath and out-breath. Giving and receiving are also meant to ebb and flow together for balance in our lives. Giving and receiving need to be in equilibrium in our lives for us to align with the energy flow of the Universe. Giving and receiving must be balanced for the energy to flow to and from us to match the flow of the Universe. We are not in balance if we give more energy than we receive. We get depleted or burned out because revitalizing energy is not flowing back to us.

Giving and receiving reminds me of a sideways figure 8 or an infinity sign. We need to be able to both give and receive well. Especially if we are heart-centered and in service to others, it is relatively easy to master the giving side of the equation and constantly give, give, give, and not receive. But giving needs to be in balance with receiving. If we over-give, our boundaries are too porous, and we will block receiving in general if this becomes a way of life for us.

In my experience, new small business owners, in particular, can find balancing giving and receiving especially difficult. The challenge is that in seeking to attract business, small business owners often engage in excessive giving, including giving their time away for free, which can actually block them energetically from receiving money. It is also possible they are acting out of lack, and when in lack energy, they attract more lack in their business and personal life. What we do in one area of our life is how we do everything else in our life.

Perhaps take a moment and consider how you receive compared to give. A simple way to do this is to observe how you receive compliments or help when others offer. If you find that you deflect compliments and help, you may also notice you have trouble asking for and receiving money. This is because receiving money from others may feel like taking something valuable from someone else, and you would rather suffer than take what you are owed or deserve.

The pre-disposition to give rather than receive is also culturally based. From a young age, many of us are taught that *it is better to give than receive*. We were raised to give because receiving is selfish. Changing our mindset about this concept is not easy, but it can be done. Awareness is the key.

> The day I realized my difficulty in receiving was a snowy Saturday in February. I was supposed to be teaching a class that day at my home. It was early in my business, and I didn't have a healing space yet. We postponed the class because of the weather. So, I decided to do a long meditation. I was lying on my yoga mat in the area where the class was to be. I meditated for a long time. I was in a complete state of bliss. I was totally aligned with my Higher Self and felt like I had no problems in the world. When I returned to the physical plane, I realized that my neighbor had come and removed the snow on my driveway and walkway. I actually flipped out. The crazy thoughts that were going through my mind were:
>
> How do I repay him?
>
> Do I write him a thank you note?

Do I get him a gift certificate for doing this for me?

What is the appropriate way to thank him?

I spent a good deal of the day in this mode of confusion and chaos. At some point, I stopped. I realized that I just needed to appreciate what he did for me. I needed to receive this gift in a positive mode. He probably felt good doing this for me. Perhaps he was looking to do a good deed for someone that day—and he chose me. Maybe he felt happy that he could do something nice for someone. Maybe he didn't want me to go into hysterics worrying about the way I needed to repay him for this kind deed. I decided that I needed to learn to receive with grace. I needed to allow people to do good deeds for me.

This experience showed me that I had a very difficult time receiving. Was this difficulty affecting my ability to receive money in my business? My conclusion was yes; my inability to receive was affecting my making sufficient money in my business. What I learned growing up is that it is selfish to receive. I must be the one giving to be a good person. This learning was so ingrained in me. "It is better to give than receive."

It has taken me years to unwind this learning and be able to say a simple thank you when someone does something nice for me. My immediate knee-jerk reaction is to do something nice for them in return. But I stop and remember that giving and receiving must be in equilibrium to be aligned with the flow of the Universe.

Letting Go

What we learn to let go of is what's going to matter significantly as we review our lives. Letting go is as significant as how much we extended love and how much we lived in peace. It is one of the most important things to do on a Spiritual Journey to discover our Divine Purpose.

To grow and evolve, we must let go of how we used to be to allow for the shifts to who we are becoming. It is harder to make changes within ourselves if we are filled up with past grievances and unresolved issues. Cleaning our slate helps us move forward with ease.

I Let Go Today

I let go of fear today,
And love flowed in.

I let go of judgment today,
Then acceptance moved in.

I let go of criticism today,
And I moved into praise.

I let go of anger today,
And peace surrounded me.

I let go of confusion and chaos,
Clarity showed forth.

I let go of darkness today,
Light illuminated my world.

I let go of guilt today,
And I understood innocence.

I let go of grief today,
Sadness was reversed.

I let go of shame today,
And realized magnificence.

I let go of resistance today,
Willingness showed up.

I let go of apathy today,
And connected to the joy within.

I let go of suffering,
And witnessed the world as Divine Wonder.

I let go of trauma,
And discovered the lesson.

I let go of challenge today,
And embraced the opportunity.

I let go of pain and suffering,
I was enlightened to who I really am.

I let go of pride today,
And became one with the Divine.

Anne M. Deatly

Letting go of emotional issues or misaligned paradigms of life is a major issue for many people. It is hard to let go of issues with other people because we think we have lost that argument. We need to be right. However, we don't realize that holding onto low-vibrational frequencies keeps us in low-vibrational frequencies and blocks us from moving forward. If we are sensitive to messages from the body, we may feel a tightness or constriction in the heart area, gut area, or some other place when we think of a disturbing situation. It could come to our senses with a specific memory in mind. The area of constriction or tightness is actually the energy of a stuck or unresolved emotion. This *truth center* is letting us know that energy is stuck and not flowing well in that particular location. The *truth center* can be in different physical places in different people. The *truth center* can be in different places with different emotions, self-limiting beliefs, and thoughts.

Optimal health is associated with the optimal flow of energy in the body. So, any constriction is associated with less-than-optimal health. A constriction can occur in the *truth center* when the body is not aligned with a decision we've made. The lack of energy flow reflects a lack of resonance with a decision, situation, person, or business deal. I encourage people to let go of these stuck emotional issues because they can create a ripple effect in our energy fields that can cause restrictions in myriad ways—internally and externally. The problem is we don't associate the feeling of restriction in our physical body with the stuck emotional issue.

I worked with a client who was experiencing excessive worry. In our discussion, I learned that from a young age, he had been exposed to his father's pattern of excessive worry. The energetic imbalance of worry did not show up in energy testing for several sessions. However, fear did come up as an imbalance in the five rhythms energy system (see Section One). We worked on fear, finally releasing it, and balance was restored. In the next session, the imbalance of worry showed up by energy testing as an imbalance in a different aspect of the five rhythms energy system. So, the ripple effects of worry became fear. There appears to be a layer effect and a ripple effect of energetic imbalances. Like a stone dropped in a lake sends ripples in the water, a core issue sends ripples throughout our energy field. The presence of fear had blocked the detection of worry. So, we had to release the fear first.

As an Energy Medicine practitioner, I was aware that the body would only show an imbalance when the body was ready to let it go. We aren't shown everything that is out of balance in the present moment, which may be why it usually takes several sessions to work through all the layers and get to the core issue. In this particular client, the core issue of worry led to fear. Likely, the presence of worry and fear in the client's field attracted more experiences of worry and fear since what we transmit, we receive.

Most of us are not aware of the many layers of imbalance that precipitate or trigger our less desirable responses to what is happening. When I conduct energy tests on my clients, I am aware that I am seeing only the imbalance their bodies are ready to release. Often, energy imbalances are layered from a buildup of the effects of events or imbalances stacking up in our energy fields. I find it an extraordinary demonstration of the body's intelligence to reveal these different layers of imbalance only as they are ready to be released. That is why I can clear an imbalance in one session in one person's fields, and it takes several sessions to clear the same type of imbalance from another person's field. It is like the ripple effect of a stone dropped into the lake—the stone representing the core issue, or the original event, could result in emotional stress or shock. While my goal is to uncover the core issue that caused all the ripples or domino effect of imbalances in the energy field, my client's energy only shows the ripples at first.

Another helpful analogy for understanding the body's intelligence in revealing imbalances is the game of pickup sticks. If we try to remove the core stick first—the one in the center of all the other sticks—it is likely that the whole pile of sticks will destabilize and fall as we remove it. Likewise, energies would also become destabilized if we removed the core issue without removing the ripples first. To have real freedom in life, we need to shed the energy imbalances by letting go of old thoughts and patterns holding them in place; otherwise, we get stuck repeating what happened in the past. We are unable to move forward when we are held back by unresolved emotional issues of the past. If we are held back, it is unlikely that we will discover our Divine Purpose. We would not be in a state that resonates with our highest mission in life.

In letting go, we also must forgive. We must forgive ourselves and others by focusing on the gift of the lesson a challenging situation offers rather than our reactive or negative feelings. From this empowering perspective, we can be grateful for having the golden opportunity to learn something new with the understanding that we chose the challenges we experience. This ability to focus on learning and growth is an important part of our Spiritual Journey.

Letting go of grief is another important opportunity for growth and restoring balance. If we don't let the grief go after a period of processing loss, it remains in our energy field and holds us back, permeating all aspects of our lives. We can end up seeing our entire life through a lens of sadness, loss, and grief.

> A client came to me with excessive grief. Several people she was close to had died successively in a short period, and she could not process the grief of one loss before the next occurred. This onslaught of grief and loss left my client feeling like she was sinking into an unmanageable well of grief. But with time, energy clearing, and releasing her grief, she rose above the ashes of all the loss and decided to help others dealing with excessive grief. She realized she needed to take better care of herself through this process of letting go of her grief.

Fear is another emotional issue that holds people back and can be a game-changer when we let it go. We have fears about all kinds of things. For example, clients have come for help with all manner of fears about driving: fear of driving on the highway, driving in the dark, driving to unfamiliar places, driving over bridges, and driving in inclement weather. Fear of flying is another common issue. Whatever the fear, it is likely controlling us in ways we may or may not be aware of and preventing us from connecting with our True Selves. Fear keeps us from flowing with the Universe. There is a saying that fear is an acronym for *false evidence appearing real*, and I believe that to be very true. If we are in fear, we aren't living from our heart. If we are living in fear, we think it is all about us—that we are in it all by ourselves. We are only alone if that is our choice.

Understanding our Divinity should help us let go of fear. If we are in fear, we are disconnected from the Divine. The source of fear is thinking we don't have any support. We not only have support; we have the support of the Divine. How can we possibly feel separate and alone when we are part of the whole Universe?

One of the teachings in *A Course in Miracles* workbook is that we think there are many problems in life. But there is really only one problem. The one problem is our separation from the Divine.[135] We can choose to be ONE with the Divine or go it alone and take full responsibility for what happens in our lives. Having been on both sides of this issue, I can say that life is much better when connected with the Divine. Life is easier, happier, and more peaceful. There is no struggle. Life unfolds naturally without judgment or attachment to any specific outcome because we are in the energy flow of what we want rather than being blocked by what we don't want.

We need time to process our experiences and emotions, but holding on to them without exploring the gifts of the lessons offered limits our growth and true potential. At the right time, we can let go and move forward, having gained truth and learning from the experience. Everything in our lives happens for our greatest good, even if we don't see it right away. We have all had the experience of something happening that appeared bad at first but ended up being exceptionally amazing and helped us grow tremendously. It is all about learning, growing, and then letting go!

If we hold onto things in the past, it blocks us from moving into the future. What is done is done. The lessons from the event could be our main point and focus- not the event and not the hurt. If we hold on to too much of the past, we won't have the energetic space to create something new. Our new elevated Selves will not be able to emerge like the phoenix from the ashes.

> *Letting go is like the sudden cessation of an inner pressure or the dropping of a weight. It is accompanied by a sudden feeling of relief and lightness, with an increased happiness and freedom.*[136]

In his book *Letting Go: The Pathway of Surrender*, Dr. David Hawkins created a mechanism to help us let go. The letting go mechanism helps us understand why we hold on to low-vibrational thoughts, feelings, and beliefs. This mechanism is about connecting to the feeling of the negative emotional state by not resisting it. We carry around a huge reservoir of accumulated negative feelings, attitudes, and beliefs. The accumulated pressure makes us feel miserable and is the basis of many of our illnesses and problems. We are resigned to the negativity and explain it away as the human condition. We seek to escape it in lots of ways. The average human life is spent trying to avoid and run from the inner turmoil of fear and the threat of misery. Everyone's self-esteem is constantly threatened, both from within and without.

Allowing the thought, feeling, or belief to be is the key. Our resistance to the feeling is what holds the energy in place in our physical bodies in our *truth center*.

Once we decide to allow it to be, we can let it go. We are now open to discovering what the lesson is for us.

When we allow the feeling to be, it may be possible to let "out the energy behind it [the feeling]."[137] While letting go, ignore all thoughts. If there is no resistance, the emotional state and the feeling will decrease. It may not be immediate, but if practiced over time, we can let go of these emotional states or levels of Consciousness. I also suggest holding one hand over the area of negativity and the other hand over the heart to engage higher-vibrational energy to support the letting go process. I have also added chanting, "Let go, let go, let go," to the process. Then, take a deep breath because the breath helps to move energy. Continue for several minutes, paying attention to any changes in the negative feeling. Practicing this over and over every day will allow the energy to dissipate and release completely.

Using a particular method helps us to consciously and frequently let go at will. Utilizing a conscious process enables us to be in charge of how we feel. We are no longer at the mercy of the world and our reactions to it. We are no longer victims. Inspired by Dr. David Hawkins's *Letting Go Mechanism*, I developed the following process shown in Figure 1 to help with letting go.[138]

Figure 1: The Letting Go Process

1. Think of a specific emotional issue to let go.

2. Letting go involves being aware of a feeling, letting it come up, staying with it, and letting it run its course without wanting to make it different or do anything about it.

3. Let go any and all resistance to the feeling. Let go of any fear that is blocking the letting go.

4. Feel the feeling. Where is this feeling in the body, the truth center?

5. What does it feel like? Describe it. Give it a number between 0 and 10 to represent its level of discomfort.

6. We can touch that area in the body to connect with the energy there with one hand.

7. We can touch the heart area with the other hand to connect to higher vibration energy of our Higher Self.

8. Breathe deeply. Exhale longer than you inhale. Deep breathing helps the energy of the emotion to shift.

9. Say let go, let go, let go. Take a deep breath.

10. Keep repeating let go, let go, let go and deep breathing for 5-10 minutes.

11. Feel that area where the negative feeling was and describe the feeling now.

12. Has the feeling changed? What number is it now?

13. Repeat daily until you know the issue has been released; when that negative feeling is completely gone, and the number is 0.

14. We can try to understand that the feeling is not the truth of who we are; the feeling was created by the ego.

15. When something is fully surrendered, it disappears from our Consciousness.

Source: David R. Hawkins, MD, PhD, *Letting Go: The Pathway of Surrender*, (Hay House, Inc, 2013), 22-25.

Divine Purpose in a Nutshell

Knowing our Divine Purpose for being alive on Earth in a physical body means we realize that we are here to evolve our Souls and contribute positively to Universal Consciousness. We each have our own unique purpose, and we all share a common purpose to extend Divine Love through the Universe. We were all Divinely created. The Divine created us to become our full potential Self, the highest versions of ourselves, to realize our Divine Magnificence, and to accomplish our unique and shared missions. These are all part of the Divine Plan. We are all part of the Divine Plan. The Divine is incomplete without us, each of us. The Universe is also part of the Divine Plan, with geometric proportions, numerical sequences, and ratios within each aspect of its design so that everything is in proportion and resonant with everything else, creating symmetry, harmony, and balance.

Everything came from Universal Consciousness. Quite unknowingly, we have been co-creating with the Universe to manifest opportunities, situations, events, and people in our lives—even if we haven't been aware of it. The Universal Law of Perpetual Transmutation of Energy illustrates how something physical comes from Universal Consciousness or energy. Wave-particle duality suggests the wave and particle aspects of things are the same—as $E=mc^2$ illustrates—but are in different states. If we, as humans, have an unlimited potential or unlimited wave states, perhaps using the "observer effect" to consciously collapse the right wave of a higher-vibrational version of ourselves could help us discover our Divine Purpose and align with the flow of the Universe. Our Spiritual Journey leads us to our Divine Purpose. As we go, we learn and grow, and miraculously, life unfolds in unexpected ways to open the way to switch directions, if needed, to discover our reason for being here.

To accomplish our missions, we are invited to be in elevated states of BEing or higher levels of Consciousness. Here are some ways that help us to achieve this state so we can connect with and accomplish our mission.

- Focus on our desires, which may be our Divine Purpose.

- Live from our heart and vibrate at the level of Love Consciousness or above. Living from our hearts allows the energies of love and compassion to flow from us. We can support our hearts energetically as the gateway to optimal health, vibrancy, and resilience—physically, psychologically, mentally, emotionally, and spiritually. Developing heart-brain coherence will help us through this journey with peace, ease, and confidence.

- BE our best to fit into the Divine Plan.

- Learn how to be in equilibrium with giving and receiving to align with the natural cycles of ebb and flow in the Universe.

- Let go of lower vibrational frequency states of BEing. We must let go of who we were to allow shifts to who we are becoming. A specific letting go process will help us let go of unresolved emotional issues that do not resonate with BEing our best.

Being aligned with our Divine Mission or accomplishing it illuminates our spiritual growth. The next phase of our journey will be to awaken further to the truth and wisdom of the Universe. We recognize the fundamental need for all to understand who we truly are and align with our True Self.

Exercises

Take some time to write out your answers to the questions below. Then, think about how your answers could encompass more love and compassion and see what comes forth from within. The answers to these questions must express Divine Love and compassion if we want to live our best lives.

Exercise 1: Meditation and Journaling

How do you envision aligning more fully to your True Self and allowing a natural unfolding of your life without controlling anything?

- What are we here for?
- What am I here for?
- What is the expectation for each of us?
- What is the expectation for me?
- What is the responsibility for each of us while we are here?
- What is my responsibility?
- Write about your understanding of Consciousness.

Exercise 2: *What-if* Questions

- *What if* you identified primarily with your True Self? How would that change the way you are BEing?

- *What if* you knew your Divine Purpose? What would that be for you? What would you have to change to accomplish your Divine Purpose, if anything?

- *What if* you could let go of a major grievance or unresolved emotional issue? Do the Letting Go Process and write about how you feel after doing the process daily for one week.

- *What if* you could forgive someone completely? What would change for you?

- *What if* you could give and receive in equilibrium? Write about how well you give and how well you receive. Which is more difficult for you?

- *What if* the heart was the core regulator of the body? What perception of yourself would change?

- *What if* you could live from your Divine Purpose?

- *What if* nothing that happens to you is random? How would that change your perception of life on Earth?

AWAKENING ON THE SPIRITUAL JOURNEY

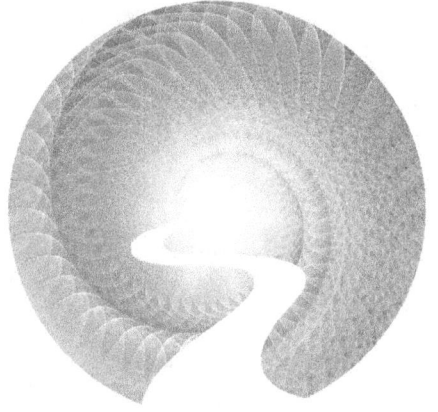

All Doors are Open

We're invited to embark on an adventure
Discovering our mission and true purpose in life.
All doors are open for us to use on this journey.
So what holds us back?

Fear stops us from moving forward.
Feeling small keeps us limited.
Not being worthy or good enough
Are messages from our subconscious we don't hear.

But these messages regulate 95% of life
And we don't know those messages are buried
Deep within regulating everything,
Our relationships, opportunities, our careers.

Our BEing-ness and focus in life
Under the control of negative messages about
Our abilities and our potential.
We are on the edge of the flow—not in the flow.

All the world is ONE, why don't we see that?
Universal Consciousness surrounds us, we ignore its nudges.
We're set on success, SMART goals our employers require
And forget about our personal needs and wants.

We're so tied up with money
We lose the value of this precious life adventure.
What a cost it is to miss the opportunities
To Be who we truly are at the very core.

All the doors are open, and we can flow to the other side of living
Focused on the Spiritual side, participating in the world like Angels.
BEing of service to others and the Universe,
We constantly put out positivity and healing.

Why do we walk past these open doors dismissing their significance?
Not realizing these doors represent a true path
A Divine Path alien to the 3D needs and desires.
Are we scared to make the 180-degree change?

Are we so lost and committed to the physical that
We can't even imagine there's anything else.
Why is it so hard to see the TRUTH?
Why is it so hard to BE the TRUTH?

All the doors are open, but we ignore the light.
We place boundaries between us and the light.
We keep ourselves protected in the limiting world
of seeing, hearing, tasting, feeling, and smelling.

We can't imagine the Universe is so wonderful, loving, and patient,
Waiting for us to wake up and see the obvious ONLY pathway
To choose and thrive as us 2.0.
To be so connected to all,
we truly need to be the ONE we intended.

Anne M. Deatly

Awakening on a Spiritual Journey

What do we need to awaken from? Awakening indicates we've been asleep or unconscious about the truth of who we are and why we are here on Earth in this lifetime. Being asleep, we focus on social status, our careers, climbing the ladders of success, money, and the material aspects of earthly life. Our thought system is *if I get more, I will be more*. We need to struggle to get our piece of the pie. We are insecure and feel unsafe in the world, constantly trying to prove that we are worthy of our existence. We are seeking things outside of ourselves to make us feel whole. We seek love, approval, and guidance from others because we simply don't trust ourselves.

Sometimes, we are living a nightmare enveloped by stress, anxiety, fear, and trauma. We must wake up to become conscious and realize that life is meant to be all about love, joy, and peace. We have free will. We are the creators of our lives and choose the nightmare or the awakened state.

Awakening is about opening to a new way of BEing and understanding to support our journey of discovering our Divine Purpose, revealing the mystery and joy of living a Divinely guided Spiritual Life. Let all the doors be open to finding our unique and specific path of BEing, living in alignment with our Divine Purpose, and unlocking the truth of our deep knowing that we all are meant to be here. We all have a significant function to fulfill that is uniquely our own. We must awaken to our separation from the Divine.

Choosing an awakening path opens us to *seeing* past what we perceive with our eyes to what appears to our inner vision. In this way, we become more available to witness the miracles happening in our lives and be present to new experiences beyond our expectations and what we may have thought possible. It's an opportunity to realize there are things beyond our current knowing that can change how our lives unfold. Once known and experienced, we can put this wisdom into practice while realizing we can't go back to our old way of BEing. We learn to be observers of who we are BEing and what we are doing. This observer guides us to stay on the path of wisdom and truth.

Perhaps the natural world also has a Divine Purpose to elevate its level of Consciousness. It accomplishes this purpose, in part, by supporting us in our Divine Purpose through the Oneness that connects all that is—us, the natural world, the Divine, everything. In other words, if we achieve our Divine Purpose,

Universal Consciousness, including the natural world, is also elevated, and we receive ideal conditions of balance, harmony, and order to support our evolutionary journey.

Embarking upon a path of awakening to our Divine Purpose transforms our lives and expands our awareness, helping us to allow and accept change rather than resisting it to conform to what we expect or think we want. Accepting and allowing enables us to see the world and each other through a different lens that allows life to unfold naturally. We begin to detach from our obsession with outcome, freeing ourselves from the need for judgment and comparing what happened to what we thought should happen. The more we surrender to what is, the more we become aligned with our Soul's Divine Purpose, changing our state of BEing, and living from a space of love and inner peace.

In these ways and more, the awakening journey aligns us more deeply with the truth of who we really are as Divine Sovereign Creator BEings. We start to see the world differently. Living a life from the form realm perspective of our physical world is very different from the spiritual realm perspective. From the perspective of the higher Consciousness of our Spiritual Nature, we can expand our awareness and understanding of how we co-create our lives, situations, and even our health through the vibrational frequency of the energy we transmit into the world. We open to seeing and experiencing a completely new dimensionality to our lives. We become aware of things we never knew before. Things and people seem different, as if hidden truths are now in plain sight. We will see patterns we never recognized before and understand ourselves in different, positive ways. It may seem that the world around us is changing, but actually, what's changing is us. We become deeply grounded in the understanding that there's so much more to life than working and paying bills and, in between, finding relief in some form of escapism.

But not everyone is ready to awaken to their Divine Purpose and Higher Guidance. Some choose instead to go through life with metaphorical blinders that block them from this higher perspective and focus instead on the mental chatter of their ego—their false self or subconscious mind—that is trying to protect them from perceived or unknown threats. This is fine. It is exactly as it needs to be, for in this realm of free will, there is no greater freedom than the sovereignty to choose, consciously or otherwise. It is just as important to accept, allow, and appreciate another's choice as it is to allow, accept, and appreciate our own. Everyone is on their own unique journey of learning their life lessons exactly how they need to learn them. Everyone is exactly where they need to be at any given moment.

When we start to awaken to our Soul's calling, opening to exploring a greater sense of Self and purpose, there can be near instantaneous moments of awareness—like a light switch being flipped on, or more gradual, like the slow turning of a dimmer switch gradually lighting a room. We may even choose to turn the light switch off and turn away from the niggling question about the purpose and meaning of our life for long periods of our life. But when we are ready, we reach a paradigm shift in choosing to follow the signs and guideposts of our awakening path where there is no turning back to living a life without connection to our Divine Purpose.

> My first real awakening was the discussion with Mike before he died when he said, "I am excited about this next step in my life. I am going to get the answers to all my questions. I think it has something to do with the String Theory."
>
> Since we'd never discussed the String Theory, I wasn't sure I knew what he was talking about. I wondered if he had gotten messages from some unseen source or perhaps from some higher experience of himself in the process of his transitioning.
>
> The next step of my awakening was a profound *knowing* that there was a healing modality I'd never heard of before that could have saved Mike's life. My body shook, opening my awareness to receive guidance to attend an Energy Medicine workshop that transformed my life. This experience also expanded my understanding that we are much more than the physical beings we appear to be. I had a sudden and profound knowing that we are energy beings. We sense and receive information from the world around us through our energy fields, and we transmit the energy of our thoughts, feelings, and beliefs out into the world.

Being on an awakening journey is learning to master our mindset, re-framing our experiences, and observing how this changes our life experiences. Consciously witnessing these changes helps us to fully grasp the significance of our choices and realize our true power to create the life we want. We start seeing life very differently from the old programming that life is all about hard work, pain, suffering, lack, and limitations.

Awakening is about living and BEing our Higher Self.

Everything Exists in Balance with its Opposite

Universal Consciousness is designed to support us in awakening to and accomplishing our Divine Purpose by maintaining a container, or space, of natural balance and harmony most aligned with creativity and connecting to our Higher Self. Nothing exists alone. Everything in the Universe is connected to and in tension-balance with its opposite—yin and yang. The existence of yin and yang opposites is like a seesaw of perpetual movement and transfer of energy, a constant flow of one becoming the other to maintain a balance that fosters growth and expansion in a vibrant dance of interconnecting and interdependent forces with each other. It is accepted in Chinese culture that the Universe was created from chaos. From that disorganized state, the yin and yang cycles were created in the natural world. We not only witness these cycles in the changing of physical form, but we can also even experience the expression of yin and yang in our bodies and our lives. [139]

Yin-Yang Balance

Yin and yang work together as interdependent and interactive aspects of one whole.[140] This tension of opposite but complementary, interconnected, and interdependent forces actually creates the rhythm and cyclic nature of how *one becomes the other*. Similar to the heart organ pumping blood through our bodies, the yin-yang tension-balance moves energies through the Universe. If we understand this, it can become a powerful new perspective for understanding all life: the cycles of the seasons, the cycle of day and night, the tides coming in and going out, the functioning of the body, problems and solutions, male and female, expanding and contracting, the breathing in and out. All things reflect a continuity or continuum of change, a rhythm, a natural flow from one aspect to another.

Another way yin-yang balance works to support our living Universe is through movement. Movement is an essential component of our living Universe. Nothing is stagnant; the Universe is dynamic and constantly moving and changing. The primordial principle of the Universe is to move forward and flow toward more life, to grow, expand, and increase its vibrational frequency. The tension of the yin-yang opposing but complementary forces create continuous movement from imbalance to balance and balance to imbalance, pushing and pulling, resulting in energetic rhythms, patterns, and cycles for Universal expansion.

Yin energy governs the internal life, grounded Earth energy.[141] Yin is the receptive inward-directed rhythm, feminine, soft, slow, and yielding. Yin is characterized as diffuse, cold, wet, and passive, associated with water, the Earth, the moon, the oceans, and nighttime. Yin energies govern introspection plus self-reflection, inner strength, and inner transformation.

Yang energy, by contrast, governs the external life and action in the world. Yang is more outward, active energy and expresses an external rhythm. Yang is assertive, masculine, fast, hard, focused, hot, and dry. Yang is associated with fire, sky, sun, and daytime.[142] Yang energies move outward, growing and expanding.

The yin-yang symbol is often described as two tear drops swirling in a circular motion, signifying the shifting flow and balance of yin energy—the black teardrop, and yang energy—the white teardrop. Opposite each other in direction, the two teardrops show that as one increases, the other decreases until, eventually, one becomes the other. The dot of the color in each teardrop represents the presence of the opposing energy within each energetic force.

Figure 2 Yin Yang Symbol

The ancient form of the symbol was an empty white circle described as the infinite possibility of undifferentiated potential. This empty circle represents the precursor to the yin and yang; the Oneness before the separation into duality.[143] From this perspective, the yin-yang symbol represents the creation of the Universe from chaotic energy—the empty circle—to order created out of opposing forces, signifying that the Universe completely changes into everything from nothingness.[144] The addition of the white and black dots is a more modern version of this symbol, representing the potential for inner transformation.[145]

Being equal in their opposing forces, when one quality, represented as one of the teardrops, reaches its peak, it will naturally transform into the opposite quality— light and dark, fire and water, waxing and waning, expansion and contraction. This is a paradox of simultaneous unity and duality.[146]

Yin and yang are sometimes perceived as the sun over a mountain and valley. The yin aspect of this vision is the shady or dark area blocked by the mountain. The yang aspect is the area where the sun is visible and vibrant. During the day, as the sun appears to move through the sky with the Earth's rotation, the yin and yang areas seem to exchange places. The sunny area becomes dark, and the dark area becomes sunny. What was blocked is now visible; what was visible is now blocked.[147] One has become the other.

Between these black and white opposites, a continuum progresses from light to dark and vice versa. Continuing the same theme discussed above, envision a moment in the day when there is no light in the sky, and then, a moment later, a little light comes into view. The light continues to expand until there is only light and no darkness. Then, in the next moment, a little darkness comes back into view and expands across the night sky until it completely engulfs the light. The complementary forces of yin and yang are inextricably connected as parts of the same whole. One opposite doesn't exist without the other. With coins, no tails exist without the head. No shadow exists without light. No palm exists without the top of the hand. No north pole exists without the south pole. No downside exists without an upside. Every advance is complemented by a retreat, and every rise transforms into a fall.[148] In and out, up and down, and back and forth equal yin and yang as complementary aspects of life.

The yin and yang are revealed in aspects of natural growth. Let's focus on the life cycle of a seed. In yang action, the seed germinates in the Earth's soil and breaks through the Earth's surface, growing upward. A yin activity follows when the seedling reaches its full height and falls back to Earth. The leaves of the seedling exhibit a yang activity in growing toward the sunlight; at the same time, the roots grow underground in a yin activity, going deep into the darkness.[149]

Yin and yang energy is also present in the human body. In Traditional Chinese Medicine, good health is directly related to the balance between yin and yang qualities within oneself.[150] If yin-yang energy becomes unbalanced, it can result in illness or disease. In human anatomy, yin energy is associated with the front of the body, such as the face, front torso, and the insides of the legs and arms. Yang energy is associated with the back of the body, shoulders, back, and the outsides of the legs and arms. Each of the fourteen meridians in our bodies also has a yin or yang quality by virtue of its direction of flow in the body. Yin meridians flow upward through the body, and yang meridians flow downward, energetically feeding the body organs connected with their respective energies. Yin organs are the dense tissue organs that constantly function: the heart, spleen, lung, kidney, and liver. Yang organs have a hollow space within their tissues and only work when processing food or fluids, such as the bladder, gall bladder, small intestine, stomach, and large intestine.

Breathing is another example of a yin and yang cycle in the body. The yin aspect is expressed when we breathe in, opening and expanding the lungs to let air in until they reach full capacity. Then, the yin flow reverses itself and becomes yang energy on the exhalation as we let the air out of the lungs and the body until it is fully expelled. As the body releases the air, it is already preparing to take in more air for the next breath in a continuous in-out cycle. Each organ and system in the body, from digestive to cardiovascular, ebbs and flows through yin and yang phases.

Understanding the rhythm of yin-yang energy offers profound insight into creating balance that we can use in practical, everyday ways. In general, our culture relates more to the yang energy of action than the yin energy of inward reflection. But if we are all yang action and doing, doing, doing, then we are not allowing for yin time for revitalization. This imbalance will lead to burnout. Too much yang activity interferes with the body's biological clock or circadian rhythm. Too much yang activity can make us more susceptible to illness. To be healthy, we must bring balance into our lives. It behooves us to create time for daily yin activities like silence, meditation, yoga, journaling, and reading. It is important for us to re-center and get back to our True Essence. Getting to bed as early as possible helps us be more balanced. Our bodies need yin time to rest and revitalize. Spending time in gratitude is also yin. Gratitude helps to keep us grounded and more present to life and calms the mental chatter in our heads. Making changes like these can open the door to vibrant, radiant health.[151] Too much yin energy expression can also cause imbalance. We need to move and be active to get our energies moving so we don't get stuck, feel pain, or block the energy flow.

The Universal Law of Polarity

Opposites in balance are such important components in the Universe that there is a Universal Law of Polarity, which states everything exists with its opposite simultaneously in equal proportions. Nothing exists alone. Opposites cannot exist without the other. The paradox is that opposites are really the same thing but different aspects. One might consider that everything has a dual nature. These different aspects come together to create a *whole* thing. For example, each side of the magnet is magnetized to opposing forces, the north and south magnetic poles, which are inextricably linked together. The magnet loses its functionality without these opposing forces working within it. Also, consider that we can't remove the north side of a magnet without having some of the south pole attached. They are so linked together; they can't exist alone. Likewise, on a planetary scale, the north pole cannot exist without being connected to the south pole, and the south pole cannot exist without the north pole. The polar ends are the opposites of the same thing—a dual nature, and in between, the opposites form a continuum.

We can add to our understanding of polar opposites by considering success and failure as being connected on the same continuum. The good news is that failure cannot exist alone. Failure must exist with the potential for success. The negative and positive are inextricably linked together. Similarly, lack exists in a continuum with abundance. Hate exists only with the potential for love. Understanding that opposites exist simultaneously on a continuum, we can see how they are just different expressions or aspects of the same thing.[152]

The Universal Law of Polarity helps us understand the value of the contrast between what we do and don't want to experience. We can be in gratitude for both. For example, when we have abundance, we can appreciate the contrast relative to lack, and the wisdom of the experience of lack helps us to appreciate and understand abundance. There are valuable life lessons available to us in understanding the continuum of contrast, making us less likely to take for granted the abundance and the positive when we have experienced lack and negativity.

We can also apply the principle of the Law of Polarity to understand the energy of problems and solutions as polar ends of the same situation. If we are focused on the negative energy of the problem, we cannot see the solution. On the other hand, if we focus only on the positive energy of the solution, perhaps we may miss an important lesson that was present in the negative energy of the problem. We have all experienced talking about our woes and what is happening to us by focusing on the problem and the negative energy. But how many of our friends, peers, and relatives share what is going well in their lives, the solutions arising from positive energy? Likely, it is not as many as those who share their problems and even less engage in conversation with a good balance of problem and solution energy.

However, according to the Universal Law of Polarity, our problems exist in the same space at the same time as the solution and in an equal proportion. Therefore, we need to focus on finding the solution rather than wallowing in the problem while staying attuned to the value of the problem as an opportunity for growth. We can understand this problem-solution duality as different aspects of the same or whole situation sending a pulsing vibration through the Universe. This pulsing or movement is the yin-yang balance. We decide not to get stuck in the problem when we focus on the solution. We are aware there is another choice right there in front of us. We need to open our inner vision to see the solution. When we focus on the solution, energy will flow away from the opposite pole of problem toward solution. Where our attention goes, the energy flows.

Taking this concept even further, imagine a continuum of states of BEing from human incarnation to our Divine Essence—one form, the other formless. There is the formless aspect of the Divine in our human form and a form aspect of our formless Divine Spiritual Nature. The human and the Divine are inextricably linked within us and cannot be separated. They are connected by the balance of yin-yang tension in a push-pull dynamic. One becomes the other. Humans become Divine, and the Divine becomes human.

The Power of Awareness

Throughout millennia, humanity has had at least some sense of higher meaning and purpose. But in these times, more than ever, we are waking up as a collective to that innate sense that we are here to make a significant contribution to human evolution by realizing our Divine Purpose. As our curiosity opens to this blossoming awareness, we begin to see that we are all connected to the Divine and have access to all the knowledge and wisdom of this energy and Consciousness to accomplish our Divine Purpose. All the wisdom and power of the Divine is within us, not outside of us. All Consciousness is within us. As Neville Goddard states, "The whole of creation exists in you, and it is your destiny to become increasingly aware of its infinite wonders and to experience ever greater and grander portions of it."[153]

Expanding our awareness of Divine Consciousness, our Divine Purpose, and the wisdom and skills we have access to for accomplishing this purpose is key to skillfully navigating the awakening journey and living our best lives—BEing the best version of ourselves. As our awareness of connection and purpose expands and deepens, we more consciously attract or magnetize the experiences we need to grow and evolve toward our highest state of BEing. We more easily discover our Divine Purpose and become aligned with accomplishing our Divine Purpose. We make better decisions to fulfill this purpose on our journey of discovery.

Awareness empowers us with new ideas, new perspectives, and different ways of BEing that would not otherwise appear to us, allowing us to soar to our highest potential for joy, abundance, and living a meaningful life with a sense of true purpose. Part of that expanding awareness is envisioning the life we are creating as overlayed with our life in the present moment—creating from an awareness of living our vision in the present moment rather than seeing it in the future.

> I spent most of my life ignorant of how the Universe really works. My life has been transformed by learning the truth about the laws governing the Universe. I now have the awareness needed to live an extraordinary life.
>
> Being aware that I was Divinely created for a specific mission is empowering. No longer do disempowering ideas about myself and my life control my behaviors.
>
> I am uplifted to live my best life and contribute at the highest level possible. I start each day with a positive attitude, knowing that I will have new opportunities to see with the vision of the Divine and think through the Divine Mind. I can pull back and see the bigger picture of my life and envision the Divine's Invitation for me. Now, I can help to improve the lives of others and give or provide accordingly.

Another key to expanding my awareness of how Universal Consciousness works in creating the world we experience was learning the principles of quantum physics. It transformed my life and my understanding of working with energy to discover and live my Divine Purpose and navigate my new life. Knowing that everything and everyone is energy made all the difference in my sense of feeling empowered to live by different principles and paradigms that completely changed my life in big and small ways.

I had broken my right wrist, and the orthopedic doctor was very impressed with my recovery and that I hadn't experienced any pain. I told him I am an energy healer, and he acknowledged it helped my amazing recovery. He said I didn't need physical therapy and even suggested that I do push-ups to build strength. *What? How am I supposed to put all my weight on the broken wrist?*

As part of my energy work to heal my broken wrist, I regularly massaged my right hand and weaved figure 8s over my right hand, wrist, and arm to ensure the energy flowed along the pathways down my arm and off my fingers. I also pulled, opened up, and twisted my fingers to enhance the energy flow in my hand. Balancing the energy of the area impacted by the injury and keeping it flowing along the affected pathway undoubtedly helped my body heal completely and quickly.

Another way my deepening awareness of quantum physics principles transformed my life and amplified my frequency was a growing understanding of how our energy fields interact with and affect each other, our surroundings, and our environment. We are one with each other, the world around us, and Universal Consciousness. Because we all share the same energies, how we exchange this shared energy affects everything and everyone; I talked about this before with the "observer's effect," but I want to address this concept with a new awareness.

An example of this connection to shared energy is testing how well the five rhythms energy of water, wood, fire, earth, and metal are balanced and flowing in our bodies. The five rhythms system is all about emotional balance. Emotional imbalance is interconnected with physical balance. Significantly, emotions are the root of physical imbalance and pain. But the five rhythms are also closely attuned to our environment.[154] Each rhythm is separate and has a different function, but the energy of all the rhythms works together to make up the whole system. In testing for the flow of five rhythms energy, the element of water is envisioned on the right hip, wood on the right waist, fire at the center just below the sternum, earth at the left waist, and metal on the left hip. The flow of energy between these points is envisioned as a clockwise circle beginning with water and flowing to wood, then fire, then earth, then metal, and then back to water in an ongoing cycle of flow.

A practiced energy healer can test for imbalances in each rhythm to determine whether one or more of the five rhythm energies are out of balance. A rhythm imbalance may reflect an emotional imbalance because the control cycle is disconnected. The control cycle is envisioned as the shape of a star beginning with water, which controls fire, fire controls metal, metal controls wood, wood controls earth, and earth controls water. If any of these energies get disconnected, their aspect of control is lost. Once the imbalanced energy is identified, we can use the energy work to restore the balance and return to an emotional state of optimal well-being.

The story of how I discovered the truth of how I affect my environment happened just a few days before I was going to put my house on the market to sell. I had asked a handyman to come and fix a few things in my house that weren't operating 100 percent. One of the needed repairs was the mechanism in the bathtub that controls the flow of water from the tub. After the handyman had *fixed* that bathtub mechanism, I took a bath, and when I let the bath water drain out of the tub, it flowed into my dining room ceiling and then down the wall into the basement ceiling. Both ceilings were destroyed. I went to bed that night feeling anxious about the delay in putting my house on the market while waiting for the repairs to be completed.

I woke up the next morning realizing I was the problem. Somehow, I realized that the water rhythm in my own energy system was out of control and had played out by flooding in my house. I immediately checked the control cycle of the five rhythms on my body. Indeed, the earth to water control was disconnected in me!

Quickly, I fixed the issue energetically by connecting the earth rhythm to the water rhythm, so the water was no longer *out of control*. No more floods! I realize that this sounds bizarre. But I didn't make this up. That was a powerful experience for me to realize how true it is that we are tuned to our environments and how we affect what happens in our environment.

All Wisdom and Power are Within You

Taking the concept that we are all connected through Universal Consciousness a step further reveals that being connected also means that all wisdom and the power of this shared energy is within us. Knowing this, we no longer need to look outside ourselves for the answers to our deepest questions or for the love and support needed to discover who we really are and why we are here. Nothing outside of us can produce any more support than what is available within us through our connection to the vastness of our shared energy with All That Is. We are more powerful and wiser than we realize.

In her book, *The Power is Within You*, Louise Hay explains that we can surrender our lives to the Divine. We can use this essential magnificent support as intended. Our lives will result in more ease, deeper satisfaction, and an understanding of our co-creative ability. The Divine Mind and our minds are inextricably connected. Divine Energy is "pure love, freedom, understanding, and compassion."[155] If we surrender, we benefit from the Divine's benevolence, support, and deep love for us.

So, what limits us from accessing, engaging with, and fully expressing this Infinite Power within us? Louise Hay suggests that to experience this Inner Power and create the lives we want, we have to believe it's actually possible to do this and "release the patterns in our lives that are creating the conditions we say we don't want."[156] I agree. We cannot be our best if we carry unresolved issues from our past. Our present and future selves need the freedom to be who we are in the present or who we are evolving to be in the future. We must release the binds that hold us back in a less desired space and time. Somewhere, I heard this car analogy: *we can't have our foot on the accelerator and brake simultaneously and expect to get anywhere.* Our foot on the brake is similar to holding onto unresolved issues. We must let go of past issues to allow the space for our future selves to evolve as intended. We must let go of the past to become a more evolved version of ourselves.

Setting Intentions

Intention setting is a powerful way to overcome our habitual negative patterns and move forward in life. But what I am suggesting here is beyond the kind of intention setting we are familiar with, like an intention to fulfill a New Year resolution to lose weight. This is taking intention setting to a whole new level of engaging the support of our Higher Self, our Inner Power—setting an intention to evolve to the higher version of ourselves. In The *Power of Intention: Learning to Co-create Your Way*, Wayne Dyer explains how intention is an energy force in the Universe. This intention energy, or field of energy, is around and within us.[157]

Focusing on intention is a way to experience aspects of quantum physics in our everyday reality. Focusing on intention is a concrete way to apply the information of wave-particle duality, and the observer effect ourselves. We can influence what is happening in our earthly lives. Setting intentions exemplifies how we can use the energy around us and within us for our benefit, the benefit of others, and the Universe.

Looking at this phenomenon from a scientific perspective, Lynne McTaggart, a renowned expert in setting intentions, has authored two books of scientific research on intentions.[158] Her goal was to determine the value of setting intentions in transforming ourselves and the world. Her clear conclusion was that "thought affects physical reality."[159] She explains that decades of scientific research from prestigious institutions around the world showed that thoughts affect everything from "the simplest machines to the most complex living beings."[160] McTaggart shows evidence of the tangibility of our thoughts and intentions as having physical aspects. Our thoughts have the power to impact the world and physicality.[161]

McTaggart's work makes it evident that setting intentions directs thoughts in a conscious way to change what is happening in our lives and attract a field of energy to support reaching the intended goal. Setting intentions clarifies our awareness of what we want and transmits that to the Universe, connecting us to Universal Consciousness and inviting its participation to create an experience that aligns with our best and highest potential. In this way, our intentions invite the power of our true potential without limiting the outcome.

Setting intentions also helps us focus our attention and energy to make more conscious decisions about what we want to happen and where we want to go on our Spiritual Journey. Once an intention is set, conscious attention to fulfill that intention intensifies the focus and magnifies the energy of the intention that naturally attracts Life Force Energy toward the intention. This provides an ideal opportunity to observe our awakening process and affirm that we are more powerful than ever imagined. Each of us has the Infinite Potential and power to bring into form what we want through conscious intention. Understanding that we also have unlimited potential to amplify the power of that intention by consciously connecting with all the energies around us through Universal Consciousness, intention setting is a valuable and powerful way to co-create our lives.

To set an intention, we direct our Life Force Energy to something positive—something we really want. To enhance the energy and strength of the intention, we can set the intention from our heart space. After the intention is set, we detach from the outcome, trusting and surrendering to the wisdom of the Universe. We then physically take action, expecting the intention is on its way. We dig the ditch and then let go of controlling what is built. Anything is possible.

It may be difficult at first to fully grasp the true power and potential of intention setting through a conscious connection to the shared energy, especially when we have been so doggedly programmed only to believe what we can perceive with our five senses: see, hear, touch, smell, and taste. But once we step into this higher level of understanding, we begin to experience how easily and quickly we can make changes in our lives to feel happy, joyful, empowered, and at peace.

> I use intentions all the time in my practice to get more specific information about issues in my clients' energy fields. For example, if I want to find the priority imbalance, I set the intention to find it. I live in a completely different world than the one I was raised in as a child. The world I grew up in was limited. There was lack. The only way to get ahead was to work hard. The harder I worked, the more tired I became. The more tired I became, the more I lashed out at people. It was a repeating cycle. But with my new awareness, I am free of these limiting beliefs and subconscious stories that life is hard and difficult. Aligning with the Divine to co-create my life through conscious intention has freed me from struggle and suffering.
>
> Curious about intention setting, I enrolled in Lynne McTaggart's Intention Masterclass, a year-long program. Participating in a Power of Eight Intention group was an exciting part of the program. These groups of eight people met weekly during the program to focus on the intentions of two or three members or their loved ones. The basic idea was that each intention was magnified sevenfold by the other members, focusing on the intention for the one. For the most part, the intention setting was successful and mirrored what McTaggart explains in her books *The Intention Experiment* and *The Power of Eight*.[162] My group of eight formed a tremendous

bond, and we are still meeting periodically to support each other and magnify the power of intentions for each other.

Conscious intention setting means becoming acutely aware of what we are focused on to create what happens in our life—*where intention and attention goes, the energy flows*. Get real clarity. Envision or visualize only what you desire with single-pointed focus and concentrate on it. Believe it and feel it as if it is already a present fact. Don't resist what we don't want. Accept what is; love what is.[163] Resistance holds what we don't want within us. Instead, renounce what you don't want and make a clear and definitive declaration of what you do want. After the declaration, don't give any more attention to what you don't want and focus solely on what you do want. Make sure your actions only match what you want; stay in alignment and do what you are able to do to bring that into reality.

What We Believe About Ourselves Matters

Another aspect of expanding awareness is freeing ourselves from believing that we do not have any power over how the external world affects our lives. As Neville Goddard explains, what happens in our lives is determined by what we believe about ourselves.[164]

Opening to the idea that we have power and influence over the outside world and grounding that belief in our everyday awareness may be more challenging than expected. For the most part, how we were raised, and our life experiences do not empower us to believe that we have a hand in creating the world we experience. Instead, we are programmed with a sense of self-doubt that shuts the door on any belief in our ability to create the life we want. The pervasive cultural, familial, and collective messaging aimed at fear-based survival that we receive from a young age imprints deep levels of fear, lack, and doubt about our self-worth that require a concerted effort to release. During our early developmental stage before the age of seven, messages from parents, teachers, and friends telling us that we are less than, not good enough, or in danger, along with our interpretation of events to support these messages, land in our subconscious mind becoming indisputable facts about ourselves and our world. Because the subconscious mind lacks any analytical capacity to process or refute information, it simply stores the data it receives.

It is not until our conscious minds are more fully developed after age seven that we can access the analytical skills needed to accept or reject the information we receive. Interestingly, as the cognitive skills of our conscious mind come online, we disconnect from our subconscious minds, leaving the old messages from our childhood unchecked and stored away in the hidden file cabinets of our mind. Despite our lack of awareness of what's in all those hidden files, it may be surprising to know that our subconscious mind regulates 95-98 percent of our lives. But, of course, this begs the question, do you really want your seven-year-old self running your life?

Since what we think about ourselves largely comes from what went into our subconscious minds before we were seven, it most likely does not align with the truth of our Divine Nature and Purpose. In other words, the immutable truth of our Divinity and our ability to access this aspect of ourselves is obscured by reliance on misaligned conceptual thought and subconscious programming that translates into what and how we experience the world within and around us. Fortunately, we can override the old programming of our subconscious and change our view of ourselves and, ultimately, what happens in our lives. I am very passionate about this. What happens in our lives is a product of our own Consciousness, so please do not criticize or berate yourself for negative beliefs about yourself. Instead, use this awareness of your seven-year-old self to let go of the old subconscious programming and make room for new understanding about who you really are and your true magnificence.

Changing our view of ourselves may take hold quickly or evolve over time. One way to look at this rich field for sowing the seeds of expanded awareness is to look at the goal of understanding and appreciating the truth of who you really are as a new goal or burning desire you are working toward. *Who do you have to become, or what do you need in your life to BE that burning desire?* Once you have a clear vision, view yourself as already BEing in that state of Consciousness and experience. This changes your vibrational frequency, enabling you to create the life and experiences you desire. You can think of this process as BEing in the spirit of your burning desires. Imagine what it feels like to be in the state of BEing you desire—feel, experience, and see it. Go further and believe that you already are that or have what you need. If you want to heal from a disease, believe you are already in optimal health. If you want more money, believe and act in ways that make you feel like you already have it. If you want a better relationship, be more loving, compassionate, and understanding of the person or persons you want to have a better relationship with.

One way of understanding why this processing of BEing the outcome we want works relates to our understanding of our inherent interconnectedness with the quantum energy field. Even if we are not consciously engaging with this powerful force, we are constantly interacting with it to create our world and experiences. As we discovered in previous sections, what we transmit into the quantum field dramatically influences what is created. So, when we visualize what we desire with clarity and strong intention, our transmission is more powerful, and energy is magnetized more quickly to affect that result. Because we can visualize it in the present moment, we can feel this is the truth in the present moment. We are changing our lives using the technology of the quantum field.

See what you desire as a single-pointed focus and concentrate on it. Believe it and feel it as if it is already a present fact. Feel the feeling of having that right now. Be in the energy of that in the present moment.

Bringing this discussion back to our Spiritual Journey, we must believe in our own Divinity to be the best version of ourselves in this lifetime and impress this awareness of BEing upon our subconscious mind. We must start telling ourselves the truth. The more often we tell ourselves the truth about our Divinity and magnificence, the less the subconscious mind will counter by subversively acting from the opposite belief. Our new belief is overriding old self-limiting beliefs. High-vibrational frequencies superimpose and deconstruct low-vibrational frequencies.

All is Happening for Us

Another level of awakening is the understanding that everything is happening for us—not to us. All the obstacles, challenges, or hardships we experience are offered as a way to learn, grow, and evolve. This is the most fundamental way we exercise our creative power. If we truly understand this concept, we can accept all that is happening as a welcome journey for the greatest growth and embrace the richness of each experience. We are no longer victims of our circumstances and challenges but rather lucky recipients of circumstances and challenges that stretch us with opportunities to learn, grow, and evolve, even if we don't see the *good* at first. We develop and trust this concept with our awakening.

You may already have some understanding of the perspective that everything is happening for us at our specific vibrational frequency. We always have the option to change that frequency to create from different states of Consciousness and awareness.

Universally shared energy has no option but to flow toward more life, growth, and expansion. It conspires with us on our journey toward more life and growth. The Universe is Divine, a benevolent, compassionate, and kind Consciousness. I invite you to awaken to this good news and flow with the Universe toward more life, accepting and allowing it to bring you what you need to grow.

Allowing Life to Unfold Naturally

Letting go of control to allow for the Universe to support us is hard to do. However, if we insist on being in charge and making decisions that we think are best for us or listening to our egos, we will limit our potential to grow, learn, evolve, and progress on our awakening journey. Clinging to the need to control slows, if not stops, our progress because it's based on a false presumption that our ego self, our force-of-will self, knows more about what we need than our Spiritual Self, our Higher Self—the Divine. Without discounting the need for an aspect of ourselves that attends to ensuring our survival, it is a mistake to put that self in the driver's seat for our Soul Journey. Instead, we need to surrender that self to the Divine within us and All That Is, allowing life to unfold naturally, in our highest interest, and in Divine Right Timing and Order. By surrendering the part of us that needs to control, we remove the blocks that prevent Divine Wisdom from illuminating what is best for our Soul Journey.

Surrendering as a form of accepting is also a positive emotional state of BEing or level of Consciousness that is just above *willingness* on Dr. Hawkins's *Map of Consciousness*.[165] According to Dr. Hawkins, the correlating attributes to the *acceptance* level of Consciousness are the view of God as merciful, a view of life as harmonious, the emotion of forgiving, and the process of transcendence. Accepting allows us to come to terms with the realization that we don't, and can't possibly, know and understand everything; if we did, we wouldn't be here because there would be nothing to learn to sustain our growth and evolution. Accepting also means that we are willing to be in the energy of the situation or event and be open to what is being offered to help us learn something new, grow, and evolve. We can trust that Universal Consciousness is carrying us in flow toward more life and expansion for our greater good and to benefit all.

In reality, we only know what we know. We don't know what is beyond our human perception capability. The more we learn, the more we realize how much more there is to know. Knowledge seems to grow exponentially and expand, leaving us with more than enough to focus on within ourselves, let alone worrying about what is happening within others. As much as we may want to shift that focus at times and dwell on the behavior of others, it's important to remember that we are all on the same trajectory of learning through life's lessons. While we may not agree with how others are behaving in the present, we can at least accept that whatever is happening for them is exactly right for their journey of learning, growing, and evolving, just as our journey is right for us. Accepting and allowing others to be who they are is freedom for ourselves and others.

Letting life unfold naturally is in the same line of thinking. It means accepting what happens without judgment or attachment. Perhaps we are attached to how things should be or outcomes because we believe it's necessary to satisfy a perceived need for safety and security. But if we stay in the safety and security of survival mode, we aren't taking risks. We aren't learning, and we aren't growing. According to David Neagle, Life Coach at *Life is Now*, safety and security are the second basic needs behind love and connection.[166] So, safety and security want to exert a strong pull in our lives, but focusing on this need holds us back from thriving and keeps us in survival mode, just barely hanging on.

Being in the low-vibrational frequency of survival mode also attracts like energy into our field, creating experiences that affirm the need for safety and trapping us in a prison of survival. Another way we trap ourselves in a cycle that prevents us from achieving the vibrational frequency of acceptance is the desire for perfection as a measure of worth in ourselves and others. It is another way of focusing on what should be that prevents us from accepting the richness of what is.

By contrast, when we operate from the thriving mode of *acceptance*, we take risks and stretch ourselves to do more and BE more of our potential. We put ourselves out there and make our way. As a result, we are more resilient and can adapt to situations as they arise. We know we can try again if things don't work out the first time. We pick ourselves up and keep going because we have learned a valuable lesson, rather than an affirmation of failure. The more we pick ourselves up and keep going, the stronger we become, and the easier it is to overcome challenges and find the gold within them. If we quit along the path of our desires, we will never win. Perhaps it was Vince Lombardi that inspired his team to never give up. Winning comes with staying in the game.

Accepting ourselves and surrendering control can be difficult, but it's a necessary step on our awakening journey and a critical first step in being able to accept others.

Allowing and Accepting

The Universe is not stagnant; it is always moving and changing, flowing effortlessly within changing patterns and cycles. What a great role model for us! Expect change. Expect uncertainty. Bless change and uncertainty.

As strong as this might sound, if we aren't moving, growing, and expanding, then we are actually in the process of dying because there is no neutral state. We are constantly flowing toward one end of the continuum of increase, growth, life or decline, decay, and death. We need change and uncertainty to stretch ourselves and stimulate growth. To make that change work for us in the most beneficial way for our awakening, we need to align and flow with the Divine, Universal Consciousness and allow it to guide our lives. When we resist change, we resist the flow of the Universe and lose its greatest power to support us through conscious co-creation. Although Universal Consciousness is always co-creating with us whether we realize it or not, choosing not to engage with this aspect of ourselves and what's available takes away the invaluable guidance and help of a powerful ally. Allowing the Universe to bring us what we want as it comes is a very evolved, joyful, and self-aware way to work with the power of Universal Consciousness and Intelligence.

Our State of BEing

BEing is more than character, values, and beliefs. BEing, in my definition, is the vibrational frequency of a person's energies, a level of Consciousness. As discussed in Section One, our vibrational frequency is always transmitting energy, regardless of our awareness of what is being transmitted. We are the sum vibrational frequency of all our words, thoughts, feelings, and beliefs at any moment. Our vibrational frequency illuminates our state of BEing.

Our state of BEing is how we express ourselves. It is the primary vibrational frequency through which we engage with and experience life. We view the world around us from the perspective of our state of BEing. We make decisions, react to situations, and set goals from our state of BEing. We are either limited and become weakened by our state of BEing or empowered and strengthened by it. To optimize our highest potential and BE the best version of ourselves, we have free will to choose a state of BEing consistent with higher-vibrational frequencies and levels of Consciousness. This choice is a fundamental part of our Spiritual Journey, individually and collectively, to evolve and expand Consciousness and raise the vibrational frequency through which we experience the world and others.

> A client and student of mine took my *Letting Go to Manifest Prosperity* course. When she started the program, testing showed that she already embodied the higher-vibrational frequency of Love. On completion of the program, test results showed her state of BEing had reached the level of Enlightenment on Dr. Hawkins's *Map of Consciousness*.[167] She had done the work of letting go of issues that were holding her back from reaching her Highest Potential.
>
> After taking my course, she began working with a healer on ascending to higher dimensional levels of Consciousness and states of BEing. She also participated with me in a small group program, *Thinking Your Way to a New Life*, in which I shared high-level wisdom teachings.

Our state of BEing is extremely significant on our Spiritual Journey and deserves a deeper exploration of how it relates to who we really are in this life. To illustrate and clarify the concept of our state of BEing, we will explore it further using the examples of BEing inner peace and BEing love.

Inner Peace

The vibrational frequency and Consciousness of inner peace is a state of BEing that exudes the feeling and presence of peace at all levels—physical, energetic, mental, emotional, and spiritual. You feel peaceful and are peaceful. Your energy body and physical body are at peace. People can feel or sense your peaceful presence and are attracted to you because you are BEing peace.

Embodying inner peace as a state of BEing is an expansive presence that permeates all aspects of life experiences beyond the momentary peace you might experience in meditation or at a spiritual retreat. BEing peace means it is your default vibrational frequency for experiencing life. You are consistently in a state of peace, feel peaceful, and transmit peaceful energy regardless of external circumstances because you know that everything is happening for the highest and best opportunity to progress on the Spiritual Path. In a state of peace, you trust and surrender to the wisdom of the Universe, knowing it is always working to support you on the path of self-discovery and growth.

> Several clients have presented similar aspects of not being in a state of inner peace based on needing to please others. For example, one client was focused on pleasing her friends by adapting her behavior to meet their approval. In most cases, these clients were disconnected from their authentic Selves and didn't realize it. Engaging in people pleasing and the lack of authenticity was blocking their True Magnificence; they didn't trust that they could decide their own value. However, valuing our differences and gifts helps us be authentic and true to our unique qualities. Taking back our personal power by BEing our true, authentic selves is an important way we find inner peace.

Most of us want to be at peace, see the world, make decisions, and create our lives through the lens of peace. We want to move through our day peacefully and meet and solve challenges easily from this peaceful state of BEing. As with all states of BEing, inner peace is a choice. It is a decision to let go of lower vibrational frequencies that attach us to experiencing anger, panic, fear, grief, guilt, and shame.

When we decide to strengthen our inner peace by seeing the world from the perspective of the Divine who created us to be peace, we can more easily step into actualizing inner peace as a state of BEing. This level of awakening brings us peace, joy, and freedom. There is an abiding sense of BEing in flow with the Universe and an innate ability to embrace every experience, pleasant or unpleasant, as perfectly aligned with our evolutionary trajectory. We can connect to this inner peace at any moment, accepting all that is happening and allowing it all to add to our serenity and resilience.

BEing in a state of inner peace also requires accepting others for who they are and their life path and understanding that we really don't know what is best for someone else. In other words, peace comes from being judgment-free.[168] Judgment is perception and not necessarily based on fact. "To judge is to be dishonest, for to judge is to assume a position you do not have."[169] We cannot be at peace. What we are judging most likely does not exist except in our minds. Especially any negative or false perception is an illusion created by ego. Even if a particular judgment is positive, it still indicates conditional acceptance based on ego beliefs. Either way, being in judgment indicates that we are basing our beliefs on something unreal and trapping ourselves and others in a prison of our own making. If we are in judgment of ourselves or others, we are not at peace.

Maintaining peace within allows the Soul to guide us and allows for non-judgment to be pervasive in our world. How can any one of us be in judgment of another's behavior if we don't know what they are trying to learn or overcome? If we are all on separate Spiritual Journeys, how can we judge each other? How do we know what journey someone else is on and what is best for them? How do we know what critical lessons someone else needs to learn? How can one Divinely created person be better than another, especially when each Divinely created individual is on a completely different life trajectory?

When we start to awaken, we realize peace and cooperation are the key modes of interaction. Our Spirits are already in sync with the essential goals of the Universe. But physically, we have bought into competition that is pervasive as a physical paradigm of life. We focus on getting our piece of the pie or more. We think that having more material wealth means we are better people, living at a higher status. If we don't understand the significance of peace and love, we equate money and things with living our best life.

Our real or Spiritual Life is way more than we can see or comprehend. Things are happening beyond the physical that affect us, but we don't always realize it. Here is a great way to look at something or someone instead of being in judgment.

> There must be something I don't understand about that person and their journey. I wouldn't have made that same choice, but isn't it interesting that they are on the pathway they're being guided to take? I hope they learn what they need to from that experience.

We could take this even further and find that we have lessons to learn from the people we have judged. If we are in judgment, we are likely living in the past. If we could let go of the past and live in the present, we would be better able to accept that each event is an opportunity for us to grow. We must establish this mindset of learning and growing from this experience to be in a state of inner peace.

Because most of us are in competitive mode, we tend to judge others based on how harshly we judge ourselves. We've learned to put others down to feel better about ourselves. We want to be perfect to overcome something lacking or deficient in us. We think we need to be perfect to be lovable or loved. If we have such high standards for ourselves, we tend to have similar standards for others. So, we judge them and ourselves if we don't meet these high perfection standards. We feel like we have failed, or they have failed. It doesn't feel good, and we try to find someone we judge as lesser to feel better about ourselves. Judgment is more about feeling a lack within us.

On the other hand, if we feel we are being judged by others, it really has nothing to do with us. It just means they are in judgment. Why do we have to live up to their standards based on how they need to feel about themselves? It has everything to do with what they are here to accomplish and whether they are on the right path to achieve it. It has nothing to do with us. We are on our own journey. We need to stay on purpose, grow, learn, and evolve our Soul in our own way.

We are invited to forgive others and allow them to be themselves and be on their Spiritual Journey without judgment. If we could just imagine that there is way more to this physical life than we can see and comprehend, we would be in awe and wonder rather than judgment. We would allow others to be themselves— their True Selves. We would be able to be our True Selves from a place of inner peace.

Love

A state of BEing that operates primarily at the vibrational frequency of Love means experiencing and engaging with the world through a deep sense of loving others even when they are not acting loving toward us. However, even more fundamental to this state of BEing is self-love. Love and connection are top needs for all of us. Love feels good, especially when shared with other people and pets. We want to feel and experience love for our spouses, families, friends, pets, and church communities. Love exists when we extend it from us. From the spiritual perspective, when we give what we value highly, we keep it in our mind. This is the law of extension.[170] But we don't always think about feeling love for ourselves or how important that is to our ability to love others. By extending love to others, we are receiving love from the Universe for ourselves.

Some may feel that self-love is selfish. But to fully live and express oneself through love, we must first accept and love ourselves, understanding that our experiences, mistakes, and all are how we learn and evolve. We need to go within to discover how magnificent, unique, and extraordinary we are. Viewing ourselves from our Soul's Perspective—our Divine Perspective—is necessary to awakening to the state of BEing love. Loving all, as the Divine intended, includes loving ourselves. Loving ourselves reveals our Divinity.

In her book, *The Power is Within You*, Louise Hay discusses self-love. Hay feels that loving ourselves can heal the root of all our problems. Loving ourselves improves relationships and opportunities at home and work.[171] Hay also says that the wisdom of self-love is that it is the most significant gift we can give ourselves. When we love ourselves, it is easier to love others and the world around us. Self-love or love "is the most powerful healing force there is."[172] We can choose to love ourselves; we can choose to love others. The more love we extend, the more love comes back to us.

Self-love may be hard for some people because of trauma or early childhood programming. Perhaps they did not get permission to be themselves at a young age; being told what to think about themselves went into their subconscious as truth. But it wasn't true then and is not true later in life. So, the subconscious untruth has to be overridden with a new truth of self-love and acceptance. Letting go of negative patterns from the past, living in the present moment, and using positive mantras and affirmations can effectively re-wire the subconscious to the truth of love.

The state of Consciousness of love is a constant state of BEing love, not just random acts of kindness or feeling love when we are with our children or significant other. It is a state of loving kindness that permeates all aspects of our life. BEing love extends to all people. BEing love extends to all situations of life. The Consciousness of love affects our every encounter with others, whether they are loved ones or not. It is the extension of Divine Love within us.

The vibrational frequency of love is the energy of the Universe or the language of the Universe. It is Divine Intention for us to come from our heart energy, be loving, and extend Divine Love. We are invited to see ourselves as the Divine sees us. We are invited to see others as the Divine sees them.

> My experience of true love was when I gave birth to two children. I knew I loved them before they arrived. But I didn't know real love until I cared for them, and they responded with love back. I know I can't really explain this phenomenon.

My two children opened my heart. Maybe I had closed my heart because of something that happened. Perhaps my heart was hurt emotionally, so it felt unsafe to be open. But my two children opened my heart and increased the capacity for my heart to love. Maybe my heart felt safer to open with them. Maybe the feeling that I helped to create these two miracles connected me to Divine Love that I hadn't experienced before. Nonetheless, something miraculous happened in my heart because of my two children.

Love Consciousness is not limited to an emotional state. Love Consciousness is a state of the Spirit or the eternal energy BEing that exists on its own in Universal Consciousness. It is available for us to tap into at any given moment. It is unlimited and unconditional. It transcends fear, anger, panic, worry, and grief—any low-vibrational frequency. Conscious love is infinite, always expanding into the higher realms of peace, joy, and enlightenment. Understanding the true nature of Love Consciousness may even be at the base camp of enlightenment. I believe Universal Consciousness is Divine Intelligence, unconditional love, and enlightenment all rolled into one. Conscious love is the reflection of the Divine in our hearts.

Love—and beyond—is where we are all headed on our Spiritual Journeys. We seek to understand Love Consciousness in relationship to ourselves, others, the Divine, and the Universe. I believe our journeys are meant to intersect at some point with the overriding hope of the Divine for us to feel love, act with love, and BE LOVE. We are meant to experience Divine Love through our adventures and our journey. From these experiences, we have the knowledge of this infinite connection and high-level frequency to guide us.

Most importantly, what we learn about love, we share with others. What we share gets magnified through Universal Consciousness. Love is whole in and of itself. No aspect of love is different. There are no individuated *parts* of love. Love cannot be divided. Love surrounds us and is within us—unless we choose to block it and live in the false belief that we are separate from it. Perhaps we can ignore the truth that we *are love* or focus on other aspects of ourselves, but love is always there. We always have the choice to remove the veil that shrouds us from the truth of who we truly are and why we are here having this human experience so we can experience love. We are all connected through the unconditional love of the Divine. Love is the Soul language through which we broadcast and transmit messages of love throughout this world and beyond in myriad ways.

> One of the ways I experience and live in love is through my work helping people see the Universe differently and opening them up to a new way to see and enjoy life. I am passionate about sharing my journey of exploring, learning, and awakening to higher Consciousness and the unfolding of greater awareness about how the Universe works to support us. Knowing the Divine is everywhere in everything and sharing that awareness with others created a major shift within me, revealing that BEing love translates to and permeates all aspects of my life.

Having a greater understanding of the awakening process allows us to grow and expand our Consciousness in ways that were not previously accessible. We begin to realize that we are empowered Beings. Within us is all the wisdom and power to do and BE who we are meant to be—our authentic Selves. We do not need to look outside ourselves for the truth or wisdom. The Universe's wisdom inside us knows what is in our highest and best good. It is up to us to allow and accept what is unfolding as opportunities for growth and learning, understanding that what we believe about ourselves becomes the lens through which we experience our lives and see the world. Knowing the truth about who we really are as Divine Souls transforms everything, making us more conscious and aware that we are here to learn, grow, and expand, and in doing so, we benefit the whole Universe.

Knowing that, like us, everyone else is also here to grow and evolve gives us the grace to allow and accept that each person is on their own journey of discovering their Soul Path. Understanding these concepts from an awakened state elevates our state of BEing as the filter through which we see and operate in the world. Our state of BEing affects what happens in our lives and how we can grow. The next step of our journey is to see beyond the physical reality. We are starting to cross the bridge from the physical to the Spiritual. What lies ahead is more miraculous than what you can imagine.

Exercises

To apply this information to your life, sit with these questions in quiet contemplation or meditation and allow the answers to unfold before you begin journaling.

Exercise 1: Your are Divine Creation

- Write what comes to mind when you sit with the thought *I am as the Divine created me.*
- Next, observe how knowing this truth changes how you think about yourself and how you show up in the world.
- Write what comes to mind when you meditate on God's will.

Exercise 2: Invitation to Connect to Your Inner Wisdom

I invite you to look back on some of the greatest challenges in your life and ask yourself the following questions, considering how your answers connect to your True Self.

- Am I able to see the benefit of the challenge?
- Am I able to see how my life improved because of the challenge?
- Am I able to see how much I grew from the experience?
- Am I able to say that I am grateful for the growth from the experience?

Exercise 3: Going Deeper

- How would you describe your current state of BEing?
- Do you have inner peace?
- Are you vibrating at Love Consciousness?
- Do you live in an open-door or closed-door reality of life?
- What is your ultimate goal in life?
- Do you live free? If not, what is restricting you?
- What do you want from your awakening?

- How does understanding the Universal Law of Polarity help you focus on the positive?
- What is the Divine's Invitation for you?
- Are you able to take responsibility for your life—what is happening in your life?
- What are you setting as a new intention of BEing?

Exercise 4: *What-if* Questions:

- *What if* you understood that all the power and wisdom you need is within you?
- *What if* you believed in yourself and completely trusted yourself?
- *What if* you could allow life to unfold naturally rather than forcing things to happen?
- *What if* you could vibrate at Love Consciousness?
- *What if* you could elevate your state of BEing?

CROSSING THE BRIDGE
FROM THE PHYSICAL TO THE SPIRITUAL

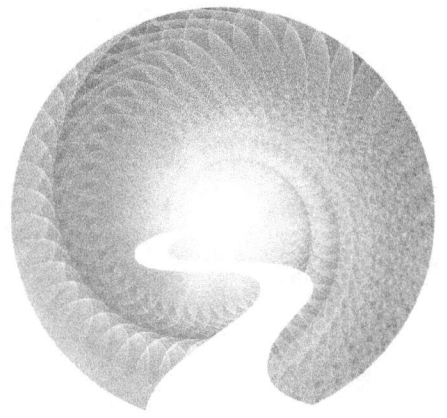

Crossing the Bridge from the Physical to the Spiritual

We are more than a physical body. While our physical body exists in the form world of the third-dimensional plane as our everyday life experience, we also have other aspects of our BEing—energy body or Spirit Body—that exist in both the third-dimensional plane and beyond. There is no clear answer about the number and nature of other dimensional planes. Some schools of thought suggest there are fifteen dimensions, and others suggest even more. Physicists postulate that there are eleven dimensions, including a dimension of time, based on String Theory research and mathematics.

Regardless of our understanding of multi-dimensionality, there are other realms of experience beyond what we perceive in the form world of the physical realm. To live at our highest potential, we can tap into the higher levels of Consciousness that open our awareness to *see* or *know* an existence beyond the limits of the physical realm. Seeing beyond the physical is seeing through our mind's eye into the unlimited nature of the energetic and Spiritual Realms. Seeing beyond the illusions, or what appears to be real in the physical world, and moving toward knowing the truth and wisdom of the Spiritual Realm and our Spiritual Aspect is a major discovery in self-actualization.

Physical Realm and Spiritual Realm Paradigms

To explore this more deeply, we can develop an understanding of life experiences from the different perspectives of the physical and Spiritual Realms by examining their relative paradigms. In this context, I am referring to paradigms as lifestyle patterns, principles, and belief systems associated with different perspectives. As I was writing about the physical and spiritual realm paradigms, I was asking myself what I really mean by the principles and paradigms of the physical and Spiritual Realms. I had a general understanding of the feelings or sense of energy related to each set of principles or paradigms but never actually spelled them out until I examined the differences more closely and created a side-by-side comparative list.

It was incredibly revealing to see just how much our outlook, perspectives, and choices squarely land us in one paradigm or the other. Of course, nothing is perfect, and we easily slip back and forth from one paradigm of experience to another. But at least if we recognize when we are creating our experience from a physical realm perspective, we can make a conscious choice to remain there or shift into the higher perspective of the Spiritual Realm.

Here are some examples of the experiences and perspectives on the list I created. I have included the full list in Table 5, located in the Appendix. I encourage you to spend some time with the full list to get a deeper appreciation for the differences between these two paradigms in creating the life you want to live and get familiar with the choices available to you for shifting into the Spiritual Realm paradigm.

Table 5 (abbrv.): Physical and Spiritial Paradigms for Living

Physical Realm Paradigms	Spiritual Realm Paradigms
• I see life through the lens of fear.	• I see life through the lens of love.
• I must fear the next trauma that will inevitably happen in my life.	• I have challenges to face in order to learn, grow, and evolve into higher vibrational frequencies and higher levels of Consciousness. I embrace the challenges because they bring me closer to my ultimate goal, to evolve my Soul.
• I must control everything around me and protect myself from danger, I am in charge of what happens to me.	• I surrender to invitations from the Divine and respond in deep gratitude by being the best version of myself and performing at my highest potential, realizing that I am working for a reason way beyond me.
• I was procreated by my parents out of sin.	• I was Divinely created. I am an idea in the mind of the Divine. This idea is immutable.
• I make mistakes and commit sins, which makes me feel bad about myself.	• No matter what I do, my essence or core is still the immutable Divine idea. Sinlessness is guaranteed for all. This empowers me to be the best version of myself as I Iearn and grow.
• I see myself as unworthy, and I struggle in life. I am not good enough.	• I see myself as Divine, and I am working to accomplish my Divine Mission in life. My goal is to do what will benefit the Universe.
• My false self or ego is in charge, and I feel stuck. I have pain and disease in my body. I don't know who I really am.	• Divine Energy flows through me easily and I feel free to be my True Self. I am healthy, happy, and whole as my True Divine Self. I identify primarily with being a Soul.

Although they are fairly comprehensive, the list above and in Table 5 are not an absolute or exclusive itemization of the possibilities for expressing in either realm. Still, they capture what I believe to be some of the key experiences relative to each paradigmatic realm. We are rarely fully expressing or experiencing life solely in one realm or another. Someone who identifies more profoundly with the physical realm may not exhibit all these principles or perspectives and vice versa.

I invite you to use Table 5 to understand better the principles or paradigms you have adopted as part of your lifestyle and way of living. It may be helpful to identify the paradigms you are familiar with in the physical realm and compare them with the corresponding spiritual realm paradigm to see where you currently identify most predominantly. It doesn't matter where you are right now. The point is to make some helpful observations without judgment. If you have oriented more toward the physical realm paradigms, you may want to consider what you can change or heal in your life to align with the spiritual paradigms more fully if that is your desire. It may become apparent that some aspects of your lifestyle, patterns, or belief systems require healing to enable you to shift into certain spiritual realm paradigms. This is an important realization and part of the Spiritual Journey, as we can only heal what is being revealed to us. The goal is to become more Self-aware.

Healing physical realm experiences to open the door for higher alignment with the spiritual realm paradigms can start with simply setting an intention to heal. A major part of our collective healing and what we need most, individually, is releasing the limiting beliefs and patterns that keep us from realizing our Divine Nature as powerful, sovereign creator BEings. So, we can set an intention to start aligning with who we really are as our authentic selves—True Self, Higher Self, Soul. We can stop aligning with old stories about not being good enough and letting go of feelings of lack and limitations. These are self-limiting beliefs that come from the ego, not the Soul.

I invite all of us to explore where there are opportunities in our lives to adopt spiritual realm paradigms as our way of living and BEing. Adopting the spiritual paradigms into our physical existence will help us live more extraordinary, miraculous lives with ease and peace.

Using Our Inner Vision

Developing our inner vision of intuition helps us see and visualize beyond the physical realm. The energies of our third eye and the third eye chakra strengthen and support our ability to connect with and expand our intuitive skills.

Intuition and Knowing

What is intuition? Intuition bridges the gap between the conscious, subconscious, and superconscious mind. Intuition is our Inner or Innate Wisdom, a knowing beyond the limits of the physical world. We don't have any intellectual knowledge about the content or the context of the intuitive message. We just know. Intuition can guide us in every aspect of life. We could even call it our internal GPS. Even though you may not realize you are receiving intuitive messages or haven't yet grown to trust them when you do, you can develop these skills with practice and intention.

When we engage with life through intuition, we connect to our Core Essence, everything around us, and our Divine Wisdom. We have a sense there is something beyond our limited ability to understand that is more powerful and wiser than us, helping us make our way in the world. Using our inner knowing can help us overcome feelings of being separate, alone, or unsupported. When tuned into my intuition, I feel part of a flowing movement of energy and love.

Because we are wired to the cosmic web or Universal Consciousness, we can receive information from sources beyond what our physical senses can perceive through our intuitive senses. There are seven different senses involved with intuition: instinct, feeling, seeing, hearing, knowing, smelling, and tasting.

Each of us has the capability to use all seven senses. All seven senses are weaving together at all points—but some will be more active in us than others. Although we possess all seven intuitive senses, one or two may be more prominent or available to us than the others. As we get more familiar with one intuitive sense, another may arise in our awareness. Over time, we receive a broad range of information through our six intuitive senses plus instinct.

Here is a brief explanation of instinct and the six intuitive senses, sometimes called the *clairs*.[173]

1. Instinct is a natural or innate state of BEing, behaving, or thinking. Instinct is more related to our sense of survival exhibited at a very young age. It's not learned; it's part of our makeup. When we are young, less than seven years old, we use instinct and intuition to interpret and understand the world. Instinct and intuition can come into play again in our teenage years.

2. Clairvoyance is clear-sightedness beyond the physical sense. Clairvoyance is seeing images through inner vision, like a movie trailer. Images can appear as symbols, metaphors, or archetypes. Clairvoyants use intuition to see the shimmering vibrations, colors, and images with their inner vision. Clairvoyants can sometimes see future events.

3. Clairaudience is clear hearing of something imperceptible to others. It is hearing from your inner ear. The intuitive message may come as an inner voice, music, or an external sound inaudible to others. Hearing internally could be interpreted as hearing your own thoughts, or one could hear the voice of intuition. Sometimes multiple clairaudients can hear the same thing from a non-physical source. For example, some clairaudients can hear pitches or tones in a room and translate the energetic vibrations into words. Clairaudience may be the most common type of intuition.

4. Clairgustance is clear tasting of something that is not physically present. Some clairgustants can taste a specific meal or essential oil that isn't physically present. Some clairgustants experience a bad taste in their mouth.

5. Claircognizance is clear knowing in your body. This knowing lands in every aspect of us- down to our cells. One example of claircognizance is waking up in the morning with a clear knowing of something not known the night before. Claircognizants don't question this knowing. It is deeply rooted in their BEing—there is absolutely no doubt. It is a resonance with knowing as a deep truth.

6. Clairsentience is clear feeling, a very common form of intuition. Like tuning forks, clairsentients' bodies receive and interpret energetic vibrations. The messages are experienced as what we might know as *gut* reactions, feelings, or hunches that correlate to a physical sensation.

7. Clairalience is clear smelling of something not physically present. Some clairalients can associate smells with memories of relatives who have transitioned. Clairalients can also smell vibrations of health or physical imbalance, such as disease or death, or distinguish a truth from a lie through smell. We even have phrases that indicate clairalience, like *follow your nose* and *sniff out decisions*.

Being intuitive or sensitive to our own energies and the energies of others is also a natural state of BEing as a Divine Gift. Intuition is a result of our connection to

Divine Wisdom. If we really use our instinctive and intuitive gifts for the highest purpose, we can have the most amazing life and reach our highest potential. Our intuition guides and empowers us to align with our Divine Plan.

When we are intuitive, we work with our deep Inner Wisdom and relate it to the external world. Using our intuition, we can have a continual exchange with Divine Wisdom that is seamless, intact, complete, and protective, making us feel like a co-creative or active partner with the Universe. Or the connection can be blurry, leaky, and messy, making us feel more like a victim rather than a co-creative partner.

Extrasensory perception and intuition can keep us in the flow of the Universe, flowing toward growth and life and removing the strictness or rigidity of life to experience joy. This freedom is living from our core, our most magnetic place. If we live from this space within us, we benefit ourselves and others by awakening and inspiring the core energy within them.

The bottom line is everything is energy, and we're all connected to the cosmic web of life. The more we understand this, the more we will be in balance within ourselves and with Universal Consciousness. Even though society has bought into the idea that success is all about hard work, some very successful businesspeople think otherwise and attribute their success to their powerful intuition. In a research study, CEOs from thirty-six major corporations were asked to name the most important element in their decision-making. Eighty-five percent responded with *intuition* or *gut feeling*.[174]

Both Albert Einstein and Steve Jobs attributed their success to their intuition and believed their intuition was more powerful than their intellect.[175] Steve Jobs credited his intuitive mind as having a significant impact on his work. Jobs shared that trusting his intuition has made a significant difference in the way he makes decisions. His intuition positively affected his life and career. Einstein also believed his accomplishments and scientific discoveries stemmed from his intuition; sometimes, he knew that his intuition was right without understanding how.

Others have chimed in with a similar view. Bruce Kasanoff writes, "Intuition is the highest form of intelligence."[176] Joining the chorus, Richard Branson adds statistics don't represent the whole picture. Branson uses his instinct more when making significant decisions in business. Intuition helps us know when to take risks and when not to.

What does the scientific community think about intuition?

Most scientists base their decisions on data. They have worked hard to develop a critical mind to interpret their findings accurately with precision, critical data points, and statistics. Yet, despite Albert Einstein's revelation, the scientific community generally is not focused on intuition.

People using their intuitive and perceptive gifts may be the best decision-makers and the most successful people, perhaps because their developed intuitive senses are highly specialized for their intentions. In contrast, poor decision-makers and money managers who don't learn from their mistakes are thought to have less connection to their intuitive abilities because either the skill was never developed or it's weak from lack of use. Intuitions can wither away if people don't believe in their intuitive abilities. If we don't use it, we could lose it!

Unclear or cloudy intuitive messages could result from being depressed, anxious, emotionally blocked, or simply not feeling our highest and best. Intuitive messages can also be muted by loud and overbearing ego-mind chatter. Quieting this superficial *monkey mind* is the key to unlocking our deeper and far more powerful subconscious and superconscious minds where we connect with our intuition.

Our intuitive link may have been broken, but that doesn't mean it has to stay broken. If the conscious mind can be quieted down, the disruptive effect of mind chatter or negative emotional states can become a non-issue, giving us easier access to our deep-thinking subconscious mind and even our more creative superconscious mind, and intuition flows more easily.

We've all had experiences being guided by our magnificent inner compass, even if we didn't realize it. We can learn to harness this amazingly powerful innate ability and develop trust in it by using it regularly. Having well-developed intuition helps us on our inner discovery to get the answers specific to us and our own Spiritual Journey.

Here are some steps to access, develop, and amplify our intuition.

1.   Grounding to be in the present moment and focused.

2.   Connecting and strengthening our energetic core.

3.   Paying attention to our energies.

4.   Paying attention to our gut responses.

5. Slowing down enough to hear our *inner voice* and respond to it.

6. Practicing mindfulness, meditation, silence, and other ways of counter-acting the busy-ness of life.

7. Celebrating the differences in how humans approach learning, thinking, and doing based on their past experiences, preferred styles, and interests and acknowledging that we're all on our own journeys of understanding.

8. Trusting our *inner voice*, or gut, as a credible source of information and a way of *knowing*. It is a gift to be treasured.

9. Trusting our hearts as having deep wisdom.

10. Practicing what social scientists call *empathic accuracy*—an intuitive awareness of what other people think and feel or using cues such as body language and tone of voice to help hone our skills and respond with kindness and care.

Open the Third Eye to Connect to the Spiritual Realm

The third eye, located between the eyebrows, is an energetic area where the invisible world is perceived, which helps with spiritual awareness and connection. The true third eye is visible to the clairvoyant as a radiant aura with moving electrical light.[177] The third eye opens toward the crown chakra and beyond. Like the first two human eyes, the third eye has the capability to focus light through an opening and observe different colors.

The third eye interacts with the pineal gland, an endocrine gland in the brain's center believed to aid in non-physical perception, such as intuition. The third eye is likely located in the aura of the pineal gland. Many traditions believe the pineal gland connects the physical and Spiritual Realms. Similarly, activating and enhancing the third eye helps bridge physical and spiritual awareness. Rene Descartes referred to the pineal gland as the seat of the Soul.[178]

According to Drunvalo Melchizedek, the size of the pineal gland has decreased from the size of a ping pong ball to the size of a dried pea over time, possibly due to the fall in Consciousness following the destruction of Atlantis approximately 13,000 to 16,000 years ago.[179] This has contributed to making us less aware or less conscious of the Spiritual Realm than our ancient counterparts. Relative to ancient cultures, who could perceive beyond the physical more easily, the decrease in the size of the pineal gland over time has limited our inner vision.[180]

If we identify primarily as a physical form and allow the ego to regulate our life, then the gifts of the third eye can be obscured even more or possibly closed. Opening the third eye allows us to see and know beyond what our physical senses can sense through extrasensory perception. Opening the third eye also increases our ability to sense the abstract and navigate our lives with greater insight, intuition, clearer Self-expression, and decisiveness. It is easier to make the right decisions if we are connected to the hidden truths of the Spiritual World.

Donna Eden uses a simple technique for opening the third eye by touching your forehead with your middle finger just above the nose, moving your finger slowly up the center of the forehead like raising a window shade to allow the sun to come into a darkened room. You can also move your middle finger from your nose to the top of your head and crown chakra.[181]

Clearing the Third Eye Chakra to Transcend the Physical Realm

The third eye chakra is the energy of transcendence. The psychological theme of the third eye chakra is sensory perception, extrasensory perception, intuition, abstract thought, inspiration, imagination, and Self-realization. As the seat of intuition, its role is to be the center of an individual's wisdom, conscience, and Higher Consciousness. In Sanskrit, the third eye chakra is Ajna, which means perceiving and beyond wisdom. Physically, the third eye chakra spirals over the forehead, eyes, ears, and nose, aiding in vision, hearing, and smelling—including the same inner senses. The third eye chakra also includes the forebrain, skull, and hypothalamus.

As the conduit of intuition and psychic awareness, the third eye chakra helps us to *see* with our inner vision. Its perceptive abilities regulate Self-awareness, higher wisdom, visualization, clarity, discernment, imagination, and creative dreaming. When the third eye chakra is open, aligned, and balanced, it can help us become aware of the Spiritual Realm and our interconnectedness or Oneness.

The third eye chakra can be obstructed by congested or built-up energetic residue, limiting our ability to use our inner vision and extrasensory perception. A closed or congested third eye chakra can result in headaches, sinus, or vision issues. On the emotional and spiritual levels, a blocked third eye chakra can lead to confusion, headaches, vision problems, lack of purpose, pessimism, uncertainty, and disconnection from our Higher Self or the Divine.[182] Balancing the third eye chakra to release the obstructing energy can be accomplished in several different ways: meditating, visualizing light going into and out of the third eye, using aromatherapy, or using blue or purple crystals or healing stones like purple fluorite, amethyst, labradorite, citrine, azurite, sodalite, turquoise, tanzanite, and lolite.[183]

Clearing or balancing the third eye chakra can also be done with a simple hand technique. This clearing method removes anything blocking the full functioning of the third eye chakra without affecting the memories or other cognitive connections to the past, significant life stories, and lessons learned. To do this technique, put your left hand over the eyes, eyebrow, and forehead and circle in the direction your left fingers are pointing or counterclockwise. To help understand this counterclockwise movement, imagine the clock is on your forehead, facing the space in front of you.

Next, slowly circle your hand about two to four inches above the area over the whole width of the forehead to entrain the third eye chakra energy with your hand. This circling will release congested energy in the area through attraction to the electromagnetic points on your fingers and hands. You may feel tingling, dense energy, or static energy on your hands, which indicates you are picking up the congested energy, like a magnet. Continue the circling motion for about two to three minutes or until you sense the congestion or blockage has lifted. To ensure the released energy does not go back into the third eye chakra, move to a healing crystal, like selenite, and throw the released energy from your hand onto the crystal. The healing crystal, especially selenite, will clean the energy of the space. Next, clap your hands to remove any energetic residue on your hands. Then, take your right hand and circle similarly, slowly, in the direction your fingers are pointing, or clockwise, for one to two minutes to integrate the energetic shift.[184]

Sensing the Invisible

> *Nothing real can be threatened.*
> *Nothing unreal exists.*
> *Herein lies the peace of God.*[185]

Sensing the invisible or Spiritual Realm means we understand that the Divine is in everything. Instead of listening to or paying attention to our egos, we can decide to perceive and sense others and the world through the loving lens of our Soul, seeing the Divine in everything and seeing everyone as love, guilt-free, and sinless. Changing our perspective shifts us from living in fear to living in love. We create miracles when we shift from a fear-based existence to a loving one. We are living from the spiritual realm paradigm. We are living as the Divine intended us to live.

If we could see ourselves and others for the truth of who we are as Divine BEings, we would be in awe of each other. Since nothing created in the mind of the Divine can be changed, no matter what we do, the truth of who we are never changes, just our ability to perceive it

Sensing the invisible opens our hearts to see the world through the filter of love. Seeing through the lens of the Divine makes it easier to forgive.

Forgiveness is the Function of the Light

Forgiveness opens our hearts.

Forgiveness neutralizes negative energy.

Forgiveness allows new possibilities, reconciliation, and a deeper connection.

Forgiveness is the acceptance of another just as they are.

Forgiveness is seeing the goodness rather than the faults.

Forgiveness is seeing the Divine aspect rather than the mistake.

Forgiveness means I care more about the relationship than the issue.

Forgiveness says you are very special to me.

Forgiveness lets go of the need to be right.

Forgiveness is seeing through a different lens.

Forgiveness is without judgment.

Forgiveness aligns with peace.

Forgiveness allows the radiant light to shine through the darkness.

Forgiveness fosters new beginnings.

Forgiveness is a declaration of true love.

Forgiveness is a breakthrough.

Anne M. Deatly

> *For forgiveness literally transforms vision, and lets you see the real world reaching quietly and gently across chaos, removing all illusions that had twisted your perception and fixed it on the past. The smallest leaf becomes a thing of wonder, and a blade of grass a sign of God's perfection.*[186]

Forgiveness is one of the most significant and loving things we can do for ourselves and others. Forgiveness is a pillar in *A Course in Miracles.* Forgiveness allows freedom, happiness, and peace to thrive within us.[187] Knowing how the Divine views all of us will help us view each other in loving and forgiving ways.[188]

Holding onto things that bother us can bring us down emotionally. It literally drains us of energy, weakening and disempowering us. Whether we realize it or not, if we hold onto any negativity, like unforgiveness, we transmit that vibrational frequency into the Universe, including colleagues, friends, and family.

The unforgiving mind is fearful. It has no space for perceiving through love because the lower vibrational frequency of fear blocks awareness of the love frequency. An unforgiving mind stays in the dark, sad, without hope, and expects to witness danger in the world, experiencing misery, doubt, and confusion. Its fear magnifies sounds, the ominous feeling of the darkness, despair, and is terrified by the threat of something bad happening. An unforgiving mind cannot let go, relax, rest, or sleep and is stuck in negativity and anxiety. Without acknowledging mistakes, it seeks out the sins of others and sees only the sin and sinful in all places. An unforgiving mind believes in its judgments, knows it's right, and that there is no other way to experience the world around it.[189]

But through learning to forgive, we are forgiven. Giving and receiving forgiveness are the same. Forgiveness is the Divine Plan for salvation.[190] It offers peace, happiness, certainty of purpose, a quiet mind, care, safety, protection, deep abiding comfort, and perfect rest.

> *What could you want that forgiveness cannot give? Do you want peace? Forgiveness offers it. Do you want happiness, a quiet mind, a certainty of purpose, and a sense of worth and beauty that transcends the world? Do you want care, safety, and the warmth of sure protection always? Do you want a quietness that cannot be disturbed, a gentleness that never can be hurt, a deep abiding comfort, and a rest so perfect it can never be upset?*[191]

All this forgiveness offers you, and more. It sparkles on your eyes as you awake and gives you joy with which to meet the day[192] *. . .Changelessly, it stands before you like an open door, with warmth and welcome calling from beyond the doorway, bidding you to enter in and make yourself at home, where you belong.*[193]

Forgiveness is the extension beyond third-dimensional programming and worldview by taking us to what we know is true beyond the illusion of the physical world. Forgiveness allows us to understand and know we love each other and that we all are love. As one of the spiritual realm paradigms, forgiveness allows us to cross the bridge from the physical to the Spiritual.

To be able to forgive means we must let go of our story behind what we need to forgive and the meaning we've given to something or someone. Letting go is difficult for most people. Letting go of anger, hurt, and humiliation is especially difficult. When we feel wronged, hurt, abandoned, neglected, and even abused, it is challenging to find a place from which we can release the memories, emotions, and feelings because, at some level, we may feel we deserve the negative experience. We may also resist forgiveness if we feel that forgiving means exonerating hurtful behavior that deserves a consequence.

Sometimes, people disappoint us when they're not acting as we wish they would or showing up as *we* want or need them to be. We get upset because we want them to be different. That is not on them; that is on us. No one needs to be anything other than their pure, authentic Self on a journey to be their best. Forgiveness is realizing that our expectations are our own and cannot fairly be placed on others. We do not know their journey and are often more off-course than on-course in our projections about others.

Forgiveness is easier if we allow each other to make the necessary mistakes for growth. When we grow, everyone benefits—the Universe benefits, and the level of Universal Consciousness is raised. Forgiveness is an act of faith that knows we are all unique and different expressions of the Divine. Forgiveness realizes that everyone is an idea in the mind of the Divine. Everything another person says or does is aligned with how they need to grow.

Forgiveness is seeing the Divinity in a person who has hurt or disappointed us, seeing them as the Divine created them. We can recognize the innocence of their Divine Nature and realize they just got off track. We can decide not to hold a grudge when they don't act according to their Divine Nature.

Also, since our response to what someone else says or does reflects our internal world, we can learn about ourselves by understanding how and why we respond the way we do. In examining our responses, we are invited to view the situation from the perspective of an opportunity to learn about ourselves and others, knowing that whatever happens is always for each person's best and highest good.

Perhaps some people are here to do things that help the rest of us grow and evolve. So, yes, some people's mission is to come into this life and challenge us to be the best versions of ourselves. Do you have someone in your life who is challenging you, is in your face, or even subtly making sure you are working to be different in the way you want to be different and evolve?

We also need to forgive ourselves for our own mistakes and transgressions. Recognizing that our mistakes lead us to new understandings and lessons learned, we rise to a higher level of BEing that allows us to grow and evolve rather than devolve into negative states of mind. Forgiveness helps us transcend the illusion of guilt, knowing that the Divine celebrates our mistakes and our resulting growth.

Forgiving ourselves and others is so significant and Divinely important. We are the vessels through which the Divine brings forgiveness, peace, and salvation to the world. The ability to forgive is also part of BEing the light of the world because BEing a shining light permits others to BE a shining light. "Being the light, we can be the conduit of peace to all minds, as we forgive ourselves and others."[194] Forgiveness is one way to use and share our light with the world. It is an elevated way of BEing, a higher quality of living, and a higher-vibrational frequency that aligns us with the spiritual realm paradigm.

Forgiveness frees us up and connects us to our sacred identity—our Soul. But it takes a lot of inner work to get to this place of forgiveness.

As a role model, Jesus, the representative son of the Divine, actualized this potential in all of us. Through this realization and actualization, Jesus gained the power of the Divine on Earth. We are all invited to walk this path. If we see ourselves and each other as Souls on our own unique journeys perfectly designed for our growth and evolution, we can more easily let go of judgment, including paying attention to the judgment of others about our own Spiritual Journey.

Going deeper, we can establish ourselves to be in a state of forgiveness that opens the doorway to maintaining a continual state of forgiveness—totally letting go of all judgment. This doorway invites us not to engage with our false selves, misinterpreting what is going on with another person or us. Instead, our goal is always to see and interpret situations from our Higher Selves or Soul, creating a powerful ripple effect in the world.

Forgiveness is a gift we give and receive. It is an excellent way to let go of emotional issues, whether we are forgiving ourselves or someone else.

Remember, not forgiving someone doesn't hurt them; it only hurts us. We carry negative vibrations about them that get embedded in our energy fields and transmitted to the Universe. Forgiveness means we can let go of the past negativity and be free. Forgiveness is being the best version of oneself using spiritual realm paradigms.

Seeing Through the Eyes of Love

We are love. We were created in love, so love is who and what we are. We are love at our core. Love is what the Divine intended for each of us. But living on the physical plane, it is easy to lose connection with our true nature as love and get caught up in the lower vibrational frequencies of fear—love's opposite energy. We tend to respond to all the fear-based circumstances and stories so pervasive in the news and all aspects of life with more fear, believing that fear is real. But fear is an illusion. It is an emotion that the ego uses to keep us restricted, blocked, and suffering while obstructing our ability to access love. Fear is accepting the false self as real.

Fear is a choice to live unauthentically as someone we are not; it is not part of our authentic Selves. If we listen to the ego, we give it our power. Instead, we can tell our ego that the feelings of fear, lack, and limitation it expresses are simply not true. We can regain our power by speaking from the spiritual plane's truth and wisdom. We can regain control of our thoughts, beliefs, and lives. We can have inner peace. We can live and act from our real, authentic Selves. Seeing through the eyes of love is an important aspect of our Spiritual Journey. When we aren't seeing through the lens of love, we can easily get off-course from our Divine Mission.

The whole Universe is love. Love surrounds us and is within us. It is the energy that permeates every natural living thing and being. Love is the energy that expresses the quality of our BEing. We just need to connect to the love that we already are just by BEing. When we identify with the love within us, within our Soul, we are seeing through the lens of love. It is a choice to view life through the lens of love.

Love is the energy we broadcast to the rest of the Universe. When we extend love, we receive love. Love is a great teacher. We can be great role models to others by BEing love—compassionate, caring, and kind. We can teach love by demonstrating love and BEing love. Love is a healing energy that can transform us. There is a ripple effect with love. Celebrate Universal love within and around us. BEing love means we are radiant Divine BEings extending and sharing love. Through our loving and authentic presence, the world transforms.

Sacred Geometry Connects the Physical and Spiritual Realms

Sacred geometry represents a visible form of high vibrational frequency. Sacred geometry forms are perfectly designed to contain Spiritual Energy in the physical realm. By the perfection of proportion, structure, balance, and symmetry, sacred geometry contains high vibrational frequency Spiritual Energy of the Divine. Sacred geometry illustrates Divine Alignment. We can perceive these sacred geometry structures as dynamic, moving, vibrating energy that brings the spiritual into the physical. These sacred geometry forms hold the potential of the Divine and Consciousness in a physical form. These sacred geometry forms are crystallized Divine Energy that brings Divine Energy into the physical.[195]

Each physical form is a manifestation of energy through geometry. Different vibrational frequencies correlate with different geometric patterns. Robert Moon, the inventor of the atom bomb, invites us to perceive atoms and molecules as the energies of geometric forms rather than limited particles.[196] The higher the vibrational frequency, the more complex the geometric figures. The correlation to this concept is that intelligently designed balanced and harmonic geometric patterns create or contain higher-vibrational frequencies.

Similarly, according to Dr. Sue Morter, all physical matter is compressed energy.[197] As energy becomes more compressed or dense, the higher-vibrational frequencies of the Spiritual Realm become less aligned and cannot merge with form. Sacred geometric forms, however, provide a high vibrational frequency match for the energies of the Spiritual Realm. Sacred geometry connects the physical and Spiritual Realms by merging form with higher-frequency energy.

To understand this concept, let's consider the architecture and intentional design of a specific building—like a church, cathedral, or temple. These types of buildings are designed and created in a unique way to create a space for connecting with the Divine more easily. When we go to a service held in one of these buildings, we feel the palpable difference relative to other buildings designed for a different function. We are affected by the ease of energy flow and the high vibrational frequencies present. As a result, it is much easier to feel the presence of the Divine. We feel a sense of enlightenment, lightness, and openness. Music played in these spaces resonates at high vibrational frequency partly due to the design of the building with the right proportions, symmetry, and order. Similarly, the Spiritual Energy, perfect proportions, balance, and symmetry of sacred geometry forms can produce a similar sense of the Divine within us.

Since sacred geometry forms are the building blocks of the natural world in the physical realm, these sacred forms help us understand that the Divine is in every living thing. Understanding sacred geometry enhances our Spiritual Journey since it signifies the Divine's underlying support, love, and presence all around us and within us. Sacred geometry forms the foundation and Oneness of everything in the Universe.

Sacred geometry defines the proportions of all physical aspects of the natural world and is the blueprint of creation, the origin of form, and the templates for life. Every natural pattern of growth or movement is derived from one or more of the basic geometric shapes called the five Platonic solids: the tetrahedron, hexahedron, octahedron, dodecahedron, and icosahedron. Recently, another Platonic solid called a heptahedron was discovered by artist-sculptor Frank Chester. It is a seven-sided structure that correlates to the structure of the human heart.[198] It makes perfect sense that the Divine would intentionally create the physical heart as an idealized structure to enhance its potential to embody the energies of the Spiritual Realm. The design integrates the concept of crystallized Divine Energy with its function as the physical core regulator of the body. An example is that the physical and spiritual are inextricable.

The physical nature of sacred geometry helps us understand that the Universe is designed by mathematical relationships, bringing order and symmetry to the physical world. Sacred geometry explains the exact energetic organization of creation and the energy patterns that create and unify all things. Using these building blocks, nature creates order out of chaos. All structure and mathematical relationships that permeate the natural world induce order and stability for life on Earth. The Universe is organized according to principles, mathematical proportions, and Universal Laws that enable freedom, balance, and serenity to surround us as we traverse our Spiritual Path, transforming ourselves and others. Focusing on this concept may awaken us to the underlying principle that everything in the Universe is designed with constant scientific parameters.

Sacred geometry is an expression of Divine Love for us. Sacred geometry illustrates how the energy of the Divine Mind and Divine Intention crystallizes into physical matter. Significant to this discussion is the concept that our Universe is a mind before it becomes matter.[199] The Universe was created to be in balance, harmony, and order. Order was created out of chaos for the predictability of the natural life cycles of the world, giving us stability on our path to transform and evolve. Knowing the intentionality of the universal design will enhance our journey to realize the underlying love and support of the Divine. We understand how and why the Divine Mind created the Universe through these sacred geometric structures and how the Divine Energy comes through these physical forms.

The Platonic Solids

All life forms are created out of geometric shapes or codes: DNA, trees, flowers, shells, snowflakes, grass, bushes, pinecones, and leaf structures are just some examples. All these complex geometric shapes can be pared down to the basic building blocks of the five Platonic solids to help us understand the mathematics that highlights the shapes, templates, and structures we see in nature. The five Platonic solids are considered cosmic because they are part of everything in the Universe.

All five Platonic solids are three-dimensional and have equal angles, edge lengths, and faces that fit into a sphere. In addition, each of the five traditional Platonic solids is associated with an element and at least one chakra, as shown in Appendix, Table 6.

The newly discovered heptahedron is different because it is produced with two types of faces: triangles and quadrilaterals. The heptahedron fits into a Platonic solid, the hexahedron, at a 36-degree tilt.

Tetrahedron

The tetrahedron is the simplest Platonic solid with four equal triangular faces. This shape is symmetrical in four ways. No matter how you hold this triangular pyramid, the structure is the same. Any of the four vertices can be the top or apex of the structure. Any of the four triangular faces can be the base. As the most stable of the Platonic solids, the tetrahedron

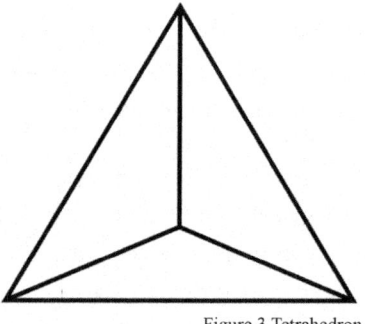

Figure 3 Tetrahedron

represents perfect balance, unity, harmony, and symmetry. This stability not only represents focus, direction, and strategy but also represents the wisdom of Soul creation in relation to the theme of personal power, self-esteem, and personal identity of the solar plexus chakra. Representing fire, the tetrahedron spiritually and symbolically combines the Divine Spark with life's energy and passion.

As a fire element form, the tetrahedron brings clarity through light and energy. In fact, the basic structure of a photon is a tetrahedron.[200] We may relate to the tetrahedron as the fire of ambition, illuminating what is necessary to bring a new idea or present goals into reality. The tetrahedron represents action, male, masculine, and yang energy that helps us move forward and complete whatever is needed for our best and highest good. Tetrahedron energy is related to expansion and Self-awareness. As yang energy, the tetrahedron represents the sun and light and becomes a channel for light energy as a source of unlimited healing energy.

The energy in the tetrahedron moves upward from the three different base vertices, shown in Appendix, Table 6. Three different energies come together at the base of the tetrahedron and rise together to get released from the apex—the top point directed toward the Spiritual Realm. The first base point represents the individual with unique and specific spiritual gifts and insights from their journey. The second base point represents partnership—cooperation and shared commitment along the Spiritual Journey with others. Significantly, the power of the individual is shared for the completion of the Divine Plan. Our commitment and willingness to work with others are key to our spiritual growth. We can help each other grow and expand to our Highest Potential by collaborating and working together. The third base point represents spiritual focus. Choosing to prioritize our time, energy, and intention on our Divine Purpose will help us overcome whatever is blocking us from our spiritual growth and a new Spiritual Consciousness.

The energies of these three base points converge synergistically within the tetrahedron to send the energy to the apex, or fourth point—the Divine Spark. This point transmits the combined energy of the individual, partnership, and focus on a new Spiritual Consciousness. This energy can be transmitted through the apex to anyone, anything, any place, or any action to bring about a higher level of wisdom and Consciousness. With this awareness, we can use the focused tetrahedron energy to make positive changes in our lives and the lives of others. The energy of the tetrahedron can be used as a tool to access and energize the Divine Consciousness to elevate ourselves and the Universe.

This sacred geometry structure also energizes the solar plexus chakra, the energy of personal power, identity, self-esteem, self-motivation, passion, and drive. This tetrahedron energy helps connect us to our worthiness, aligning us with the Divine Presence that surrounds and is within us. The tetrahedron also supports our desire to bring more wisdom and increased Consciousness to all.

Hexahedron

The cube or hexahedron contains six equal square faces. The six equal sides represent strength, solidity, stability, and order. It represents the need for patience, consistency, and allowing things to develop or happen in the right way at the right time. Three sets of parallel sides signify safety and containment with boundaries. If the cube unfolds, it becomes a cross of six squares— four vertical squares and three horizontal

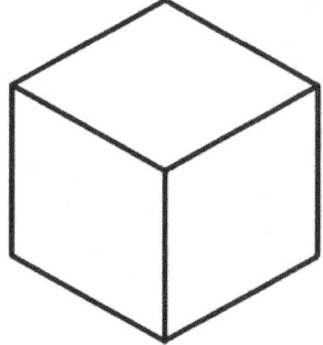

Figure 4 Hexahedron

squares; one of the squares is both vertical and horizontal. The spiritual aspects of the hexahedron are described in Appendix, Table 6.

Octahedron

The octahedron has eight equal triangular faces. Because it is connected to the heart chakra, the octahedron represents love and compassion. The octahedron can be used to connect with and honor our inner child. This sacred geometry form is about running, dancing, laughing, and playing. The octahedron is about freedom and joy.

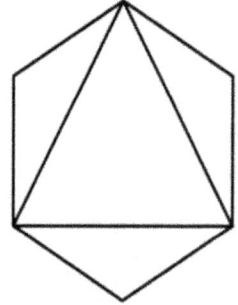

Figure 5 Octahedron

This sacred geometry structure elicits inner peace and calmness. It is a tool for connection, calmness, serenity, and forgiveness. Using this structure also offers total self-acceptance and unconditional self-love. Reflecting on this transcendental image will help with inner focus and direction. This structure helps balance the Inner Self with the outer self to increase the coherence of our inner and outer worlds. Reflecting and balancing the inner and outer selves help us determine the direction of our Spiritual Journey and how best to accomplish our Divine Mission. The spiritual aspects of the octahedron are described in Appendix, Table 6.

Dodecahedron

The dodecahedron has twelve equal five-sided pentagon faces and represents the elements of ether, Spirit, and the Universe, also known as energy, prana, or chi. Out of the original five Platonic solids, the dodecahedron is the only one connected to the Universe but not the Earth. In fact, some cosmologists are suggesting that the shape of the Universe is a dodecahedron.[201]

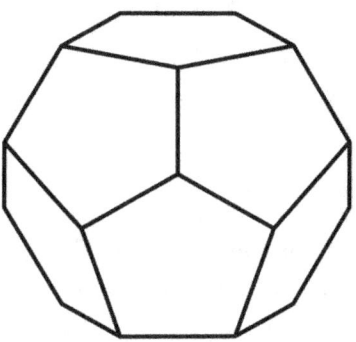

Figure 6 Dodecahedron

This structure is aligned with Spirit—the Life Force in all living beings. This force is used for healing and creativity. The dodecahedron is associated with the upper chakras—throat, third eye, and crown chakras. The dodecahedron represents what is in between existence. This dodecahedron structure helps to connect the physical and Spiritual Realms, humanity, and Divinity. The dodecahedron is like the glue that connects the visible and the invisible, the known and the unknown. The vibrations of the Spiritual Realm are more easily transported into the physical realm through this sacred geometry structure. More information about the dodecahedron's spiritual aspects is shown in Appendix, Table 6.

Icosahedron

The icosahedron has twenty equal triangular faces. The icosahedron is associated with the water element. In the spiritual sense, water is associated with emotions. This Platonic solid can be used to balance emotional upset and inner turmoil. This solid can be used as a tool to transform or transition into new phases of life. Being related to water, the icosahedron can be used to solve

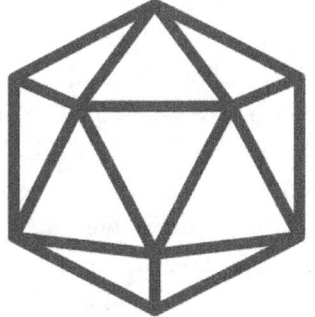

Figure 7 Icosahedron

problems. The icosahedron represents a new Consciousness, water, liquid, and yin. This structure helps you go with the Universe's flow—like water flowing in a river. The icosahedron can be used to remove blockages with creativity. The spiritual aspects of the icosahedron are described in Appendix, Table 6.

Heptahedron or Chestahedron

The heptahedron, made of four equilateral triangles and three kite-shaped quadrilaterals, was recently discovered as a new Platonic solid. Even though this form is made of two different forms, each side has the same surface area. Except for the rule of identical regular polygon shapes, the heptahedron conforms to the rules of Platonic solids in that it has three or more edges that meet at each vertex, all angles are less than 360 degrees, the structure is three-dimensional and dual, meaning it fits into at least one other Platonic

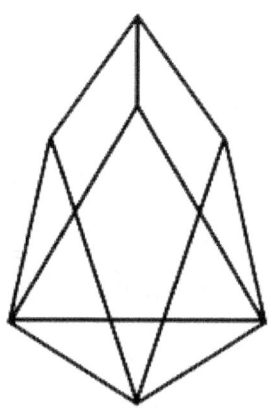

Figure 8 Heptahedron

solid.[202] The Golden Ratio is a proportion within the heptahedron creation. The heptahedron can be produced from a tetrahedron in two different ways.

We know that nothing in the Universe is at rest, everything is vibrating. The sacred geometry forms are in constant pulsing, spiraling, and transforming from one form to another. Although the chestahedron exemplifies a form resulting from the transitional dynamic vibration of a Platonic solid, the tetrahedron, it doesn't exemplify the perfect structure of one form; it has both three-sided and four-sided forms which have the same surface area.

Significantly, this heptahedron shape perfectly represents the left ventricle of the human heart. This "new" Platonic solid is also called the chestahedron after the artist-sculptor Frank Chester, who discovered it in 2000.[203] This heptahedron fits into a cube or hexahedron at a 36-degree tilt, exactly the tilt of the human heart in the chest cavity. Research on this new heptahedron implies that the heart is not a pump but a balancer of energy flow, acting more like a brake than a pump. The blood enters the left ventricle in a clockwise spiral. Then, before it leaves the left ventricle, the blood shifts to a counterclockwise spiral. The brake is needed to change the direction of blood flow. Upon further investigation, it is becoming clear that the heart is a vortex generator enhancing the intrinsic flow of the blood in a spiral.[204] This reference also explains that blood flows in a pattern not dominated by pressure. Because of the highly critical importance for blood flow for our physical health, blood has its own innate pattern of flow and a unique momentum that is supported by the structure and function of the heart. [205]

Spinning the chestahedron on its axis produces a bell-like structure that mimics the cross section of the human heart. Significantly, this bell-like structure is how Rudolf Steiner, a renowned Theosophist, explains an evolving Soul. Through inner vision, Steiner envisioned the Soul in the shape of a downward opening bell. Ancient Egyptians also represented the Soul as a bell in hieroglyphics in its descent from heaven to incarnate into a physical body. This suggests an interesting connection between the heart and Soul. More information about the chestahedron is shown in Appendix, Table 6.

Other Significant Sacred Geometry Forms

Although not Platonic solids, the sphere and triangle are sacred forms intimately associated with sacred geometry. The triangle is included in the structure of four of the six Platonic solids.

Sphere

The sphere is the simplest and most basic sacred geometry form and is integral to understanding the other sacred geometry forms discussed below. A sphere is a geometric shape with all aspects of the outer structure equidistant from the center. The sphere holds all the other sacred geometry forms. Earth, seeds, and atoms are considered spheres and represent

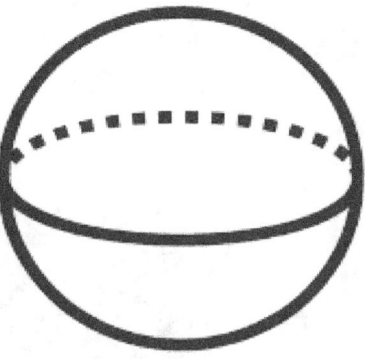

Figure 9 Sphere

wholeness and completeness. The sphere also represents the True Self, the Infinite Self, with perfect harmony and balance of mind, body, and spirit- the expression of Oneness.

Triangle

The equilateral triangle is a significant form within the tetrahedron, octahedron, icosahedron, and heptahedron. Its three equal sides and angles symbolize balance, harmony, and completion. The triangle may also represent mind, body, and spirit as one. Pointing upward, it represents elevation to higher Consciousness.

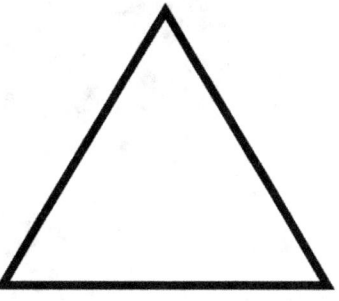

Figure 10 Triangle

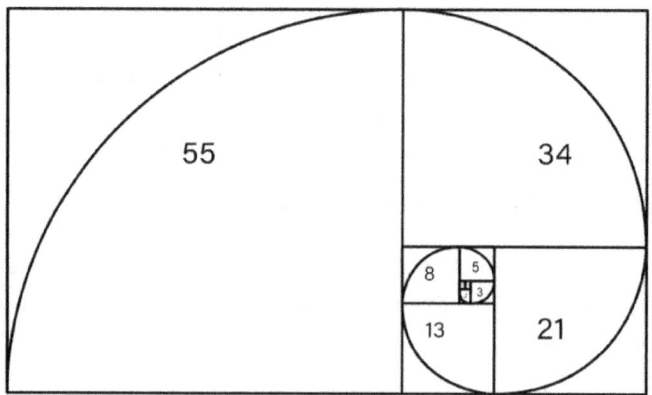

Figure 11 Golden Spiral

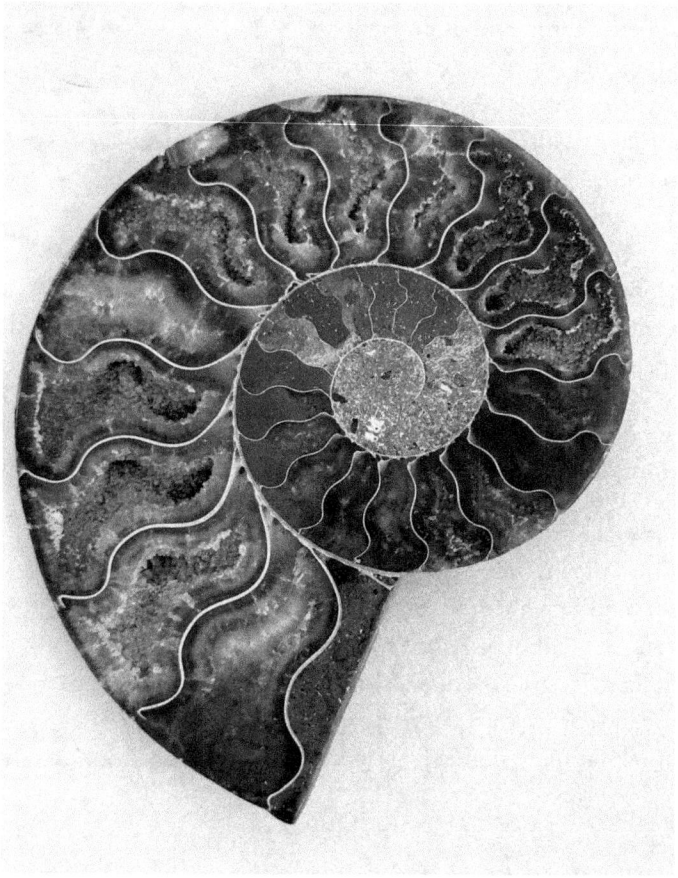

Figure 12 Golden Spiral Fossil

The Golden Spiral

The Golden Spiral, shown in Figures 11 and 12, is a blueprint for all nature, including humans, that bridges the physical and Spiritual Realms. (Appendix, Table 7 and Figure 25) This shape is present in nature, from the double helix DNA molecule to the shape of galaxies. We see this shape in nautilus shells, hurricanes, sunflowers, desert plants, pinecones, coiled snakes, fern buds, ocean waves, fingerprints, fractal properties of a branched tree, leaf patterns, riverbed formations, fossils, and human lungs. The pyramids and other famous buildings in Egypt are situated along the path of a Golden Spiral.[206]

The Golden Ratio and Fibonacci sequences create the Golden Spiral when approaching infinity. In geometry, a golden spiral is a logarithmic spiral whose growth factor is phi, φ—the Golden Ratio. This means a Golden Spiral gets wider and wider as it moves away from its point of origin by a factor of φ for every quarter turn it makes.[207] Appendix, Figure 25, provides additional information on creating a Golden Spiral.

Mathematical sequences and ratios define everything in the Universe. This awareness opens us to deep wisdom and the ability to understand life and the creation of the Universe. There was and is a Divine Plan. For example, many types of spirals follow the mathematical Fibonacci sequence pattern, which starts with 0 and 1 and then increases with the sum of the previous two numbers (0, 1, 1, 2, 3, 5, 8, 13, 21…). When we become aware of life's consistent patterns and shapes, we understand that the natural world is not random.

In the spiritual sense, the Golden Spiral represents the cosmos in ideal balance, universal harmony, and spiritual transformation. Golden Spiral wisdom helps us understand the depth of our connection to every wave, every grain of sand— literally every aspect of creation. We are part of the life flow of the Universe, the Oneness, and All That Is. There is no separateness. To emphasize the significance of the Golden Spiral in your Spiritual Journey, it is inlaid on the book cover.

The Golden Ratio

The Golden Ratio or phi, φ, numerically represented as 1.618, is considered the most beautiful number in the Universe because of its ubiquitous presence. Relative to the adult human body, the Golden Ratio is also referred to as the Divine Proportion. For example, if we divide the length from our head to our toes by the length of our navel to our toes, we will get 1.618. We get the same result if we divide the length from our shoulder to the tip of our index finger by the length from our elbow to the wrist of the same arm, the length from the top of our head to the shoulder by the length from the top of our head to our chin; or the length from the top of our head to our navel, by the length between our head and shoulder, we will get the Golden Ratio 1.618.

Do you see how these mathematical relationships show the order and symmetry of the natural world?

Similarly, mathematical sequences and ratios define everything in the Universe. These mathematical sequences further enhance our understanding that the natural world is not random, opening the door to deeper wisdom and understanding of life and the creation of the Universe.

We can comprehend that sacred geometry is the template for life. The natural world was designed using the mathematics of the Golden Ratio, the Golden Spiral, the Fibonacci sequences, and the form structures of the Platonic solids. This design's simplicity and unity create balance and order. In addition to yin-yang balance and the balance of opposites being aspects of the same thing, the physical aspects of sacred geometry add further order and balance. Superimposed on these forces are the Universal Laws. Therefore, the Universe can maintain balance in many ways while constantly changing and expanding.

Sacred Geometry of Creation

Sacred geometry is also a vehicle of the Spirit or a way to contain high vibrational frequencies of disembodied Spirits to connect with the Spiritual Realm. As the language of creation, sacred geometry forms the foundation of all that is in the Universe, including Spirit. It is the language of Oneness.

Focusing on human creation and development, we see simplicity and unity in the design of a human being and every other living thing. All life forms are based on the same geometrical patterns and start from the same structural form—a sphere or ovum, emphasizing the order of creation and the unity of all life. The diagram in Table 3 shows the sacred geometry of human development. The creation of a human from an egg cell, or ovum, is a sphere representing Oneness, wholeness, and completion.

Table 3 Source Note: https://www.UniversalLifeTools.com

Table 3: Sacred Geometry of Human Development

Day(s) After Fertil- ization	Number of Cells	Structure of Cells	Sacred Geometry Form	Sacred Geometry Image
0-1	oocyte-> fertilization-> zygotę		Sphere	
2	2 cell stage		Vesica Piscis	
2 to 3	4 cell stage		Tetrahedron	
3	8-16 cell stage (the 8th sphere is behind the central sphere)		Egg of Life or Star Tetrahedron	
4	32 to 64 cell stage		Flower of Life or Morula	
5	128 cells (early blastocyst)		NA	NA
6 to 7	256 cells (blastocyst implantation)	NA	NA	NA
7	512 cells		Torus	

When an ovum gets fertilized, the sperm and the ovum become one. This is called a zygote. This cell divides and forms a Vesica Piscis—two overlapping cells or spheres. (Table 3; Figure 4; Appendix, Table 7) After each of those cells divides, and four cells are present, the structure is a tetrahedron, one of the Platonic solids. After each cell divides again, eight cells form a star tetrahedron—two overlapping tetrahedrons, with one tetrahedron facing up and one facing down. (Figure 23; Appendix, Table 7) This structure, also known as the Egg of Life, is shown in Figure 18 and Appendix, Table 8.

These original eight cells are significant as they are always within us in this lifetime. They do not go through the standard life cycle of all the other cells in the body, getting replaced every five to seven years. Instead, they remain in an energetic opening near the perineum, where the central vertical channel or energetic core runs through both our physical and energy bodies. Each cell divides again in the zygote, forming sixteen cells and another star tetrahedron. At the 32-cell stage division, it starts to become a sphere again. There are sixteen cells in the middle and sixteen cells on the outside.

The structure then becomes a blob or hollow sphere with thirty-two more cells, or sixty-four total, called the morula, represented by the Flower of Life illustrated in Table 3, Figure 19, and Appendix, Table 8. The north side starts dropping down through the space inside, going toward the south pole. At the same time, the south pole comes up through the space to meet the north pole. The hollow sphere becomes a spherical torus at 512 cells, three more cell divisions later. (Table 3; Figure 17; Appendix, Table 8)

Every single life form goes through this stage. At the torus stage, the cells start to differentiate into cells for the heart, kidney, muscles, and other organs. The hollow space inside the torus becomes the lungs. The north pole becomes the mouth, and the south pole becomes the anus. All the internal organs form inside the central tube in the middle.

Table 4 Source Note: Drunvalo, Melchizedek, *The Ancient Secret of the Flower of Life*, Vol. 1 (AZ: Light Technology, 1998), 152-153.

Table 4: Sacred Geometry and Creation of the Universe

Day of Creation	Spheres of Creation	Sacred Geometry Form	Creation in the Gensis Story
0	1 sphere	Sphere	start of creation
1	2 spheres	Vesica Piscis/ Bi Veca Code	light
2	3 spheres	Tripod of Life or Tri Veca Code	sky
3	4 spheres	Tetrahedron	land and vegetation
4	5 spheres	NA	stars, sun, and moon
5	6 spheres	NA	water creatures and birds
6	7 spheres	Seed of Life/ Genesis Pattern	livestock animals, wild animals, creatures that move along the ground, and humans

Similarly, sacred geometry explains how the Universe was created out of the Void, as illustrated in Table 4. Like the human development theory, the Genesis story represents how the Universe was created from Consciousness, starting with one sphere with additional spheres coming into existence as different aspects of creation. Following the sequence in Table 4, the first sphere represents the start of creation. The two spheres represent the creation of light, and the intersection of the two spheres looks like an eye. The third sphere represents the creation of the sky or vault, as described in the first chapter of Genesis in the Christian Bible.[208] The fourth and next sphere represents the land with vegetation. The fifth sphere represents the stars, the sun, and the moon. The sixth sphere represents water creatures and birds. The seventh sphere represents the creation of livestock animals, wild animals, creatures that move along the ground, and humans.

The whole Genesis pattern of six spheres around the central sphere is the sacred geometry form known as the Seed of Life, shown in Figure 16. More information about the Seed of Life pattern is shown in Appendix, Table 8.

Eye of Horus

The ancient Egyptians and many religious doctrines refer to Earth as being without form when it came out of the Void—out of nothing. Ancient Egyptians and Christian religions teach that *nothing* and Spirit are the only things required to start creating the Universe. The process is started by the

Figure 13 Eye of Horus

movement of Spirit.[209] From this perspective, the Void was an infinite, dark space with nothing physical. Spirit and *nothing*, which we understand as energy, was all that was needed to create the Universe from the Void. The Spirit of God existed in the Void without anything else. Spirit needed some adventures to activate its existence in the Void.[210]

In the Egyptian mystery schools, it was taught that Spirit—depicted as the Eye of Horus, could project a sensing beam as Consciousness out from this eye into the dark Void. (Figure 13; Appendix, Table 7) To start the creation process, the Divine Spirit had to create something first to orient Itself in the Void. Consciousness, or a sensing beam, like a ray of light, is projected out into the infinite darkness, or the Void, a certain distance. But Spirit could not sense or *know* what existed beyond that point. The Spirit would project a sensing beam of Consciousness, first to the front, then to the back, then to the left, and then to the right. Then, a sensing beam of Consciousness would be projected up, and another would be projected down. The beam of Consciousness would be projected out the same distance in all directions to define space, which we refer to as north, south, east, west, up, and down—the six directions in three-dimensional space. The Egyptians believed that creation would never have happened without the ability to project these sensing beams.[211]

In the human body, the pineal gland in the middle of the brain is also a center for projecting sensing beams or rays. This sensing beam can be interpreted as Consciousness or intuition. Many traditions believe the pineal gland connects the physical and Spiritual Realms. The pineal gland is a counterpart to the third eye. In total, there are six ways to project these rays: through the third eye to the front of the head, to the back of the head, to the right and left sides side of the head, up to the crown chakra, and down toward the neck. These are also the six directions of the x, y, and z axes in geometry.

On the deepest level, Egyptian students learned and practiced the process discussed below in their mystery schools to better understand how the Divine created the Universe. The students were to envision darkness, the Void with an Eye of Horus in it. The next step was to connect the ends of the rays of the six directions forming a diamond or square shape, depending on the viewing angle. They then put a small square in the center at their point of Consciousness. From the square, they sent a ray up to the top to form a pyramid around the base of the square, then sent a ray down to form a pyramid below. In three dimensions, the two pyramids form an octahedron, shown in Figure 5. This is Spirit. With two back-to-back pyramids, they created an energy field around Spirit. [212]

The significant point is they now have an object. Kinetic energy can now move between the Spirit and the object. Kinetic energy or movement is impossible in the Void unless there is at least one other object in the space around it. Spirit can move outside the object and around it. Spirit can go out for miles and always return to this object. Or Spirit can remain in the center, and the object can move around Spirit. The object or shape can move in all possible ways, making relative movements possible.

> *Sacred geometry started when Spirit made its first projection into the Void and created the first octahedron around itself. The Void is infinite—nothing in it—and these forms being created are also nothing. They're just imaginary lines created out of consciousness. This gives you an indication of what Reality is—nothing.*[213]

The octahedron created in the mystery schools had three axes: front to back, left to right, and up and down. Then, the students spun the octahedron on one axis. The octahedron could be spun on any axis and in any direction; the result would be the same. If they spun the octahedron around each of the three axes one time, they created a sphere. They were taught to create around their point of Consciousness, or around their physical bodies, to enact how the Divine Spirit created an octahedron and then a sphere around Itself.

In sacred geometry, it is accepted that a straight line is male, and a curved line is female. Since the octahedron is comprised only of straight lines, it is considered male. When the octahedron is spun on the three axes, creating a sphere that only contains curved lines, it creates a female shape from a male shape. The metaphor of this spun octahedron is the story of Adam and Eve—Eve, the female, was created from Adam, the male.

Only two instructions were given to the mystery school students to re-create the actions of Spirit. These two instructions indicated the actions needed to create everything in the Universe from the Void. With Spirit being in the center of a sphere, the first instruction was to move to that which is newly created. The second instruction was to project another sphere exactly like the first.[214]

> That does something very special and unique. This is an absolutely foolproof system for creating Reality. You cannot make a mistake no matter what you do. All you do is move to what is newly created and project another sphere the same size as the first one.[215]

Nothing exists within the sphere, so there is nothing new there. What is newly created is the outside or the surface of the sphere.[216] Consciousness or Spirit goes to the surface of the new sphere. This is the first motion in Genesis. "And the Spirit of God moved upon the face of the waters."[217] And the next statement in Genesis is God said, "Let there be light' and there was light."[218] At this point, Spirit knows how to project an octahedron, create a sphere, and move to what's newly created. As Drunvalo Melchizedek said, "That's it, a very simple reality."[219]

Once Spirit is at the newly created membrane on the newly created sphere, it makes another octahedron, spins it through three axes, and forms a second sphere exactly like the first one. In terms of sacred geometry, this formation of a second sphere creates a Vesica Piscis where the two spheres intersect. Vesica Piscis is produced when two circles or spheres overlap. (Table 4) This is also called the Bi-Veca code when manifesting or birthing something new. (Figure 14; Appendix, Table 7)

The next sphere produced the image of the three overlapping spheres, the tripod of life, which represents the tetrahedron—one of the most important shapes of life. The tetrahedron is an icon of sacred geometry with perfect balance and symmetry. (Table 4; Figure 3; Appendix, Table 6)

The rest of the forms are simply the addition of one extra sphere following the process of Spirit projecting an octahedron, creating a sphere, and moving to what's newly created. The Genesis structure represents the sixth day of creation. Each of these different forms leading to the Genesis structure symbolizes a different day in Genesis.

> *This is not just mathematics, and it's not just circles or geometries.*
> *This is the living map of the creation of all Reality.*[220]

The Veca Codes

The Veca Codes are powerful symbols for healing and manifestation. Although these codes have many variations, the Bi-Veca and the Tri-Veca Codes are most commonly understood. As illustrated in Appendix, Table 7, the Bi-Veca code is the result of two overlapping spheres, which symbolize the past and future integrating into the present. The Tri-Veca Code represents three overlapping spheres representing the harmony or integration of the past, present, and future. Both these codes emit a certain vibrational frequency based on the high frequency infused into the codes from the higher dimensions. Visualizing these codes aids in receiving messages and manifesting from the invisible into the physical. These codes, also known as the *Sacred Keys to the Kingdom of Heaven*, open us up to Divine Energy and help bring us back to our original Divine Order and Eternal Divine Blueprint.

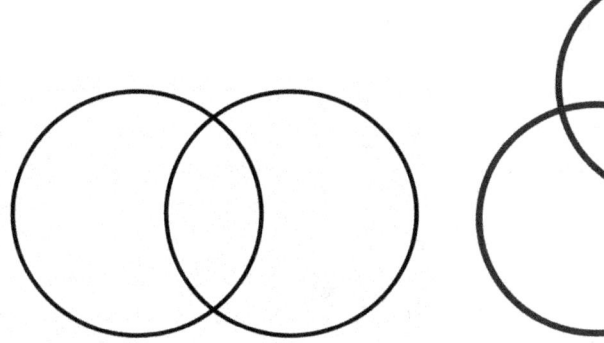

Figure 14 Bi-Veca Code   Figure 15 Tri-Veca Code

Sacred Geometry Forms that Enhance Spiritual Connection

There are still more sacred geometry forms that play a significant role in enhancing spiritual connection. Most of these forms were introduced in Tables 4 and 5. More information about how they can be used to enhance our spiritual connection is shown in Appendix, Table 8.

The Seed of Life

The Seed of Life, or the *Genesis pattern*, represents day six of the creation of the Universe with a total of seven spheres. Beyond the Genesis story, this sacred geometry form expresses the interconnectedness of the whole Universe. The Seed of Life symbolizes life on Earth as a Divine Creation. The Seed of Life represents the concept that all life originated from a single structure according to an

Figure 16 Seed of Life

intelligent plan. (Figure 16; Appendix, Table 8) The Seed of Life is derived from the center of the Flower of Life symbol. (Figures 16 and 19) The Seed of Life symbolizes all aspects of creation, which are interconnected and part of the One. Several sacred geometry forms were created from the Seed of Life structure by rotating the Seed of Life structure on one axis. As discussed in earlier Sections, the concept of one becoming the other is again evident here.

The Torus

The torus structure is a primary shape in the Universe. It is unique among other structures as it is a donut-like shape generated by a circle rotated about an axis in its plane that does not intersect the circle and has an infinitely small hole in the center. The torus is created by rotating the Seed of Life structure around one of its axes. (Figure 17; Appendix, Table 8) Its structure illustrates the continually renewing energy available to us.

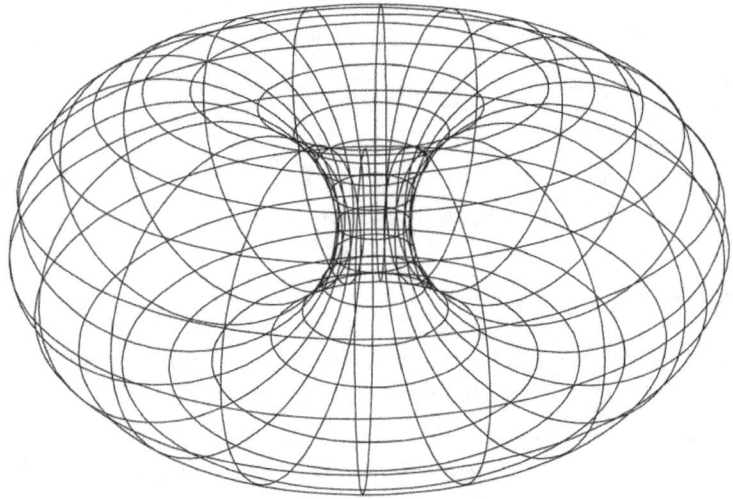

Figure 17 Torus

As the primary shape in the Universe, the torus' electromagnetic field is essentially Consciousness. This Consciousness is a sacred geometry form and is the ever flowing upward, inward, downward, outward in a continually repeating, renewing and revitalizing flow of energy. In this unique flow, the torus energy interacts with the physical and Spiritual Realm energies communicating, informing, and revitalizing with perpetual movement of information as the One Primordial Flow of the Universe. [221]

A toroidal energy field exists around everything, from the atom to the Universe: people, trees, the Earth, the sun, galaxies. Our auras may also contain nested torus fields. In addition to a torus around our physical bodies, the human heart and DNA each have a torus. The torus shape governs significant aspects of our lives, including the heart organ. Like the Genesis pattern with six spheres around a central sphere, the heart has seven muscles that form a torus. Understanding how the energy flows in the torus structure is key to understanding the fundamental energy flow in the Universe. Flowing from the center of the human body, the torus energy loops around, connecting the feet to the head in a bi-directional pattern. The energy flowing through the surface of the torus and inside the torus appears to be a spiral.

This continual repeating pattern of energy flowing or folding into itself is unique to the torus. No other shape or geometric form can do anything close to flowing, spiraling, or pulsing inward and outward, upward and downward like the torus energy. As discussed previously, the torus is the first shape that comes out of the completed Genesis pattern. Among all forms in the Universe, the torus is exclusively unique, emphasizing its significance in creation.[222]

The torus energy flow depicts how energy from the Spiritual Realm can come into the physical realm and how matter can ascend to the Spiritual Realm, showing how the two realms are intimately connected. The torus also represents how we can connect to the invisible world beyond the physical.

The Egg of Life

The Egg of Life is the second shape that comes from rotating the Seed of Life structure. In the Egg of Life, the spheres are not overlapping. Six more spheres in the Egg of Life structure are behind the two-dimensional depiction of it, for a total of thirteen spheres connected to the central sphere. Significantly, The Egg of Life is similar to a developing zygote or embryo, representing life's start, revitalization, rejuvenation, and rebirth. (Figure 18; Appendix, Table 8)

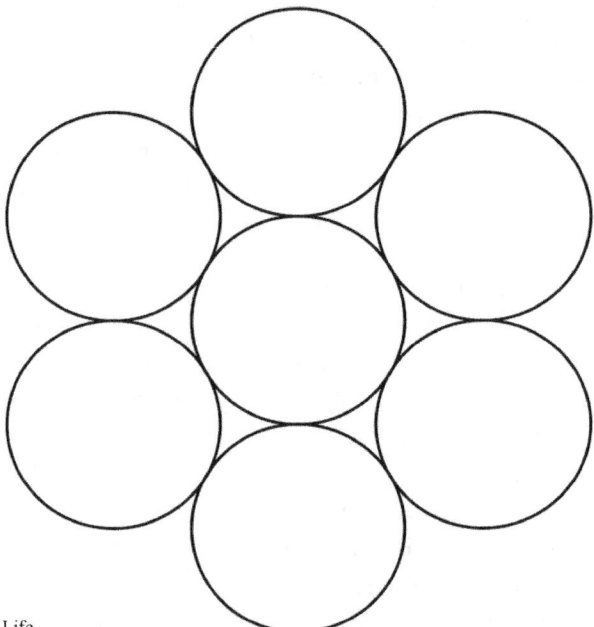

Figure 18 Egg of Life

The Flower of Life

The Flower of Life is a sacred geometry form of nineteen overlapping spheres that depicts the blueprint and wisdom of the Universe with the matrix of all matter and information. This form is an iconic sacred geometry form representing the creation of the Universe. The Flower of Life is created by creating a sphere, moving to the new surface of the sphere, then forming a new sphere. All spheres are the same size. This repeated pattern of overlapping spheres aligns with the basic building blocks of the Universe, the Platonic solids. These formations suggest intelligent and intentional design and illustrate the interconnectedness of the whole Universe. (Figure 19; Appendix, Table 8)

Figure 19 Flower of Life

The Flower of Life is an akashic information system, meaning it contains records of all that was, all that is, and all that will be.[223]

The Flower of Life symbol has been found in ancient temples worldwide, including the granite walls of the Osirion, the Temple of Resurrection in Abydos, Egypt, and eighteen countries worldwide, from Turkey to Tibet and China to Yucatan.[224] It is unlikely that all these ancient civilizations learned about this symbol from each other since great distances separated them, and they didn't share the same language. This suggests that the information came to these civilizations through Spiritual Channels.

The Fruit of Life

The third rotation of the Seed of Life form produces the Fruit of Life, symbolizing all creation. "This third rotation is extremely important relationship in the creation of our Reality."[225]

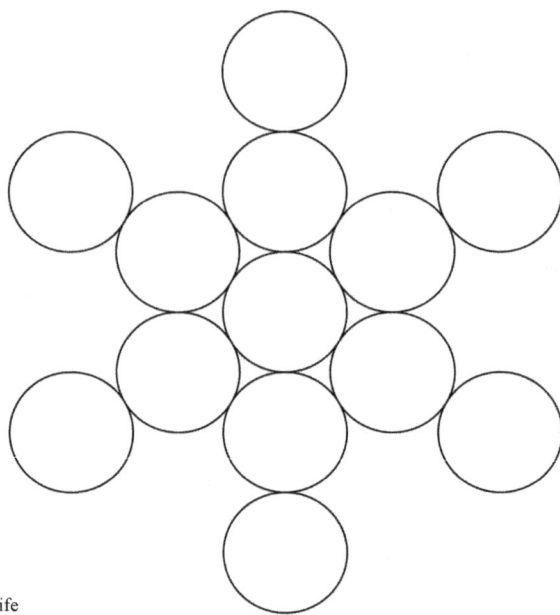

Figure 20 Fruit of Life

> *This pattern of the thirteen circles is one of the holiest, most sacred forms in existence. On Earth, it is called the Fruit of Life. It is called the fruit because it is the result, the fruit, from which the fabric of the details of the Reality were created.*[226]

The Fruit of Life has thirteen spheres that are connected but not overlapping. The Fruit of Life can also be created from a completed form of the Flower of Life. It is also contained within the Flower of Life symbol and is related to abundance.[227] The Fruit of Life is inherent in the cut-off spheres that don't overlap in the Flower of Life form. Like music, the thirteenth sphere of the Fruit of Life represents a higher octave or, in spiritual terms, a higher level of Consciousness. According to Drunvalo Melchizedek, thirteen informational systems are associated with the Fruit of Life pattern, each producing enormous knowledge. (Figure 20; Appendix, Table 8)

Metatron's Cube

Metatron's Cube is created from the Fruit of Life structure by drawing straight lines from the centers of all thirteen spheres. The combination of the arced circles and the straight lines is the joining of female and male, respectively. This joining is to create something new. This form also illustrates the perspective of sacred geometry at the beginning of the Universe and Consciousness. (Figure 21; Appendix, Table 8)

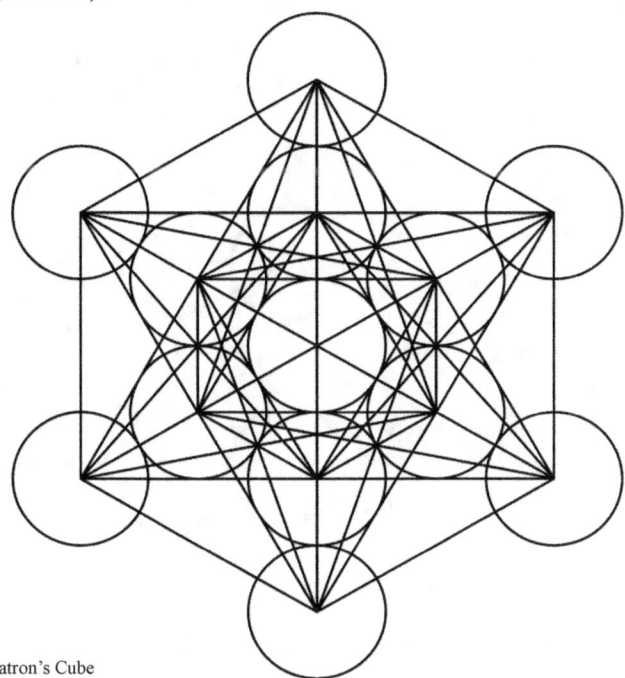

Figure 21 Metatron's Cube

Metatron's Cube is "one of the basic creation patterns of existence."[228] It contains five shapes of the Platonic solids and the star tetrahedron. These are three-dimensional objects that come out of the thirteen circles or spheres of the Fruit of Life.[229] Metatron's Cube is fundamental to the creation process at the quantum level. In essence, Metatron's Cube awakens Consciousness and heals the heart.[230]

The Tree of Life

The Tree of Life represents the path to the Divine. Two paths are illustrated in the Tree of Life structure: one starts in the Spiritual Realm and comes into the physical realm, and the other starts from the physical realm and transcends to the Spiritual Realm.

The Tree of Life also comes from the Flower of Life form. (Figures 19 and 22; Appendix, Table 8) It represents many aspects of the connection between the physical and Spiritual Realms. In the Buddhist traditions, it represents enlightenment and existence. It also represents abundance, connection, unity, and the stages of an inner journey.

The Tree of Life also symbolizes how we are all connected in the circle of life. In general, trees symbolize growth in the continuous cycle of life, changing and blossoming with time and the seasons, and strength and stability. The life cycle of a tree is a simple representation of the language of creation. A seed from a tree falls into the soil and germinates under the right conditions. The seed contains all the information to make a tree. First, there is a sapling. The sapling grows into a small tree. The tree grows, producing leaves and flowers. The center of the flower produces a fruit that contains more seeds. As the fruit ripens, it falls to the ground, opens, and the seeds germinate in the soil. The cycle repeats over and over again in nature, showing that life is created to produce more life.

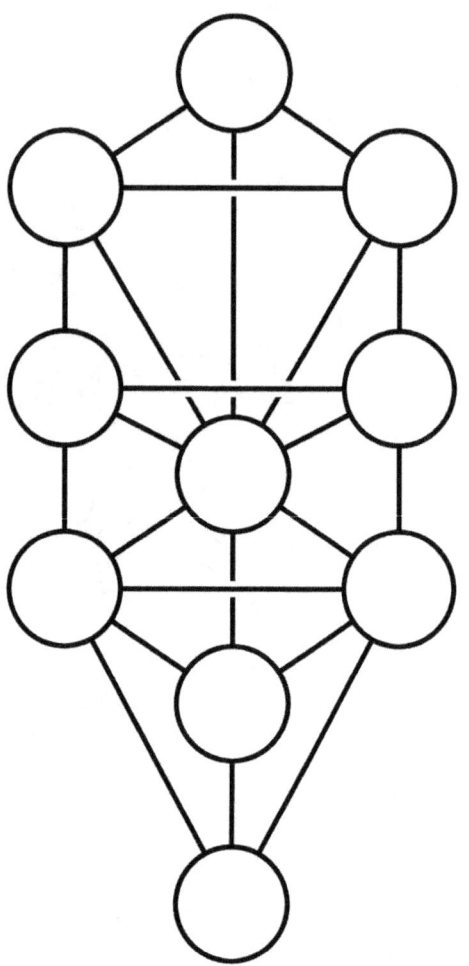

Figure 22 Tree of Life

The Merkaba

The Merkaba is a star tetrahedron with two overlapping tetrahedrons, one pointing up representing male and fire energy, and spins counterclockwise, pulling energy down from the Spiritual Realm. (Figure 23) The other tetrahedron points down, representing female, water, and the chalice, and spins clockwise, pulling energy up from the Earth. Together, the two spinning tetrahedrons produce a harmonic balance between the physical and Spiritual Realms.

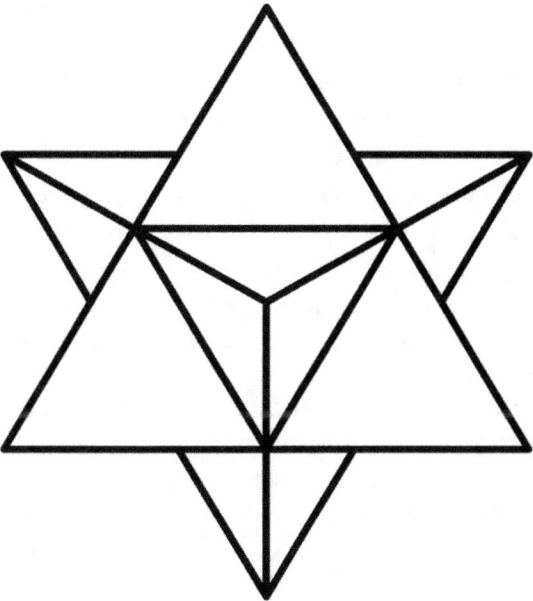

Figure 23 Merkaba

In ancient Egyptian, the word Merkaba translates to light, Spirit, and body. Mer means light, ka means spirit, and ba means body. The Spirit or ka represents the infinite Life Force in everything. The Merkaba sacred geometry form is a light body surrounding our physical form that connects a gridwork of light and sacred geometry, bringing the physical, emotional, mental, and Spiritual bodies into balance. The Merkaba can also be a container for our auric fields. The apex of the top tetrahedron of the Merkaba is a hands-width above our heads, and the apex of the downward-pointing tetrahedron is one hand's width below our feet.[231]

This star tetrahedron form is a powerful symbol that represents our pure, unlimited potential when connected to the Divine. The Merkaba is an energy matrix surrounding the aura that strengthens the alignment between the mind, body, and Soul. It offers protection and aligns us more fully with our Higher Self. The Merkaba sacred geometry is a tool for bringing in more light to the new living light body and crystalline body matrices.[232]

Through the practice of meditation and breathing techniques, anyone can access their Merkaba body. We can consciously and intentionally activate our Merkaba by visualizing this symbol surrounding us during meditation.[233] This visualization will help raise our vibrational frequency, enable us to receive Divine Insights and Wisdom, and gain powerful, intuitive knowledge through our multi-dimensional Self.

When activating the two tetrahedrons of the Merkaba sacred form, visualize them spinning in opposite directions. This spinning energy or light acts like a vehicle for transportation to higher realms of Consciousness or from one-dimensional plane to another. This lattice of light and sacred geometry radiates light energy out from us to link our multi-dimensional Self to the infinite Universe. The light radiating out often resembles a flying saucer in the Merkaba surrounding us. This light lattice is a powerful protection energy that can extend fifty to sixty feet from our physical bodies.[234] When activated as a Merkaba body, the star tetrahedron can help us expand our Consciousness to reach the outer limits of human potential by direct access to our Higher Self and Universal Wisdom.

Another important aspect of this activation process is expanding our hearts, extending our love out to the Earth and beyond so that we are living in Divine Love. Experiencing Divine Love helps move us from one dimension to another.[235] By doing this, we tap into our multi-dimensional aspects and feel the Oneness of the Universe. We are guided by unconditional Divine Love for the Merkaba to become a *living field of light*.

The Vitruvian Man

The iconic image of the Vitruvian Man drawn by Leonardo da Vinci illustrates the *Divine Proportion* and holds the secret of the Divinity of humans. This drawing contains the entire system of sacred geometry: the Golden Ratio or phi, the human energy field, the star tetrahedron, and the Merkaba. Some scholars believe that the Vitruvian Man was constructed by understanding the Flower of Life's sacred geometry form. Looking at this famous drawing, the man appears to have two sets of legs and two sets of arms. If you look carefully, one set of arms extends to the circle's edge, and one set extends to the square's edge. The same observation can be made with the legs. What is depicted in this drawing is the figure of a man with a circle around it superimposed over the figure of the same man with a square around it. If the square represents the physical realm, and the circle represents the Spiritual Realm, as historians have noted, this illustrates that the spiritual aspect of humans is superimposed over our physical aspect.[236] Another interpretation is the BEing aspect is superimposed over the doing aspect of the human body.

Historians believe that da Vinci was illustrating the human as the bridge or the connection between the physical and Spiritual realms. It has also been suggested that da Vinci knew that the human form mirrors sacred geometry structures such as the Merkaba or star tetrahedron and the Flower of Life. Da Vinci's drawing of the human body matches the proportions of sacred geometry and is in harmony with the building blocks of the Universe. This conclusion is drawn from other drawings of the Vitruvian Man with sacred geometry forms superimposed over the human form.[237]

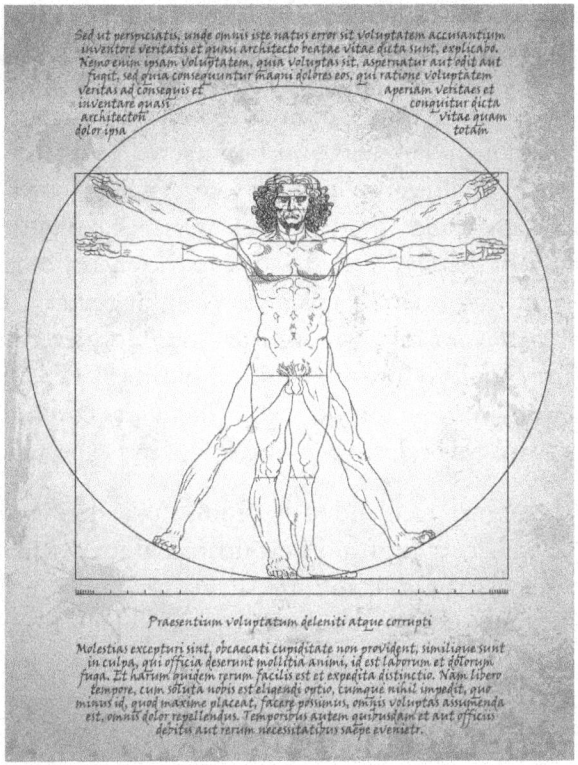

Source Note: Shutterstock, Royalty-free stock vector ID: 1014370468.

Figure 24 Vitruvian Man

Try the Vitruvian Man Exercise at the end of this Section to experience putting your physical body into a star tetrahedron and connecting to the Spiritual Realm. You may find that you feel more grounded and present.

Before I knew anything about sacred geometry, I attended a conference led by Gregg Braden and Dr. Bruce Lipton in New Mexico. I saw two purple books on the sales table, *The Ancient Secret of the Flower of Life* by Drunvalo Melchizedek, Volume 1 and Volume 2. Even though these books were at the back of the sales table, I had a strong pull to them, and they jumped to my visual perception as if there were no other books on the table. I was always acknowledging my intuition or *magnetic pulls*. I received the message that I needed to learn about sacred geometry and bought the books. As soon as I returned home, I began reading Volume 1. It was not an easy read. Volume 2 wasn't any easier. I had to learn the information in layers. The books contained a lot of math and geometry, and the concepts at the time were difficult to imagine as the truth.

Even after reading both volumes, I still hadn't grasped the significance of these books and how sacred geometry would play a role in my life and Spiritual Journey. Since then, I have come to understand the way Soul messages come to me is important. In this situation, I wasn't in the energy of learning a new field, nor was I particularly thinking that I needed something new for my own Spiritual Journey. Nevertheless, I had a strong pull to buy the books, indicating to me that the enlightening information offered in them was coming to me from a source beyond my own intention and expectations.

I have benefited tremendously from surrendering to that magnetic pull coming from beyond me. I am fascinated by these types of events in my life. It wasn't until much later, when I was writing this book, that I was able to understand the multi-faceted significance of sacred geometry more fully, from its role in creating physical balance and harmony in the Universe to support our Spiritual Evolution.

Although it may be obvious how the Platonic solids represent the structure of the physical world, the amazing and wondrous aspect of these basic geometric shapes is that they are also doorways to inner realms. When we are in the presence of these sacred geometry forms, we can raise our vibrational frequency. These geometric shapes and solids help us to enter a new way of BEing and a new way of seeing through our inner vision. Events naturally happen for our growth and well-being.

Looking at or for these different geometrical structures within sacred geometry forms, such as Metatron's Cube and the Flower of Life, is a left-brain experience. In contrast, the right brain experiences the shapes emotionally. Just experiencing sacred geometry shapes affects us emotionally and spiritually without our full awareness. Understanding this concept can help us to use these structures and forms as tools on our Spiritual Journey.[238]

The sacredness of these geometrical forms lies in the foundational belief that the patterns, mathematical formulas, and structures indicate intelligent design or Divine Creation and even evidence of creation by a higher power. Ancient civilizations believed that sacred geometry was significant in the education of the Soul. In these belief systems, geometric patterns and codes were symbols of our internal BEing and were significant to higher Consciousness and Self-awareness. As an ancient science or sacred language, sacred geometry helps us understand the design of the Universe to aid in our Spiritual Journey. The study of waves and vibrations connected with these forms and patterns helps us understand our connection to realms beyond the physical third-dimensional world. When we understand the significance of these sacred geometry shapes representing the blueprint or the structure of the Universe, as well as the proximity of Divine Energy, we know there is no separation. We are One—both physically and spiritually.

As discussed, meditating or healing with these iconic sacred geometry symbols like the Platonic solids, the Genesis or Seed of Life Pattern, Merkaba, or the Flower of Life is powerful and transformative. These symbols heighten or connect us to our True Essence and can be used to balance human energy fields in the physical world to open to higher-vibrational frequencies that help us ascend to higher dimensions of BEing.

Because each geometric shape has a specific high vibrational frequency, as well as a specific intention and specific feeling of energy, these symbols help us to connect more deeply to our internal Selves or our Souls. These sacred geometry forms or vibrational frequencies help us harmonize the world around us and within ourselves by inducing energetic shifts in our physical bodies and Consciousness that create balance and healing. Sacred geometry is also referred to as *sacred architecture* because it underlies everything and is literally woven into the fabric of all creation as the foundation of the Oneness of everything in the Universe. The consistency of mathematical relationships within all things and between all things illustrates the Oneness or the inseparable relationship between everything and everyone. This Oneness, physical and spiritual, embodies the whole Universe. These forms contain cosmic truths and wisdom. Francene Hart explains sacred geometry as the "new science of compassion," the "blueprint for all creation," the "harmonic configuration of the soul," and the "divine rhythm which results in manifest existence."[239]

The sacred geometry forms are like codes assisting us in our life journey but can also be used more consciously to bring about deep Soul awakening and connection to our True Divine Essence. Sacred geometry can open pathways or doorways to the infinite as well as the Oneness of all life. As with other sacred geometry structures, the Merkaba helps us shift from duality Consciousness to unity Consciousness, which is love, compassion, and heart connection. These aspects of our spiritual growth are the key to seeing beyond the physical and help us cross the bridge from the physical to the spiritual.

By studying sacred geometry images, we see how all the forms, Seed of Life/Genesis Pattern, Fruit of Life, Tree of Life, and Metatron's Cube, all fit into the Flower of Life, illustrating how they all relate to each other and fit together. We have discussed how sacred geometry images unfold one by one during early human development. This represents the inside of our bodies with the original eight cells in the center of our bodies. We discussed the use of sacred geometry images as illuminating a process for the creation of the Universe.

Consciousness is Based on Sacred Geometry

"Nothing—absolutely nothing—occurs without a reason."[240]

Therefore, nothing in nature is random, not even Consciousness. As Drunvalo Melchizedek states, "All consciousness, including human, is solely based on sacred geometry."[241]

> *. . . all levels of consciousness in the universe are integrated by a single image in sacred geometry. It is the key to time, space, and dimension as well as consciousness itself . . . even emotions and thoughts are based on sacred geometry.*[242]

Different levels of human Consciousness show differences in at least three areas: the number of DNA chromosomes, physical form, and the interpretation of reality. First, we will focus on the physical form as it pertains to sacred geometry. Let's return to the concept of the circle and square around a physical form, as illustrated in the Vitruvian Man drawing, and consider how this relates to the different levels of Consciousness. Remember that each of the thirteen spheres in the Fruit of Life form contains the wisdom of an informational system. The third informational system of the Fruit of Life form is important because it represents the wisdom of the circle and square. To raise our level of Consciousness, the circle, or the spiritual aspect, must be larger than the square, the physical realm aspect. To be in harmonic resonance with each other, the difference between the circle's circumference and the square's perimeter around the human body must be very close in value to each other.

The circle and square in the Vitruvian Man drawing indicate that da Vinci understood how the human form reflects its level of Consciousness.[243] By understanding the circle and square around the Vitruvian Man, we can understand how the different levels of Consciousness can be determined. As stated, this drawing illustrates two versions of the Vitruvian Man. One with his feet firmly planted on the Earth, as illustrated with the feet at the edge of the surrounding square. Proportionally, he fits perfectly within the square. The other version of him illustrates his feet at the edge of the circle—not touching the physical ground or the square edges. This version of the Vitruvian Man fits inside the circumference of the circle proportionally and represents his spiritual aspect.

This spiritual aspect superimposed over the physical aspect of the Vitruvian Man shows the simultaneous existence of both aspects of human Consciousness. This squaring the circle or circling the square is a geometric illustration of "as above, so below," a concept of the Universal Law of Correspondence discussed in Section One. The more closely the perimeter of the square and circumference of the circle surrounding the human form match in value, the more harmonic they are—the more the physical and spiritual aspects of Consciousness of that human form are in harmony. As Drunvalo Melchizedek illustrates, humans today represent the second level of Consciousness.

Today's humans have evolved from the Aborigines, a race of reduced stature between 4 and 6 feet, which represents the first level of Consciousness. The perimeter of the square and the circumference of the circle around the Aboriginal human form were close in value, indicating their spiritual and physical aspects were in harmony.[244] The perimeter of the squares and the circumference of the circles around our human forms today, with statures between 5 and 7 feet, do not closely match—meaning we are disharmonic. Nonetheless, this stage of development is an important stepping stone to the third level of Consciousness, Christ Consciousness.

An interesting correlation with the differences in Consciousness as it relates to the physical form is the concept of reality that each level of Consciousness can understand.

For each level of consciousness there is an associated geometry that completely defines how that specific level of consciousness will interpret the one Reality. Each level is a geometrical image or lens that spirit looks through to see the one Reality, resulting in a completely unique experience. Even the spiritual hierarchy of the universe is geometrical in structure, copying nature.[245]

As we observe the issues and the state of affairs in our physical world today, we can relate to the disharmony in our collective human Consciousness. As our physical forms keep evolving, so will our collective perception of reality evolve. The energy flowing through our evolving physical forms will create a new, more loving lens to view the world around us. As we further evolve physically, we will move toward a more loving Consciousness or Christ Consciousness. Our physical and spiritual aspects will be more in harmony. We will be living more from the spiritual realm paradigms than the physical realm paradigms.

Removing the Veil

As we cross the bridge from the physical to the Spiritual Realm, the veil between the two realms gets thinner and thinner. We are witnessing how closely our human physical forms are associated with the sacred geometry forms, which are crystallized Divine Energy. The sacred geometry forms indicate how close the Divine is to us and express the abiding love of the Divine. In our new awareness, everything created by the Divine is a form of sacred geometry to add stability, balance, harmony, symmetry, and order. We can transform our lives, grow, and expand our Souls, and increase our level of Consciousness through sacred geometry. This understanding helps us remove the veil that obscures the spiritual realm perspective. Removing the veil replaces the illusions of our physical world and self-limiting programming with an abiding trust in Universal truths, and we perceive the Universe through the lens of love.

We can understand a whole new way of BEing. The more we remove the veil between the physical and Spiritual Realms, the more clearly we see and know how to live our best and most radiant lives. Once we completely remove the veil, it opens us up to understanding that we are all Spirits or Souls on a Spiritual Journey, each significant to contribute to the whole.

Recognizing that there are two worlds or realms and that each uses a different set of paradigms is key to the growth and evolution of our Souls. By shifting our focus away from the singular view of the physical realm and adapting spiritual realm paradigms, we more easily express the best versions of ourselves and live at our highest potential. Perhaps more accurately, both realms are different aspects of one realm and the Oneness, as the Universal Law of Polarity suggests. On our Spiritual Journey, we are shifting from living according to the physical realm perspectives to adopting more and more of the spiritual realm perspectives.

Our third-dimensional Earth-bound programming within the physical realm paradigm often contradicts who we really are. What we witness in the physical realm may be an illusion and not the truth because of how we are programmed to think. Because of this programming filter, we see through the distortions of our thoughts and limiting beliefs—what we think is what we see.

What if we could see life through a Spiritual Realm filter?

This new filter would help us to know without a doubt that we were all created out of love; we are love at our core. When we align with and vibrate at the love frequency, we ARE LOVE. When we come from and offer love, we change our life experience at the root. Our experience changes because its cause has changed.

Physical world problems arise when we separate ourselves from the Divine. There is only one solution to all problems: aligning with the Divine through Divine Love, Divine Grace, and Divine Presence. Everything we need to know will be given to us from that place. We do not need to stress or go into our fear and anxiety mode. Turning to Divine Grace is effortless living.

Our miracle is on its way when we are aligned with the Divine. When we come from love, our miracle is on its way. When we live from our Soul, the miracle is on its way. If we are BEing love and don't experience a miracle, something is out of alignment. Perceiving guilt or any other low-vibrational frequency blocks the miracle. But when we perceive innocence, we attract or perceive the presence and possibilities of love. BEing in a state of grace makes us ready to attract and accept miracles, rather than repel them.[246]

A core principle of *A Course in Miracles* is to make the conscious shift in perception from fear to love, which is another way of removing the veil.[247] The shift from fear to love perception opens the channel to connect with the Divine and metaphorically step beyond physical reality. According to this approach, a *miracle* means a shift in perception to experience and express love. A miracle occurs when the frequency of love overrides low-vibrational frequency experiences and becomes our predominant vibrational frequency. We visualize our lives and the world around us through the lens of love.

If we show love to another person, we show love to ourselves. It is ultimately a gift to us, as well as another person. If we are attacking another, we are also attacking ourselves. If we do not attack, we are safe. It is only what we give that we can keep.[248] Removing the veil means we see and understand both the physical and spiritual paradigms and consciously choose how we show up in this world.

Removing the veil is accepting that the spiritual realm paradigms are keys to living a life designed by the Divine. Removing the veil removes the blocks to the wisdom and truth of the Universe that is available to us. We can create miracles in our lives by living more and more with the spiritual realm paradigms and BEing the highest versions of ourselves.

In this part of our Spiritual Journey, we started to cross the bridge from the physical to the Spiritual to understand the differences between these two realms of existence. We learned how to open specific energies like the third eye and third eye chakra to help us use our inner vision to see beyond the physical. We now understand that the Universe was created with a small number of forms of sacred geometry, the Golden Ratio, the Golden Spiral, and the Fibonacci sequence of numbers. We learned how to view the creation of the Universe as a mirror of the creation of a human being. This adherence to the blueprint or template of life offers us simplicity, order, and organization. This sacred geometry was intended to surround us with the stability and certainty of this blueprint or template of life. Surrounded by repeated cycles, rhythms, and patterns, we can change ourselves from the inside out. This template for life offers clarity for who we are in this grand Divine Plan. Sacred geometry of the forms, shapes, and patterns act as doorways to higher levels of Consciousness. We are motivated to raise our level of BEing and transform our lives to be more in flow with the Universe and more aligned with our Divine Purpose.

Exercises

To help you go deeper on your Spiritual Journey to connect to your True Self, I offer you several exercises. These exercises are meant to help you identify more closely with your Soul as your True Self. These exercises are meant to help you bring the spiritual paradigms of living into your physical life.

Exercise 1: Meditation Using the Tetrahedron

Here is a simple meditation practice for using the tetrahedron to achieve higher states of Spiritual Wisdom and levels of Consciousness. Select three healing crystals, some string, and a pair of scissors. For this meditation, you could select the healing stones that help open the third eye chakra or healing stones that open the solar plexus chakra. Healing stones that help open the solar plexus chakra include pyrite, yellow tourmaline, agate, tiger's eye, sunstone, amber, and citrine.[249] Then, sit in a quiet, comfortable space for meditation and follow these steps:

1. First, create the base of a tetrahedron by cutting the string into three equal-length pieces large enough to create an equilateral triangle around your body in either a sitting or kneeling position.

2. Then, place a crystal in each vertex or intersection of the triangle. Bless each crystal to invoke its power and energy to clear the space and focus the energy. Here is a recitation you may use for blessing the crystals.

   "I bless the energy of this crystal to energize its healing power and radiant light to assist with connecting to Divine Presence. With the help of the tetrahedron structure, may I align with the Divine and the Oneness of the Universe."

3. To create a meditative experience, you can light candles, play spiritual music softly, diffuse essential oils, or burn incense. Some people also like to cleanse the space before and after by burning sage. You can also clap your hands or use a Tibetan Singing bowl to cleanse the space. Choose what works for you.

4. Now, sit or kneel in the middle of the triangle created by the string and close your eyes. Connect to the energy of the space you have created. You become the tetrahedron. Your crown chakra or your head becomes the apex of the tetrahedron.

5. Take several deep breaths to relax and let go of stress, worry, or emotional turmoil. Make sure you slow your breathing to get your brain to slow down to a theta state. You could also use mantras or affirmations to help you relax and be present with your goal for this meditation.

6. Once you have achieved a peaceful state of mind, invoke the power of the tetrahedron.

7. Become aware of the Divine Presence all around you and within you. Set an intention that you will receive the Divine Messages specifically for you.

8. Choose a base point to represent you as an individual. Visualize, imagine, or sense the light energy and healing energy emerging from the crystal at that base point and surrounding you. Reflect on your unique empowerment, gifts, and Spiritual Journey. Inhale and exhale from your solar plexus chakra—between your navel and sternum. Feel your solar plexus chakra open and become available to join with the energies of the other vertices. Feel the energy opening and flowing in your solar plexus.

9. Next, align with another base point or crystal and think about your partners on your Spiritual Journey. Who has helped with your spiritual growth and expansion? Send those people gratitude and feel the revitalized flow of energy in your solar plexus. Let the light grow and expand with increasing strength.

10. Next, align with the third base point. Direct your attention to your spiritual focus, spiritual direction, and where you are on your Spiritual Journey. Visualize or sense the energy emerging from the crystal at this base point. Become aware of what spiritual practices have strengthened your connection to the Divine and your purpose. Allow this energy to fill and flow through your solar plexus chakra.

11. Now, visualize or sense the energies from each healing crystal as light. All the energies from the three crystals have expanded and merged together. Then, sense that those energies become part of your energies. Using your inner vision or primary intuitive sense, sense the energy as rays of light converging at your solar plexus chakra between your sternum and navel.

12. You may feel a strong energy flow—like a roaring flame in your solar plexus. As this energy expands, it will flow from your solar plexus chakra to your other chakras.

13. You may also feel a tingling as the energy expands from your chakras through your energy field and into your aura. Allow the energy to build up, in and around you, until it is ready to be released.

14. Channel this energy and allow it to start to flow through the other chakras up to your crown chakra, down to your root chakra, and into the Earth.

15. Feel the energetic buildup as your body becomes an energy channel. Surrender to the power of the energy flowing through you as the energy moves up to the crown chakra to be released. You may sense the release of energy as a ray of light radiating from your crown.

16. This whole process may only take a few moments. When finished, stay in a meditative state and be receptive to your Higher Self and Divine Wisdom.

17. Be conscious of the thoughts or messages you may receive from BEing the channel of the tetrahedron energy. Recognize your connection to higher levels of Consciousness and sense the Oneness of the Universe.[250]

Exercise 2: The Vitruvian Man Exercise for Grounding and Being in the Present Moment

Knowing the Vitruvian Man sacred geometry concept, we can use it as a tool for grounding to Earth energy, as well as stabilizing and anchoring our Souls more completely in our physical bodies. As we do this exercise, we open up to become a conduit of energy from the Spiritual Realm to the physical realm.

Using a stance simulating a five-pointed star, like the Vitruvian Man image, with our feet shoulder-width apart with our arms extended out to each side, right and left, we are more connected to the Earth, which creates greater stability for Spiritual Energy to flow through our body. We become a star tetrahedron.

This simple exercise helps us properly align the polarity of our energy body and aura with the Earth's magnetic polarity. In alignment with the Earth, our heads will have a north polarity, and our feet will have a south polarity. This proper magnetic polarity alignment means we are grounded. We can connect to the Earth through our feet with a south polarity and magnetize or attract energy into our feet from the north polarity of the Earth's surface. Attracting the energy from the Earth helps us to revitalize the energy flow in our body. When we are ungrounded, our feet likely have a north polarity, and our feet would not be able to attract energy from the Earth. The north polarity of our feet would repel the north polarity energy of the Earth's surface.

To do this exercise, we envision our head as the apex of the top tetrahedron, and the space between our feet becomes the apex of the downward-facing tetrahedron. We open our left palm up to receive high vibrational energy from the Spiritual Realm, and we turn our right palm down to give to the Earth or release any stagnant or stuck energy. Giving and receiving are in equilibrium. With our heads naturally straight over our necks, not jutted forward, we become the conduit of energy between Spiritual and physical realms by taking five slow, long, complete, deep breaths—no shallow breaths. We inhale and exhale slowly, taking fresh energy in and releasing stagnant energy.

Exercise 3: Forgiveness Exercises

Here are several ways to engage with the energy of forgiveness:

1. Journal about the situation or event and ask for forgiveness. Journaling engages the ability to understand the event or the situation from a different and higher perspective. If we can step back from the event or situation, we become an observer of what happened. We may consider writing about how we could have done things differently. We could ask how we could have seen the situation differently from our hearts. It is important to learn as much as we can from the situation. Learning is how we grow. We can then decide how to handle the situation better the next time.

2. Write yourself a letter of forgiveness to acknowledge something you could do better next time. Firmly embed the lesson you learned from the experience. By writing a letter outlining your reaction to the event and how the event has changed your perspective, you acknowledge moving to a higher level of BEing and a higher level of seeing yourself in the world.

3. Write a letter of forgiveness to another person. You don't necessarily have to send it to them. You are creating the energy of forgiveness around the situation by seeing their Divinity and acknowledging and accepting that either you or they were off track in this situation. This puts you in a healing mode, changing yourself at your energetic core that transmits out a high vibrational frequency instead of the low-vibrational frequency of grievance.

4. Journal or outline how you would handle a situation or person differently the next time. This shifts the focus from the grievance to

deciding on a better way to show up in the future. As you journal, hold the perspective from a higher version of BEing. For example, see the situation through the lens of love.

5. Focus on your role or responsibility in a challenging experience or situation. Accept responsibility for how you contributed to creating the situation. We can ask ourselves questions:

    • What did I do or say that precipitated the event or situation?

    • Did I misinterpret something?

    • Did I react too quickly?

    • How could I have reacted differently?

    • How does my behavior in this instance align with who I want to BE?

    • Was I able to see the positive at the moment?

    • How could I stop my reaction and see the positive?

    • What if my brain and heart were in coherence?

    • How could I have reacted in love?

    • Isn't it more important that I come from my heart?

    • Am I coming from my physical self or my Spiritual Self?

6. Write about someone who has hurt or betrayed you. Write about them through this different lens of the Divine. See if you can go beyond the physical realm and see them from the spiritual realm perspective.

7. Write about a person who is particularly challenging to you, realizing they may be your greatest teacher. See if you can identify with them using the paradigms of the Spiritual Realm. Try to envision them as a Divine BEing created by the Divine to BE their True Selves and write about their Divinity. Write about how they could be a teacher for you. Write about how they have helped you learn and grow. Acknowledge that your growth in the situation is the most important aspect and the reason for the situation.

8. Consider whether your expectations of others come through your lens and not theirs. See if you can understand how not forgiving them would be an expression of them not living up to your standard. Now,

see if you can see them on their own journey through the lens of the
Divine.

9. Ask how your Soul would handle the situation and write what comes
    to mind.

Exercise 4: Apply the Wisdom to Your Life

- Explain what it would mean for you to shift from fear to love.
- What physical realm paradigms are holding you back on your Spiritual
  Journey?
- What spiritual realm paradigms do you aspire to?
- What intuitive senses do you have? Do you dismiss your intuitive sense
  as real?
- What does it mean to you that if you forgive, you are forgiven?
- What does it mean to you to see through the lens of love?
- Do you understand how the physical and Spiritual Realms are inextricable?

Exercise 5: *What-if* Questions

- *What if* you could be more grounded and in the present moment? How
  would that change things for you?
- *What if* you could forgive someone and set yourself free?
- *What if* Consciousness is based on sacred geometry?
- *What if* only love is real in the Spiritual Realm?
- *What if* you could come from love in the physical realm?
- *What if* you could see beyond the physical? What do you see?
- *What if* you could live from the spiritual realm paradigms in the physical
  realm?
- *What if* the Universe was created with Divine Intelligence to be ordered,
  balanced, symmetrical, and stable?

- *What if* you could become open to being a better host to the Divine in your physical body?

- *What if* you could see yourself as God created you?

- *What if* you could see others as God created them as Divine Souls?

- *What if* the Divine was learning and expanding through your life experiences? What is the biggest area of growth for expansion of the Divine?

AFTERWORD

What has crystallized for me in writing this book is that we are in physical bodies for the purpose of impacting the world we live in. We are each here to participate in making a difference in how we are functioning presently. We are meant to create a life of harmony on Earth. We are here to honor and respect the Divinity in each living BEing. We are here to come from loving kindness with compassion as our authentic leading energy. We are here to be honorable and share benevolence. We are meant to create this together as ONE humanity, as a reflection of our Spiritual Counterparts and co-creators. We are here to reflect the Spiritual Realm or Heaven. All the power, fame, success, and wealth that we achieve on Earth means nothing compared to the Spiritual achievement or evolution of our Souls.

Many Spiritual Missions are available to us for growth and learning during this lifetime. Some help us learn through challenges as opportunities for growth. Others focus on connecting with the truth of who we are to express as our True Self, knowing and radiating our Divine Magnificence. Yet, others have a mission of helping others awaken to their Spiritual Journey. Whatever the Spiritual Mission, all paths lead us on a journey of coming together in peace and joining as ONE humanity to raise the vibrational frequency of ourselves and the Universe.

As you have joined me in this part of your Spiritual Journey, perhaps you have had realizations connecting challenges and shifts in your life that reveal your Divine Purpose or Mission, evoke a new perspective about the nature of your existence, or give new meaning to your life. I encourage you to reread those parts of the book that stirred an awakening and consider going deeper in your understanding through meditation and the exercises offered. As new insights naturally unfold, you may experience new shifts in energy that draw you to other parts of the book you hadn't connected with as much previously. If you consistently apply each new and unfolding wisdom to your everyday life, you are in Divine Flow, easily advancing on your Spiritual Journey.

Amazingly, we aren't on this journey alone. We are supported, loved, and guided by Spiritual BEings who care deeply about the evolution of life on Earth. We all have the opportunity, an invitation, to play a significant role in this magnificent endeavor where every living BEing benefits. The more you are connected to your Soul, your True Self, the better you will be able to function in this amazing and joy-filled way.

When we recognize the Divineness in ourselves and each other and treat each other with that understanding, we will be able to create the kind of world we all deserve and hope for. It is time we awaken to the truth of our existence and understand our ultimate reason for being here now. It is time we start viewing life through the lens of the Divine, seeing that we are all Divinely created for a special purpose, with no one person, race, religion, country, or gender being better than another. We are here to put our differences aside and revel in the Divine Magnificence that each of us expresses authentically as our True Selves.

What will it take to get everyone aligned with this as our united, enlightened purpose? It starts with viewing our lives on Earth from a new perspective. Exploring new ways for growing, learning, and expanding Consciousness through reading books like this and engaging in the suggested spiritual practices and exercises open us to new perceptions and new ways of living and BEing.

The Divine offers new invitations to help us grow into a higher state of BEing. The invitations are specific and unique for each of us. They may bring situations or challenges that help us shed past regrets, grievances, shame, blame, unforgiveness, and unworthiness. These invitations help us accept the call to focus on love, witnessing the goodness in others rather than looking for their inadequacies and placing blame. It is time to reach out and help each other get to a higher level of Consciousness that will impact the whole Universe. It is time to discover, own, and live from our Divine Magnificence.

As part of your journey of discovery, you may want to reread parts of this book or repeat the exercises to experience them through the new stages of growth. BEing comes from learning through life experiences, just as wisdom comes from doing and experiencing. You can use this book as a guide to monitor your growth and evolution over time by how your experiences and answers change to the questions and prompts offered in the exercises.

Be intentional. Allow space for your Spiritual Journey to be a priority in your life. It is the most important aspect of your life and the sole reason your Soul decided to experience life through your physical body at this time. It is the accomplishment we will most treasure when our Souls leave our bodies.

> Where would you like to be on your Spiritual Journey one year from now? Don't wait. Make it happen.

I hope you've benefited from the wisdom shared with you, revealing what's always been true to awaken you to who you really are. I hope you will apply the wisdom to your life and way of BEing. It is my wish that you have been inspired to feel, know, and connect with your expanded Self, your True Self, at a higher level of Consciousness. Most importantly, I want you to know and experience the truth and wisdom of your Divine Magnificence.

The learning, growing, and evolving don't stop here. There is always more to learn and experience. As our journey continues, it will awaken you to new concepts and new ways to adapt and BE. In this book, we went on a journey of discovering your True Self. In my next book, *Journey to Oneness: Align with Your Divine Magnificence,* we'll explore how we can align our life path with the Universal flow of Infinite Divine Potential from the perspective of our Higher Self.

We are all One. Together, let's create a world of Oneness that illuminates our Divine Magnificence.

Live radiantly!

My True Self

Now that I've opened the door
And removed at least some of the blocks
to my True Self and Divine part of me,
I feel on fire- the passion is flowing- I want more!

I am more than I've ever let myself BE.
I am expanding into higher realms of Consciousness.
I'm increasing my inner potential.
I feel safe, vulnerable, and more truly me.

My real and True Self—my eternal Self.
The Self that knows love and compassion are energies that flow.
They flow in me and around me, but I don't always connect.
I set the intention to do so more and more.

Life is about discovering this True Self.
Life is about discarding the false self.
Life is about BEING the True Self.
Life is about the journey to choose the right path for me.

Discovery, growth, expansion.
This is my truest journey.
Shedding all falseness and being my deepest part
That is so often hidden and ignored.

Letting go and surrendering.
Trusting my True Self is my Wisest Self.
Trusting my True Self will guide me to my true mission.
My True Self knows how I need to evolve.

Anne M. Deatly

APPENDIX

Figure 25: How to Create a Golden Spiral
(Section Four, Sacred Geometry)

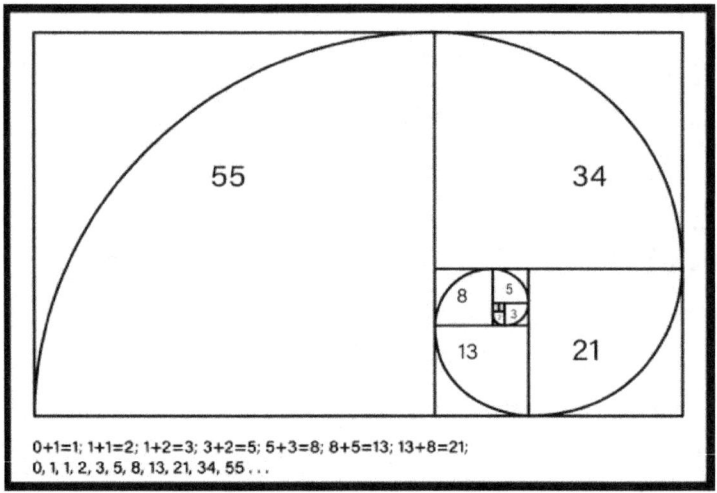

55

34

8

5

3

13

21

0+1=1; 1+1=2; 1+2=3; 3+2=5; 5+3=8; 8+5=13; 13+8=21;
0, 1, 1, 2, 3, 5, 8, 13, 21, 34, 55 . . .

To create a Golden Spiral, start with a rectangle in which the ratio of the length and width is 1.618, the Golden Ratio. From that larger rectangle, create a square like the one with the number 55 in the figure and a smaller rectangle like the one on the right side of the figure with the 13, 8, and 5. These are Fibonacci numbers. Keep dividing the rectangles in a similar way to create a square and a similar but smaller rectangle. After continuing to divide the rectangles successively, the result will be an almost complete partitioning of the rectangle into squares into infinity. Adding quarter circles to the corners of the squares will result in a Golden Spiral.

Source: https://en.wikipedia.org/wiki/Golden_spiral

Table 5: Physical and Spiritual Paradigms for Living

Physical Realm Paradigms	Spiritual Realm Paradigms
I am a random creation.	There is nothing random in the Universe. Universal Laws and sacred geometry govern the Universe. I am not random. I have a specific Divine Purpose to be here.
I was procreated by my parents out of sin.	I was Divinely created. I am an idea in the mind of the Divine. This idea is immutable.
I make mistakes and commit sins which makes me feel bad about myself.	No matter what I do, my essence or core is still the immutable Divine idea. Sinlessness is guaranteed for all. This empowers me to be the best version of myself as I learn and grow.
I see myself as unworthy and I struggle in life. I am not good enough.	I see myself as Divine and I am working to accomplish my Divine Mission in life. My goal is to do what will benefit the Universe.
My goal is to survive this life.	My goal is to thrive and be the best version of myself and live my best life. I can accomplish this by focusing on my Divine Plan to accomplish my specific mission.
The world is limited. I am limited.	I create everything in my life and see the world as abundant, unlimited, and full of prosperity, possibility, and potential. Whatever I need is made available to me. I choose to see the miracles around me by being in awe and wonder.
I have no abilities, talents or gifts so I struggle and suffer.	I was gifted specific Divine qualities and Divine Soul Energies to carry out my mission. I am not alone, I can ask for Divine help.
I have to work hard and compete to survive.	I surrender and trust as I flow with the Universe.
I am limited by what I can do and how much money I can earn.	I have unlimited potential and am connected to Universal Consciousness that contains all the wisdom and knowledge there ever will be.
My false self or ego is in charge and I feel stuck; I have pain and disease in my body. I don't know who I really am.	Divine Energy flows through me easily and I feel free to be my True Self. I am healthy, happy and whole as my True Divine Self. I identify primarily with being a Soul.
I operate from my head and ego only. I am cut off from the rest of my body.	I tap into the wisdom of my heart to make decisions with love and acceptance. My mind and heart are in coherence. I am guided by my Soul.

Physical Realm Paradigms	Spiritual Realm Paradigms
I make poor decisions and have negative thought patterns. Life is hard and I struggle through it.	I am positive and am on a path to enlightenment. Life gets easier and easier and I am at peace.
I am not good enough so I have to overcompensate for that. I don't love myself, let alone others especially perfect strangers.	I come from love and peace. I share love, compassion, and peace with others and the world. I see that everyone is a Divine Soul like me.
I see life through the lens of fear.	I see life through the lens of love.
I must fear the next trauma that will inevitably happen in my life.	I have challenges to face in order to learn, grow and evolve into higher vibrational frequencies and higher levels of Consciousness. I embrace the challenges because they bring me closer to my ultimate goal—to evolve my Soul.
I am stressed, overwhelmed, and anxious because I can't control what is going to happen to me.	I am Divine and I trust the inner guidance of my Soul and Spiritual Guides.
I don't feel safe. I feel alone.	I am never alone. I have the love and support of the whole Universe supporting me on my Spiritual Journey.
Nothing works out for me; the world is against me and punishes me.	I know whatever happens in my life is happening for me, not to me. Whatever happens is for my best and highest good.
When someone hurts or harms me or says mean things about me, I hold onto the negative feelings and unforgiveness.	When someone hurts or harms me or says something mean about me, I forgive them and move on....knowing they are Divine but off track in the moment. I work on blessing them after I let go of the grief.
I have to find guilt and shame in others so I don't feel bad about myself.	I see the Divinity in all people and accept they will make mistakes which will help them grow and learn.
I hold onto my past hurts and problems because they define me. I get attention when people feel sorry for me. I am a victim of my circumstances.	I let all negativity go so I can be at the highest vibrational frequency possible at all times.
I hold onto grievances.	I let go of grievances and focus on the miracles of life. I choose to have a miracle rather than a grievance.

Physical Realm Paradigms	Spiritual Realm Paradigms
I condemn others because I can't accept my sins. When I condemn others, I feel better about myself.	I focus on the good in everyone and myself. I see everyone as innocent as the Divine sees them. I allow myself to make mistakes so I can face the not so good within me and change.
I can't forgive others for hurting and harming me.	I forgive others even if they hurt or harm me because I know it was necessary for them to grow and sometimes for me to grow.
I see through a lens of lack and limitation. I am struggling to survive. I give more than I receive. I deplete myself.	I see that the Universe flows with an equilibrium of giving and receiving. I am learning to give and receive with grace in a balanced way. I have an equal compassion for myself as I do for others.
The more stressed I am, the more things show up in my life to stress about.	I create my own sense of peace and serenity.
I am consumed by my problems.	I focus on finding solutions to all my problems. Connecting to the Divine helps me to find the right solution. When I align with the Divine, I have no problems.
Negativity is my default.	Positivity is my default.
I see the guilt in myself and others.	I see the Divine in myself and others.
I live in fear, stress and anxiety.	I live in peace, joy, love and freedom.
I must control everything around me and protect myself from danger, I am in charge of what happens to me.	I surrender to the invitations from the Divine and respond in deep gratitude by being the best version of myself and performing at my highest potential, realizing that I am working for a reason way beyond me.
I have to do, do, do.	I just need to be.

Table 6: The Physical and Spiritual Aspects of Platonic Solids

Platonic Solid	Image	Number of Sides	Vertices	Edges
Tetrahedron		4 equilateral triangles (pyramid)	4	6
Hexahedron		6 equilateral squares (cube)	8	12
Octahedron		8 equilateral triangles	6	12

Element	Chakra	Spiritual Aspects and Meaning
fire	solar plexus	The tetrahedron is about basic survival and the joy of living. The tetrahedron structure has a grounding aspect of the triangle at its base, while the other triangles point up toward the Spiritual Realm. The grounding base triangle roots us in the physical while connecting us to the Spiritual Realm. The energy comes together at the base and synergistically focuses on Divine connection. Not surprisingly, the tetrahedron acts as a doorway to the Spiritual Realm and is important for Spiritual Awakening and physical manifestation. Meditating in the presence of this structure aligns us and ignites the passion and desire for new creation, motivation, and expansion of ideas, basic existence, and joy. *Note: the three base vertices are the intersections of the triangles at the base of the pyramid illustrated as 1, 2, 3.*
earth	root	The cube, a hexahedron, represents the physical symbol of creation—the element of Earth, Mother Nature, and the physical body. It is connected to the root chakra and helps with survival and grounding to the Earth. This sacred geometry shape helps us with wholeness, essential well-being, and being centered. The hexahedron helps us to be rooted to the Earth while being rooted in who we really are as Divine BEings. If used in meditation, we can place a cube or hexahedron near us. This shape can be used to help us get out of a situation that boxes us in or restricts us too much. It can also help to change our perspective about a situation, seeing it differently, perhaps from a spiritual perspective.
wind, air	heart	The octahedron represents the element of air, wind, and Spirit. Therefore, the octahedron also represents thought, perception, and intelligence. Air or wind is required to breathe and for inspiration. The octahedron helps us be unlimited, enhancing our ability for limitless thinking and self-empowerment to ascend to higher states of BEing. In the spiritual sense, meditating with or on the octahedron sacred geometry form will help to bring in a new perspective that could help move us forward in life.

Platonic Solid	Image	Number of Sides	Vertices	Edges
Dodecahe-dron		12 pentagons	20	30
Isocahedron		20 equilateral triangles	12	30
Heptahedron or Chestahe-dron		4 equilateral triangles and 3 equilateral quadrilaterals - all with same surface area	7	12

Element	Chakra	Spiritual Aspects and Meaning
Uni-verse/ Spirit/ ether	throat; third eye, and crown	The dodecahedron is aligned with Spirit, the Life Force in all living BEings. The dodecahedron embodies Divine thought or will and is the archetype of life and fecundity. It is female, energy, deep, inward, and heaven. The dodecahedron connects Divine thought with the awareness of the universality of Oneness. Breathe and connect to the wisdom in this shape to help move into the unity of all life. Become part of the Oneness of creation as it was designed.
water	sacral	The icosahedron can be used in meditation to balance the mind and heart. The icosahedron is connected to the sacral chakra for emotional support and freedom of emotional expression. As water, it flows to find the right path. Use the icosahedron to gain a new perspective and to see things differently, beyond the physical. We might have been contemplating something for a while and are unable to move forward. Meditate with or on the icosahedron to gain a new and different perspective on a situation.
NA	NA	"Rudolf Steiner reported that the evolving soul, before it becomes living matter as you or as me, is apparent to the inner eye as the shape of a downward opening bell. The bell shape has been used in ancient Egyptian paintings to represent the human soul, coming down to earth from the heavens to incarnate into flesh. These bell shapes, seeds of spirit, are the geometric templates for growing a human heart."[251]

**Table 7: Golden Spiral, Eye of Horus,
Star Tetrahedron, and Veca Codes**

Name	Image	Spiritual Significance
Golden Spiral		The Golden Spiral also acts as a bridge from the physical to the Spiritual Realm. It contains the energy of acceleration of Consciousness. The spiral represents expansion outward from a single source, which can grow, expand, and gain power. This iconic shape connects us to the primordial vortex of creation and the cosmic soup of the beginning of Consciousness from which the Universe emerged. (The photo in the column to the left is a fossil of more than one million years old. I use it in my healing practice to release stuck energy in muscles.)
Bi-Veca Code		The Bi-Veca Code, also referred to as the Vesica Piscis, is two overlapping spheres. This code comes from the 12th dimension, which contains Christ Consciousness. This energy is golden liquid light.[252] This Veca Code focuses on the etheric and celestial body making it a very powerful tool in healing and manifesting. It also represents the past and future time coming together and integrating into the present. The Vesica Piscis is also thought of as a birth portal.[253] It represents the male and female coming together to form something new. This can be a baby or an idea. In the creation of a baby, it can represent the first cell division of a fertilized egg. The intersection of the two overlapping circles looks like a football or oval shape. This shape of the two intersecting circles or spheres represents the geometric shape from which light was created. Your eyes were also created from this shape; your eyes take in light. Your emotions are also connected to this shape. Most significantly, the basic geometry of the electromagnetic field is the Vesica Piscis.[254]

Name	Image	Spiritual Significance
Tri-Veca Code		The Tri-Veca Code represents three overlapping spheres and is also referred to as the Tripod of Life. The Tri-Veca Code comes from the 15th dimension or the Rishi dimension and focuses on the etheric and celestial body.[255] The Tri-Veca Code represents the harmony or integration of the past, present, and future. Because of the high vibrational frequency of this code, it can be used for energy healing and for manifesting what you want. While visualizing the code, the Tri-Veca Code can be metaphorically or intentionally inhaled, through a breath to move the energy. Then this code can be exhaled and imagined or projected to the third eye, between the eyebrows, to connect to the Spiritual Realm. The Tri-Veca Code is also powerful in clearing energetic blockages.
Star Tetrahedron		The star tetrahedron is one of the most important sacred geometry forms with two overlapping tetrahedrons, one with an upward facing apex and the other with a downward facing apex. This figure illustrates the three-dimenstinal form of the overlapping tetrahedrons. The star tetrahedron represents perfect balance and symmetry and the energy of the human body. It is the same form as the Merkaba. Hidden within the two tetrahedrons is the complete Divine Self and Divine Knowledge. All life and creation relies on the equilibrium of the star tetrahedron.
Eye of Horus or Spirit		From Egyptian mythology, Horus was an ancient sky god with one eye representing the sun and the other representing the moon. This image represents the third eye. In the myth, Horus lost his eye in a battle with Set or Seth. Horus's eye was put back by Thoth. In ancient Egypt, this eye symbol is referred to as Wadjet, which means whole, after the healing or restoring of the eye to Horus. It represented protection and wholeness in ancient Egyptian hieroglyphics.[256] We are using this symbol here to represent the Divine Creator or Spirit in the context of creation of the Universe.

Table 8: Sacred Geometry Forms that Enhance Spiritual Connection

 **Seed of Life/ Genesis Pattern**

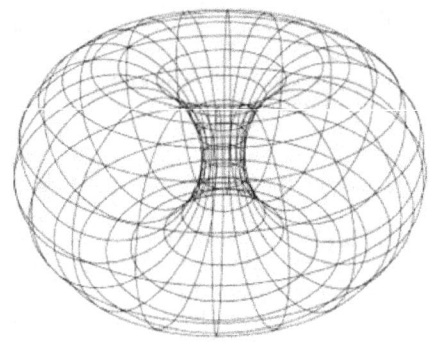 **Torus**

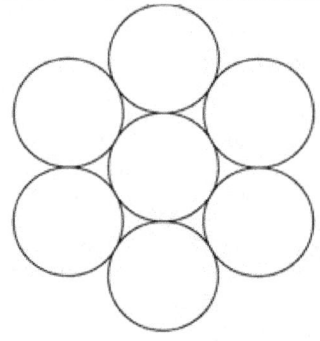 **Egg of Life**

The Seed of Life symbol has six spheres around a seventh in the center that overlaps all six. These seven interconnected spheres symbolize the interconnection of life on Earth and Universal existence. The Seed of Life symbol depicts life on Earth as a Divine Creation. The spheres of the Seed of Life pattern represent that all life was created from a single source, a seed, in the Divine Plan.[257] The central sphere represents Divine Consciousness.[258] If the Seed of Life structure is rotated one time around its central axis, it creates the torus.[259] If rotated one more time, it creates the Egg of Life.[260] With a third rotation of the Seed of Life, the Fruit of Life structure is created. Using this symbol can help with the beginning of a change or transformation. It helps us understand the accessibility and expansion of new energy or light as it enters Consciousness. The symbol can also be used for blessing and protection. Wearing the Seed of Life enhances the flow of energy and connection to the flow of Universal energy, revitalizing fresh energy to help release negativity and overcome difficult or challenging issues. Using the Seed of Life symbol in meditation can help us establish or re-establish Spiritual connections as well as create or manifest ideas and desires into physical reality.

Rotating the Genesis pattern, or the Seed of Life, around its central axis creates a donut shape with an infinitely small hole in the center.[261] In addition to being a source of continual flow or revitalizing and ever renewing energy, it also represents how we can connect to the invisible world beyond the physical. The torus represents how something from the Spiritual Realm can descend into the physical realm as well as how something material can ascend to the Spiritual Realm. The energetic movement of the torus inward and outward and perpetually moving signifies the connection between the physical and Spiritual Realms. The descension and ascension between realms occur through a central channel of light, energy, or Consciousness. This energy can only go so far in one direction, up or down, before it folds on itself and reverses direction. The concept is the energy must turn back to the Divine to obtain revitalization and increase its energy to continue forward once again and then reach a certain height or depth before returning to the Divine again for renewal. This back-and-forth movement is reminiscent of the push and pull of the yin-yang balance. This inward and outward movement represents constant renewal and revitalization from the Spiritual to the physical. When humans are balanced and functioning optimally, their energy is thought to be in toroidal energy flow. The energy of a person not in alignment with Universal energy flow eventually stops flowing and becomes stuck or blocked. The lack of energy movement is unhealthy. Eventually, the Universe corrects the flow, but not always in the same lifetime. A person is invited to work through any situation to live life in a balanced, compassionate, and detached way promoting a harmonious connection between the physical and Spiritual.

The second shape that comes from rotating the Seed of Life structure or the Genesis pattern is the Egg of Life.[262] In this structure, the circles or spheres are not overlapping, but they are connected to the central circle of the sphere. Once Consciousness projects the first seven spheres and completes the Genesis pattern of spheres, it then continues moving in a rotational pattern from every consecutive innermost place until it completes its second vortex motion, as can be imagined with another six spheres behind the original six. With its thirteen circles or spheres, The Egg of Life symbolizes Oneness. The Egg of Life depicts the three essential things for continued life: health, stability, and fertility. The significance of the Egg of Life form is that it's the geometric structure that created the human body. Your whole physicality was created through this geometric structure.[263] Every physical aspect of the physical body was created from the Egg of Life form, including your height, hair color, the length of your legs and feet—everything.[264] The Egg of Life births the Flower of Life.

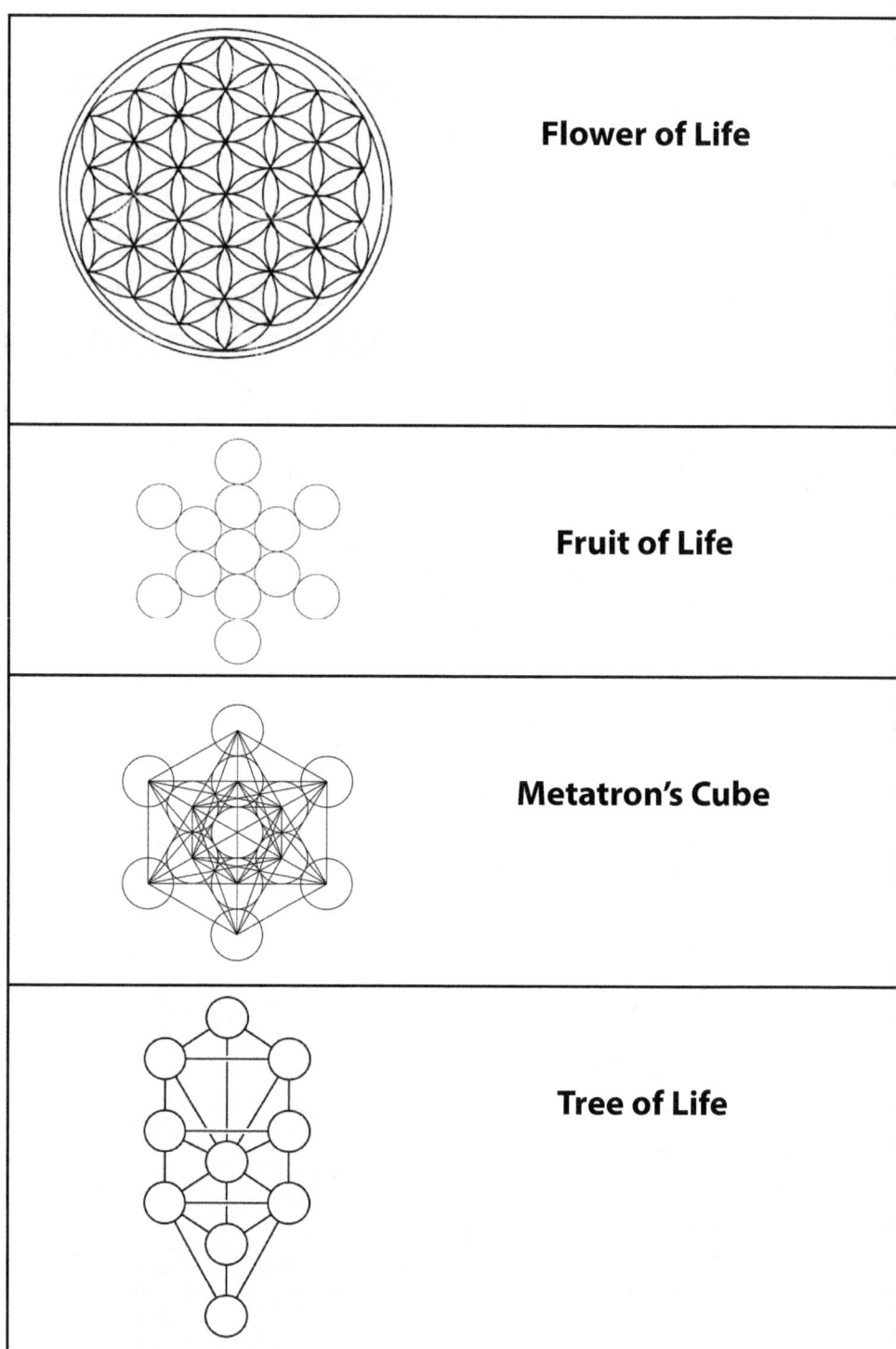

Flower of Life

Fruit of Life

Metatron's Cube

Tree of Life

The Flower of Life symbol is an iconic image of sacred geometry. Some consider the Flower of Life to be the actual blueprint of the Universe that imprints the wisdom of the Universe and the matrix of all matter and information.[265] The Flower of Life can continue forever in its design of rotation and overlapping spheres. It represents the basics of all atomic and molecular structures and all life forms—essentially everything in existence. The secret of the Flower of Life is that it produces the Fruit of Life. Out of the flower comes the fruit. The Flower of Life is an information system that holds the information of the past, the present, as well as the future, like the Akashic Records.[266] the Flower of Life symbol appears to be incomplete. The outer spheres or circles in this diagram are cut off or partial. Completing the circles or spheres creates what looks like a complete pattern.[267] If we were to rotate that structure one more time from the innermost places of the perimeter, we would get the pattern of thirteen circles or spheres. As illustrated, these circles or spheres are connected but not overlapping. This is the Fruit of Life structure, which can be extracted from the Flower of Life pattern. These sacred geometry forms are interconnected—one becomes the other by simple rotations or manipulations. Just like in human development or the life cycle of a tree—the basic cycles of living things.

Fruit comes from flowers. The Fruit of Life symbol contains 13 spheres. It is within the Flower of Life symbol and is a symbol of abundance.[268] The third rotation of the Seed of Life form produces the Fruit of Life. The rotation causes a third group of six spheres behind the original Genesis pattern of spheres for a total of thirteen spheres: two groups of six spheres around a central sphere. The number thirteen represents unity and the transition between worlds or dimensions. By focusing on the Fruit of Life structure, one can unblock the paths to higher forms or realms. This structure embodies all conceivable structures of the Universe.

Metatron's Cube is composed of the Fruit of Life. This form also illustrates the perspective of sacred geometry at the beginning of the Universe and Consciousness. The five traditional Platonic solids, and the star tetrahedron come from the structure of Metatron's Cube. These are three-dimensional objects that come out of the thirteen circles or spheres of the Fruit of Life. Its form depicts the harmony and balance of nature and the Universe. Metatron's Cube is fundamental to the creation process at the quantum level. As a transcendental form, it illustrates the mental unfolding of a two-dimensional reality into a three-dimensional reality. This concept reminds us of the Hermetic Principle that the Universe is all mental. Quantum physics also teaches us that the Universe is mental and intelligent. Whatever exists in physical reality started out as a mental idea. All physical forms in the Universe were conceived and created by the Divine from the architectural concepts or blueprints of sacred geometry.[269] Metatron's Cube is used for inspiration as well as personal transformation.

The Tree of Life represents the path to the Divine. Therefore, it is a symbol of life, renewal, and energy. The Tree of Life also represents how the Divine created the world out of the Void. This significant symbol illuminates the path to the Divine and to connecting the Divine with the physical self. There are two significant paths illustrated in the Tree of Life symbol. One starts from the Spiritual Realm coming down to Earth or material plane. The other pathway is from the material plane to the Spiritual Realm. The two pathways are like the ascension and descension of the torus energy flow. The Tree of Life symbol is an expression of how we are connected to everything physical and invisible, including the Void. This symbol strongly signifies that we are not alone. In fact, we are part of the enormous unknown. As shown, this connection to everything is a network of interconnection. The Tree of Life illustrates the journey of the Soul. The ten spheres, or Spiritual Centers, are connected by different paths or lines. The top sphere is considered the first and represents cosmic Consciousness. The bottom sphere is considered the last, and it represents the material world. The other spheres in-between represent different qualities of the Soul.

BOOK CLUB QUESTIONS

1. In reviewing your life so far, can you identify with your life as a Spiritual Journey? How has this book helped clarify the meaning of your life? Where do you go from here?

2. What other ways has this book helped you on your Spiritual Journey?

3. Do you resonate with the fact that everything in the Universe is energy? What questions do you still have about this concept?

4. Since *Life Force Energy* is not generally understood or commonly discussed, what did you learn that helped you understand more about *Life Force Energy* that you didn't know before reading the book?

5. Scientific data was presented to provide a physical realm explanation to support some spiritual concepts, such as the wave-particle duality experiment. Did merging spiritual and scientific concepts give more credibility to the relevance of the topics discussed or deepen your understanding?

6. In what ways does merging scientific and spiritual explanations about how the Universe works expand your understanding of how to create your own life experiences?

7. Do you have a new belief in how you can create what you want in your life with your new understanding of the *Observer Effect*?

8. What is a secret, hidden wisdom, insight, or epiphany you gained?

9. Has this book helped to awaken you to the truth and wisdom of the Universe? If so, how?

10. If you had to guess what your Divine Mission is in this life, what would it be?

11. Forgiveness as a way to raise your vibrational frequency was one of the major themes of the book. What did the discussion about forgiveness reveal to you that you didn't know before? Do you agree that forgiving yourself and others is essential in raising your vibrational frequency? Why or why not?

12. In what ways have you tried to raise your vibrational frequency or level of Consciousness?

13. What exercises have you done? In what way have the exercises helped you change your way of BEing?

14. What is one Spiritual Realm paradigm that you resonate with or have applied in your life?

15. Are you better able to see the physical realm from the perspective of the Spiritual Realm?

16. Does knowing more about how sacred geometry is the building block of our reality give you a greater appreciation and understanding of how it explains the benevolent design of the Universe? Why or why not? Why is sacred geometry referred to as the language of the Universe?

17. A comparison was presented illustrating how human development mirrors the creation of the Universe using sacred geometry. How does the concept of creation mirror a developing human? Do you understand the repeating patterns of the Universe through sacred geometry?

18. Each section in the book ended with a series of exercises offered to help deepen your understanding through experience. What exercises most helped you shift to a higher frequency way of thinking and BEing or helped with understanding a specific concept?

19. Do you understand your True Self more than you did before? Are you more connected to your True Self? Please explain.

**Additional in-depth guided study questions are offered at
DrAnneDeatly.com/resources**

ENDNOTES

Section One: Life is a Spiritual Journey

1 Michael Newton, PhD, *Journey of Souls: Case Studies of Life Between Lives*, 5th Ed. (Llewelyn Publications, 2018), 213.

2 Leo Cavalier, "Think in Terms of Energy, Frequency and Vibration." YouTube video, 15:57, August 25, 2023, https://www.youtube.com/watch?v=96W6xuvQzJM.

3 https://en.wikipedia.org/wiki/Double-slit_experiment.

4 Albert Einstein, "The Nobel Prize in 1921", https://www.nobelprize.org/prizes/physics/1921/einstein/lecture/.

5 https://en.wikipedia.org/wiki/George_Paget_Thomson.

6 Buks, E., Schuster, R., Heiblum, M. *et al.* "Dephasing in electron interference by a 'which-path' detector." *Nature* 391, (1998), 871–874, https://doi.org/10.1038/36057.

7 Wheeler, J.A. "The computer and the universe," *Int. J. Theor Phys* 21, (1982), 557–572, https://doi.org/ 10.1007/BF02650185.

8 Deepak Chopra, M.D., Menas C. Kafatos, Ph.D., *You Are the Universe: Discovering Your Cosmic Self and Why It Matters*, (New York: Harmony, 2018), 3-4.

9 Three Initiates, *The Kybalion: A Study of the Hermetic Philosophy of Ancient Egypt and Greece*, (Project Gutenberg License, 1912), 7.

10 Id, 10.

11 Ibid.

12 Ibid.

13 Id., 11.

14 Erwin Schrödinger, *What is Life?: The Physical Aspect of the Living Cell with Mind and Matter and Autobiographical Sketches*, (Cambridge University Press, 1958), 129.

15 Three Initiates, *The Kybalion*, 11.

16 Ibid.

17 Id., 12-13.

18 Id., 12.

19 Id., 13.

20 Id., 14

21 Id., 14-15.

22 Mike Dooley, *Playing the Matrix: A Program for Living Deliberately and Creating Consciously*, (Hay House, Inc., 2017), 11.

23 James Allen, *As a Man Thinketh*, (TarcherPerigee, 2008), 2.

24 Lee Smolin, *The Life of the Cosmos*, (New York: Oxford University Press, 1997), 252-253.

25 Duane Elgin, *The Living Universe: Where Are We? Who Are We? Where Are We Going?*, (Berrett-Koehler Publishers, 2009), 37.

26 Ann Felid, "Dark Energy, Dark Matter" NASA Science, https://www.jpl.nasa.gov/edu/events/2019/10/17/darkness-surrounds-us-the-other-95-percent-of-the-universe/#:~:text=The%20rest%2C%20a%20full%2095,and%20expands%20the%20universe%20itself.

27 Alice Calaprice, ed. *The Ultimate Quotable Einstein*, (New Jersey: Princeton University Press, 2010), 80.

28 Elgin, *The Living Universe*, 35-54.

29 Id., 43.

30 Id., 46.

31 Id., 12.

32 Id., 43.

33 J. W. N. Sullivan, "Interviews with Great Scientists VI–Max Planck," *The Observer*, January 25, 1931, 17.

34 Max Planck, "Das Wesen der Materie" (The Nature of Matter), speech at Florence, Italy, 1944.

35 Ervin Laszlo, Jean Houston, and Larry Dossey, *What is Consciousness? Three Sages Look Behind the Veil*, (New York: SelectBooks, Inc., 2016), 32.

36 Id., 95.

37 Id., 77.

38 Id., 121.

39 Vanchurin, Vitaly, "The World as a Neural Network," *Entropy* 22, no. 11 (2020), 1210.

40 Wallace D. Wattles, *The Science of Getting Rich, The Science of Being Well, The Science of Being Great and the Law of Opulence* (Limitless Press, Inc., 2010), 8.

41 Brian L. Weiss, *Many Lives, Many Masters* (Touchstone, 2018).

42 Three Initiates, *The Kybalion*, 6.

43 Donna Eden with David Feinstein, Ph.D., *Energy Medicine: Balancing Your Body's Energies for Optimal Health, Joy, and Vitality*, (Jeremy P. Tarcher, 2008).

44 Id., 1.

45 Id., 10-11.

46 Ibid.

47 https://supernova.eso.org/exhibition/images/spheroidal-universe/#:~:text=This%20is%20a%20representation%20of,through%20space%2C%20but%20through%20spacetime.

48 Eden with Feinstein, *Energy Medicine*, 187-196.

49 Id., 196-199.

50 Id., 261-272.

51 Id., 147-186.

52 Id., 159-180.

53 Id., 109-146.

54 Id., 241-260.

55 Id., 213-240.

56 Id., 204-212.

57 Id, 199-203.

58 Albert Szent-Gyorgyi, *Introduction to a Submolecular Biology*, (New York: Academic Press, 1960), 135.

59 Bruce H. Lipton, *Biology of Belief: Unleashing the Power of Consciousness, Matter, and Miracles*, (Hay House, Inc., 2005).

60 Deb Shapiro, *Your Body Speaks Your Mind: Decoding the Emotional and Psychological, and Spiritual Messages That Underlie Illness*, (Sounds True, 2006).

61 David R. Hawkins, M.D., Ph.D., *Power vs. Force: The Hidden Determinants of Human Behavior*, (Hay House, Inc., 2014), 52-53.

62 Ibid.

63 Id., 71-72.

64 Id, 52-53.

65 Id., 218.

66 David R. Hawkins, M.D., Ph.D., *The Map of Consciousness Explained: A Proven Energy Scale to Actualize Your Ultimate Potential*, (Hay House, Inc., 2020), 36-37.

67 Hawkins, *Power vs. Force*, 52, 59-60.

68 David R. Hawkins, M.D., Ph.D., *Letting Go: The Pathway of Surrender*, (Hay House, Inc., 2012), 8-25.

69 Barbara Hoberman Levine, *Your Body Believes Every Word You Say: The Language of the Bodymind Connection*, (WordsWork Press, 2000).

70 Masaru Emoto, *The Hidden Messages of Water*, (Beyond Words Publishing, 2004).

71 Frank Outlaw, "Words of Wisdom", *Canandaigua Daily Messenger*, October 31, 1977.

72 Hawkins, *Power vs Force*, 52-53.

Section Two: Our Divine Purpose

73 Newton, *Journey of Souls*, 201-248.

74 Helen Schucman, Bill Thetford, and Kenneth Wapnick, eds., *A Course in Miracles Combined Volume*, 3rd Edition (Foundation for Inner Peace, 2007) T-20.VI.10:1.

75 Helen Schucman, Bill Thetford, and Kenneth Wapnick, eds., *A Course in Miracles Combined Volume*, 3rd Edition (Foundation for Inner Peace, 2007), W-p1.94.1:2.

76 Id., W-p1.93.6:1.

77 Schucman, Thetford, Wapnick, eds., *A Course in Miracles Combined Volume*, T-19.II.1:6.

78 Schucman, Thetford, Wapnick, eds., *A Course in Miracles Combined Volume*, W-p1.38.1:3.

79   Id., W-p2.283.2:1.

80   Newton, *Journey of Souls*, 201-248.

81   https://cosmiccuts.com/blogs/healing-stones-blog/sacred-geometry-in-nature#:~:text=Everything%20on%20Earth%2C%20no%20matter,a%20result%20of%20divine%20orchestration.

82   Drunvalo Melchizedek, *The Ancient Secret of the Flower of Life*, Vol. 2 (AZ: Light Technology Publishing, 2000), 247.

83   Id., 248.

84   Chopra and Kafatos, *You Are the Universe*, 249.

85   Id., 241.

86   Id., 222.

87   Id., 110-112.

88   Id., 112.

89   Id., 124.

90   Schucman, Thetford, Wapnick, eds., *A Course in Miracles Combined Volume*, W-p1.189.1:7.

91   Helen Schucman, Bill Thetford, and Kenneth Wapnick, eds., *A Course in Miracles Combined Volume*, 3rd Edition (Foundation for Inner Peace, 2007), C-2.2:5.

92   Schucman, Thetford, Wapnick, eds., *A Course in Miracles Combined Volume*, W-p1.189.9:4.

93   Schucman, Thetford, Wapnick, eds., *A Course in Miracles Combined Volume*, T-in.1:8.

94   Schucman, Thetford, Wapnick, eds., *A Course in Miracles Combined Volume*, W-p1.48.3:3.

95   Wayne Dyer, *The Power of Intention: Learning to Co-create Your World Your Way* (Hay House, Inc., 2005).

96   Donna Eden, *The Energy Medicine Kit: Simple, Effective Techniques to Help You Boost Your Vitality and Feel Better Now* (Sounds True, 2005).

97   Gregg Braden, *The Divine Matrix: Bridging Time, Space, Miracles, and Belief* (Hay House, Inc., 2007), 85-87.

98   Schucman, Thetford, and Wapnick, eds., *A Course in Miracles Combined Volume*, W-p2.229.1:1.

99   Hawkins, *Power vs. Force*, 52-53.

100   Ibid.

101   Ibid.

102   Braden, *The Divine Matrix*, 85-87.

103   Paul Pearsall, Ph.D., *The Heart's Code: Tapping the Wisdom and Power of Our Heart Energy* (New York: Broadway Books, 1998), 7-8.

104   Doc Childre and Howard Martin, *The HeartMath Solution*, (HarperCollins Publishers, 1999), 33.

105   W. Brugh Joy, M.D., *Joy's Way: An Introduction to the Potentials for Healing with Body Energies*, (Los Angeles: Jeremy P. Tarcher, 1979), 226.

106   Eden with Feinstein, *Energy Medicine*, 184.

107   https://edenenergymedicine.com/introduction-to-electrics/.

108   Ibid.

109   Eden with Feinstein, *Energy Medicine*, 290.

110   Id., 96.

111   Id., 213-240.

112   Id., 234.

113   Hawkins, *Power vs. Force*, 52-53.

114   Childre and Martin, *The HeartMath Solution*, 9, 23.

115   Song, L., Schwartz, G, and Russek, L., "Heart-focused attention and heart-brain synchronization: Energetic and physiological mechanisms," *Alternative Therapies in Health and Medicine.* 4(5), (1998):44-62.

116   Childre and Martin, *The HeartMath Solution*, 33.

117   Pearsall, *The Heart's Code*, 65.

118   https://www.livescience.com/44460-heart-facts.html.

119   Childre and Martin, *The HeartMath Solution*, 9.

120   John I. Lacey and Beatrice C. Lacey, *Physiological Correlates of Emotion*, (New York, Academic Press, 1970), 205-227.

121   Childre and Martin, *The HeartMath Solution*, 10.

122   Pearsall, *The Heart's Code*, 73.

123   Childre and Martin, *The HeartMath Solution*, 28.

124   Ibid.

125   McCraty, Rollin, *Science of the Heart: Exploring the Role of the Heart in Human Performance*, Vol. 2, (HeartMath Institute, 2015), 5.

126   Childre and Martin, *The HeartMath Solution*, 33-34, 46.

127   Ibid.

128   Id., 51.

129   Id., 137.

130   Id., 17-18.

131   Id., 39-40.

132   Id., 64-79.

133   Id., 17-18, 47-48.

134   Id., 67.

135   Schucman, Thetford, and Wapnick, eds., *A Course in Miracles Combined Volume*, W-p1.79.1:4.

136   Hawkins, *Letting Go*, 8.

137   Id., 20.

138   Id., 19-22.

Section Three: Awakening on the Spiritual Journey

139   https://en.wikipedia.org/wiki/Yin_and_yang.

140   Ibid.

141   https://www.mindbodygreen.com/articles/yin-and-yang-meaning.

142   Osgood, Charles E. and Richards, Meredith Martin, "From Yang and Yin To and Or but," *Language* 49.2 (1973): 380–412.

143   https://en.wikipedia.org/wiki/Yin_and_yang.

144   https://www.mindbodygreen.com/articles/yin-and-yang-meaning.

145   Ibid.

146 https://en.wikipedia.org/wiki/Yin_and_yang.

147 Ibid.

148 Ibid.

149 Ibid.

150 Li CL. "A brief outline of Chinese medical history with particular reference to acupuncture," *Perspect Biol Med.*, Autumn;18(1) (1974):132-43.

151 https://www.mindbodygreen.com/articles/yin-and-yang-meaning.

152 https://www.tcmworld.org/what-is-tcm/yin-yang-theory/.

153 Neville Goddard, *The Power of Awareness*, (Devorss Publications, 1952), 42.

154 Eden with Feinstein, *Energy Medicine,* 229-230.

155 Louise L. Hay, *The Power is Within You*, (Hay House, Inc., 1991), 4.

156 Id., 3.

157 Dyer, *Power of Intention*, 4.

158 Lynne McTaggart, *The Intention Experiment: Using Your Thoughts to Change Your Life and the World*, (Free Press, 2007); Lynne McTaggart, *The Power of Eight: Harnessing the Miraculous Energies of a Small Group to Heal Others, Your Life, and the World*, (Atria Books, 2017).

159 McTaggart, *The Intention Experiment*, xxi.

160 Ibid.

161 Ibid.

162 McTaggart, *The Intention Experiment*; McTaggart, *The Power of Eight*.

163 Byron Katie, *Loving What is: Four Questions that Can Change Your Life*, (Harmony/Rodale, 2003).

164 Goddard, *The Power of Awareness*, 4.

165 Hawkins, *Power vs. Force*, 52-53.

166 https://www.lifeisnowinc.com/.

167 Hawkins, *Power vs. Force*, 52-53.

168 Schucman, Thetford, Wapnick eds., *A Course in Miracles Combined Volume*, W-p2.313.2:1.

169   Helen Schucman, Bill Thetford, and Kenneth Wapnick, eds., *A Course in Miracles Combined Volume*, 3rd Edition (Foundation for Inner Peace, 2007), M-4.III.1:2.

170   Id., T-7.VIII.1:1.

171   Hay, *The Power is Within You*, xiii.

172   Id, xvi.

Section Four: Crossing the Bridge from the Physical to the Spiritual

173   https://www.holisticism.com/journal-library/so-you-think-youre-intuitive-understading-the-six-clairs.

174   https://lead.fiu.edu/resources/news/archives/decoding-intuition-leads-to-better-decision-making.html.

175   https://www.cnbc.com/2017/06/29/steve-jobs-and-albert-einstein-both-attributed-their-extraordinary-success-to-this-personality-trait.html.

176   https://kasanoff.com/blog/2020/5/18/intuition-is-the-highest-form-of-intelligence.

177   Manly P. Hall, *The Pineal Gland: The Eye of God*, (CT: Martino Publishing, 2015), 5.

178   Ibid.

179   Drunvalo Melchizedek, *The Ancient Secret of the Flower of Life*, Vol. 1, (AZ: Light Technology Publishing, 1999), 3-4.

180   Ibid.

181   Titanya Dahlin, "Opening up Your Third Eye Chakra for Stronger Intuition," YouTube video, 0:52, Jan. 25, 2023, https://www.youtube.com/watch?v=kkq9hHsRqMU.

182   https://www.anahana.com/en/wellbeing-blog/yoga/third-eye-chakra-crystals.

183   Ibid.

184   Eden with Feinstein, *Energy Medicine*, 184.

185   Schucman, Thetford, Wapnick, eds., *A Course in Miracles Combined Volume*, T-In.2:2.

186   Id., T-17.II.6:2.

187 Schucman, Thetford, Wapnick, eds., *A Course in Miracles Combined Volume*, W-p1.121.13:6.

188 Id., W-p1.46.5:5.

189 Id., W-p1.121.5:1.

190 Id., W-p1.122.6:3.

191 Id., W-p1.122.1:1.

192 Id., W-p1.122.2:1.

193 Id., W-p1.122.5:3.

194 Id., W-p1.63.3:4.

195 Michael Angelo, "Using Sacred Geometry to Evolve Consciousness Part 2," YouTube video, 15:13, May 24, 2022, https://www.youtube.com/watch?v=mQCw4JCwoKw.

196 http://www.tjfh.club/newsinfo/927396.html.

197 Dr. Sue Morter, *The Energy Codes: The 7-Step System to Awaken Your Spirit, Heal Your Body, and Live Your Best Life*, (Atria Books, 2019), 13.

198 Williams, Kaye, "The Remarkable Seven-Sided Form: A Discovery by Frank Chester," *Lilipoh Magazine*, Spring 2009.

199 Michael Angelo, "Using Sacred Geometry to Evolve Consciousness Part 2," YouTube video, 15:13, May 24, 2022, https://www.youtube.com/watch?v=mQCw4JCwoKw.

200 Cathal O'Connell, "What share are photons? Holography sheds light," *Cosmos Magazine*, July 20, 2016, 59.

201 https://physicsworld.com/a/is-the-universe-a-dodecahedron/.

202 Melchizedek, *The Ancient Secret of the Flower of Life*, Vol. 1, 161-164.

203 http://frankchester.com/profile/frank-chester/.

204 https://www.cosmic-core.org/free/article-197-human-ap-part-4-the-geometry-of-human-life-the-heart/; https://humansbefree.com/2014/09/the-heart-is-a-sacred-geometry-vortex.html.

205 https://www.cosmic-core.org/free/article-197-human-ap-part-4-the-geometry-of-human-life-the-heart/.

206 Melchizedek, *The Ancient Secret of the Flower of Life*, Vol. 1, 109-110.

207 https://en.wikipedia.org/wiki/Golden_spiral.

208 Gen. 1:1, *The Holy Bible* (New Revised Standard Version).

209 Melchizedek, *The Ancient Secret of the Flower of Life*, Vol. 1, 147.

210 Id.,149.

211 Id., 148.

212 Id., 148-151.

213 Id., 150.

214 Id., 150-151.

215 Ibid.

216 Ibid.

217 Gen. 1:1, *The Holy Bible* (New Revised Standard Version).

218 Ibid.

219 Melchizedek, *The Ancient Secret of the Flower of Life*, Vol. 1, 151.

220 Id., 154.

221 https://www.zfabrique.com/torus-vortex-creation-story/.

222 Melchizedek, *The Ancient Secret of the Flower of Life*, Vol. 1, 155.

223 Francene Hart, *Sacred Geometry Oracle Deck*, (Bear & Company, 2001), 87.

224 Melchizedek, *The Ancient Secret of the Flower of Life*, Vol. 1, 40.

225 Id., 159.

226 Id., 160.

227 Hart, *Sacred Geometry*, 93.

228 Melchizedek, *The Ancient Secret of the Flower of Life*, Vol. 1, 160.

229 Id., 161-163.

230 https://www.andarastars.com/sacred-geometry-the-root-of-all-languages-in-the-universe/.

231 Melchizedek, *The Ancient Secret of the Flower of Life*, Vol. 1, 3.

232 https://www.orgoneenergy.org/blogs/news/merkaba-star-tetrahedron.

233 Melchizedek, *The Ancient Secret of the Flower of Life*, Vol. 2, 346-356.

234 Melchizedek, *The Ancient Secret of the Flower of Life*, Vol.1, 4, 55.

235 Id., 5.

236 Leah Russel, "Circling the Square: Uniting Heaven and Earth Through Personal Incarnation," *Watkins Magazine*, Oct. 15, 2009, https://www. watkinsmagazine.com/circling-the-square.

237 Melchizedek, *The Ancient Secret of the Flower of Life*, Vol. 2, 237-248.

238 Melchizedek, *The Ancient Secret of the Flower of Life*, Vol. 1, 222.

239 Hart, *Sacred Geometry*, 3.

240 Melchizedek, *The Ancient Secret of the Flower of Life*, Vol. 2, 229.

241 Id., 225.

242 Ibid.

243 Id., 225-230.

244 Ibid.

245 Id., 225-226.

246 Schucman, Thetford, Wapnick, eds., *A Course in Miracles Combined Volume*, T-1.I.3:1.

247 Schucman, Thetford, Wapnick, eds., *A Course in Miracles Combined Volume*, W-p1.46.6:5.

248 Id., W-p1.108.7:3.

249 https://tinyrituals.co/blogs/tiny-rituals/solar-plexus-chakra-stones.

250 https://www.spiritualunite.com/articles/tetrahedron-spiritual-meaning/.

251 Williams, Kaye, "The Remarkable Seven-Sided Form: A Discovery by Frank Chester," *Lilipoh Magazine*, Spring 2009.

Appendix

252 RKSeekerofTruth, "High Veca Codes Technique for Healing," YouTube video, 28:05, Nov. 1, 2021, https://www.youtube.com/watch?v=dkYte6DI5tA.

253 https://mandalachakra.com/2017/09/15/vesica-piscis/.

254 Melchizedek, *The Ancient Secret of the Flower of Life*, Vol. 1, 152.

255 RKSeekerofTruth, "High Veca Codes Technique for Healing," YouTube video, 28:05, Nov.1, 2021, https://www.youtube.com/watch?v=dkYte6DI5tA.

256 https://en.wikipedia.org/wiki/Eye_of_Horus.

257 https://www.uniguide.com/seed-of-life-number-7-sacred-geometry.

258 https://www.outofstress.com/seed-of-life-meaning/.

259 Melchizedek, *The Ancient Secret of the Flower of Life*, Vol. 1, 155.

260 Id., 158.

261 Id., 155.

262 Id., 158.

263 Ibid.

264 Ibid.

265 https://dailydish.co.uk/the-flower-of-life-an-introduction-to-sacred-geometry/.

266 Hart, *Sacred Geometry*, 87.

267 Melchizedek, *The Ancient Secret of the Flower of Life*, Vol. 1, 159-160.

268 Hart, *Sacred Geometry*, 93.

269 https://www.rareearthgallerycc.com/blog-entry/91/introduction-to-sacred-geometry.

RESOURCES

Double Slit Experiment

Hui Peng, "Universal phenomena of single slit, double slit, cross double slit, triple slit, disc ring, 1D grating and 2D grating wave experiments —Non-interference patterns evolving to orthogonal interference patterns". 2023. hal-03932202.

Young, Thomas. "I. The Bakerian Lecture. Experiments and calculations relative to physical optics." *Philosophical Transactions of the Royal Society of London* 94, (1804): 1–16. doi:10.1098/rstl.1804.0001.S2CID 110408369.

Feynman, Richard P., Leighton, Robert B., Sands, Matthew. The Feynman Lectures on Physics, Vol. 3 (1965) https://www.feynmanlectures.caltech.edu/.

Davisson, C. J. "*The diffraction of electrons by a crystal of nickel,*" *Bell System Technical Journal 7 (1928): 90–105.* https://doi.org/10.1002/j.1538-7305.1928.tb00342.x.

The Observer Effect

Weizmann Institute Of Science. "Quantum Theory Demonstrated: Observation Affects Reality." ScienceDaily. www.sciencedaily.com/releases/1998/02/980227055013.htm.

Ira Pastor, Big Questions: The Multiverse: Cosmological Neural Networks and Space Noodles (Ira Pastor interview with Vitaly Vanchurin, YouTube video- 1.02.22 min), Sept. 23, 2020, https://www.youtube.com/watch?v=bmyRy2-UhEE.

Gaia Staff, Is The Universe One Big Interconnected Neural Network?, *Seeking Truth, General Science, Science & Technology*, April 21, 2021.

Azarian, B. The case for why our Universe may be a giant neural network, June 12, 2023. https://bigthink.com/hard-science/the-universe-may-be-a-giant-neural-network-heres-why/#:~:text=Where%20Hossenfelder%20described%20the%20 structural,of%20neurons%20inside%20our%20skulls.

Health and Our State of Well-being

Dr. John F Demartini, *The Breakthrough Experience: A Revolutionary New Approach to Personal Transformation* (Hay House, Inc., 2002).

Thoughts Become Things

https://www.tut.com/product/thoughts-become-things/.

How the Heart and Brain Communicate

Paul Pearsall, PhD, *The Heart's Code: Tapping the Wisdom and Power of Our Heart Energy* (New York: Broadway Books, 1998), 65, 66.

Doc Childre and Howard Martin, *The HeartMath Solution* (HarperCollins Publishers, 1999), 28-29.

Heptahedron or Chestahedron

http://www.frankchester.com/wp-content/uploads/2009/08/Lilipoh-article.pdf.

PERMISSIONS

Excerpts from *The Living Universe* by Duane Elgin used by permission of Berrett-Koehler Publishers.

Excerpts from *What is Life?: The Physical Aspect of the Living Cell with Mind and Matter and Autobiographical Sketches* (1958) by permission of Cambridge University Press.

Quotes from *Canandaigua Daily Messenger* by Frank Outlaw (1977). Used by permission of Gannett Co.

Excerpts from *The Power of Awareness* by Neville Goddard, ISBN 9780875166551, DeVorss Publications, www.devorss.com. Used with permission.

Excerpts from Donna Eden's website: https://edenenergymedicine.com/introduction-to-electrics reprinted by permission.

Excerpts from *Energy Medicine*, by Donna Eden, reprinted by permission of Schulman Literary Agency, and TarcherPerigee, a division of Penguin/Random House.

All quotes from *A Course in Miracles*, copyright © 2007 by the Foundation for Inner Peace, 448 Ignacio Blvd., #306, Novato, CA 94949, www.acim.org. Used with permission.

Excerpts from *The Intention Experiment: Using Your Thoughts to Change Your Life and the World* by Lynne McTaggart (2007). Reprinted by permission of Simon & Schuster, and Scovil Chichak Galen Literary Agency.

Excerpts reprinted by permission from Bruce Kasanoff's blog: https://kasanoff.com/blog/2020/5/18/intuition-is-the-highest-form-of-intelligence.

Excerpts from *The Ancient Secret of the Flower Life, Vol 1* by Drunvalo Melchizedek (1998) by permission of Light Technology.

Excerpts from *The Ancient Secret of the Flower Life, Vol 2* by Drunvalo Melchizedek (1998) by permission of Light Technology.

Interview with Max Planck in 'The Observer' (25 January 1931), p.17, column 3

https://en.wikiquote.org/wiki/Max_Planck

https://creativecommons.org/licenses/by-sa/4.0/

Quotes from *The Kybalion: A Study of the Hermetic Philosophy of Ancient Egypt and Greece of* Project Gutenberg (1912). Used with permission.

ACKNOWLEDGMENTS

My first acknowledgment is to my spiritual guides, who invited me to write this book. If it were not for this nudge and inspiration, it wouldn't have been created. I also acknowledge that I was prepared to be a Spiritual Guiding Light with the infusion of my primary Divine Soul Wisdom energy. I am grateful that I connected to my True Self in this lifetime. I know we are always working together, the physical and Spiritual, and I am deeply grateful for this expanded connection.

I am deeply indebted to Michael Angelo Ludas for his cryptic guidance for me to be on a different life's journey. I only wish we could have shared the experience of bringing the invisible or Spiritual into the physical together. I feel your presence around me often. I am in total awe that I recognize you as Spirit from knowing you in the physical.

I sincerely thank Angela (Andi) Rosenau, creator of Sacred Dragon Publishing Services, for being on this journey with me as my editor to make this book happen. Andi guided me in ways beyond my wildest imagination by asking me key questions. I am indebted to her guidance, kindness, conviction, and wisdom. She is dedicating her life to bringing the truth to the world. In that goal, she has gone above and beyond what I expected as an editor. I am grateful for the guidance to meet you and work with you. You have shared this journey of the evolution of this book with me, and you will always be a part of my life because you have shared the unfolding of my True Self as I continued to go deeper in writing this book to address your insightful and inspiring questions.

I acknowledge Donna Eden, the pioneer of Energy Medicine, who opened a whole new world for me in terms of understanding the energy body. I find your radiance and joy a gift, and you are treasured in my heart. With what I have learned from you, I have been able to help optimize the health and well-being of many clients. Your guidance is unprecedented. Thank you for who you are and what you have shared with the world.

I acknowledge *A Course in Miracles*. It has transformed my perceptions of the Universe, the Divine, and myself. I have connected to my True Self because of the course's teachings.

I thank my energy medicine clients for encouraging me to write this book. It is for you and all others who are seeking more from this physical realm or who want to participate in bringing the Spiritual Realm into the physical realm.

I acknowledge Ida Janssen for the design of the book cover. Ida, you were given a lot of conceptual ideas that you transformed uniquely into images that symbolize the deep messages in the book. Your creative genius revealed the perfect design.

I acknowledge Ryan Forsythe for his creative design of the book's interior format. There were a lot of different expressions of the content, and your recognition that each needed a unique look shows your illustration genius.

I acknowledge Sharon Castlen for her help and brilliance in helping to market the book so the people who need this book on their Spiritual Journey will certainly find it.

I am deeply grateful to Mary Brophy for her proofreading expertise. Mary helped tremendously with the very hard job. Her dedication and commitment to this book were authentic and admirable. I am very appreciative.

ABOUT THE AUTHOR

Anne M. Deatly, PhD, is the CEO and Founder of E Quantum Breakthroughs (EQB.) Her mission through EQB is to share her experience using *Life Force Energy* to help people break through and transcend limiting barriers holding them back from living a joyful life and achieving their highest potential.

Bridging science, spirituality, and human potential through Consciousness, Dr. Anne shares how to tap into the wisdom of the body to transform your energies to be the highest version of yourself and live your best life. She is known as the Radiant Energy Doctor on the popular show "Energy Medicine and Optimal Health" on the VoiceAmerica Talk Radio Network, Health & Wellness channel.

With a PhD in Microbiology from the Vanderbilt School of Medicine, Dr. Anne's professional career spanned several decades in the scientific community studying viruses, including positions as a Principal Research Scientist at Wyeth and Pfizer. Dr. Anne is also an Eden Energy Medicine Advanced Certified Practitioner. She brings her full background in science and energy healing to her healing services, programs, books, and speaking engagements.

Dr. Anne is the creator of five energy healing programs: Energy is All There Is: Master the Flow to Enhance Your Life; How to Manifest Anything You Want in Life, Letting Go to Manifest Prosperity, Achieve Your Burning Desire: Energy Guide to Break Through Blocks, Lack and Limitations to Live in Freedom; Joy, Growth and Abundance; Conscious Leaders Journey to Creating a Prosperous and Abundant Life.

The author of *Journey to True Self: Discover Your Divine Magnificence,* Dr. Anne's next book, *Journey to Oneness: Align with Your Divine Magnificence*, continues the trilogy with an expected release in 2025. Her joy is to read, discover, and explore through learning, growing, and expanding into deeper connections with her True Self. Living on a small lake, she is guided by the natural world and lake population into peaceful resonance and coherence with the Oneness of this quiet community.

For more information about Dr. Anne's services, programs, and books, visit her website at DrAnneDeatly.com.

ABOUT THE SPEAKER

Dr. Anne is passionate about exploring the wisdom of the Universe. She shares secrets of the Universe to reveal there's so much more to life if we elevate our thinking and perceiving. Her sessions, programs, and books engage people who want to become the best versions of themselves and live their best lives. She inspires her audiences to increase their vibrancy, vitality, and radiance by discovering their magnificent uniqueness in a profound, bold way that expands Consciousness and awakens their True Self within.

Dr. Anne's inspirational wisdom appeals to a broad range of interest groups: business leaders, women's groups, religious small groups, not-for-profit organizations, networking groups, and libraries.

She delivers her messages through multiple formats: keynote addresses, workshops, seminars, mastermind groups, conferences, and panel discussions.

To inspire and empower audiences with new wisdom and understanding for living a more meaningful life in these challenging times, Dr. Anne is excited to speak on a range of uplifting topics, including:

- Your Consciousness Determines Your Best Self and Best Life
- Understanding Mind-Body-Spirit Connection for Health, Wholeness, and Well-Being
- Living Together Peacefully as One Humanity
- Owning Your Divine Magnificence
- Secrets of Your Inner Wisdom
- Do You Really Know Who You Are and Why You Are Here?
- Connecting to Your Inner Wisdom, Your True Self
- Harnessing the Power of Your Life Force Energy
- Using the Power of the Placebo Effect to Heal Your Life
- How to Primarily Identify with Your Soul, *Not* Your Physical Body

To learn more about Dr. Anne, receive a review copy of her book, *Journey to True Self: Discover Your Divine Magnificence*, and schedule her to speak at your event, please visit her website DrAnneDeatly.com/speaker.

INVITATION TO CONNECT

Thank you so much for taking this Spiritual Journey with me. I hope you enjoyed and benefitted from *Journey to True Self: Discover Your Divine Magnificence*. Each of you who takes a journey like this will help uplift the whole Universe. We are working together for the benefit of the whole. I am delighted to be One with you in this amazing and lofty endeavor. We are making an impact in the world.

Please share your comments about *Journey to True Self* on your favorite book review sites and social media groups. The more people that take this journey and apply the principles and secrets in this book, the more the Universe will benefit. The time is now to raise the vibrational frequencies of the Universe. We can do this together. I would love to connect with you, so don't hesitate to contact me. There is strength in numbers.

For continuing support and inspiration on your journey, I invite you to listen to my Divine Wisdom Moments video series on my YouTube channel or website.

> https://www.youtube.com/@AnneDeatly

> https://www.DrAnneDeatly.com

For more information about my Energy Medicine practice, sessions, and programs, connect with me on social media.

> https://www.facebook.com/EquantumBreakthroughs/

> https://www.linkedin.com/in/annedeatly/

> instagram.com/deatlyanne/ @deatlyanne

I am excited to hear about your journey and hope our paths cross in person or online.

Live radiantly!

225

www.ingramcontent.com/pod-product-compliance
Lightning Source LLC
Chambersburg PA
CBHW060914120626
46553CB00001B/324